SPOT⸱ ⸱ıE
A ⸱ ⸱ır

In a full and varied life Michael de Larrabeiti has worked in the film industry, as a travel guide in France and Morocco, as a shepherd in Provence, as an English teacher in Casablanca and as a travel journalist for the Sunday Times. He read French and English at Trinity College, Dublin, won a scholarship to the École Normale Supérieure, Paris and began a D.Phil at Oxford which he abandoned to take up writing full-time.

He is the author of the much admired *Borrible Trilogy*, recently reissued, as well as several other books. He has three grown-up daughters and lives in Oxfordshire.

SPOTS OF TIME

A Memoir

Michael de Larrabeiti

First published in Great Britain 2006 by Tallis House
www.tallishouse.co.uk

Copyright © Michael de Larrabeiti 2006
www.michaeldelarrabeiti.com

British Library Cataloguing-in-Publication Data
A catalogue record for this book is available on request from the British Library

ISBN 978-0-9554622-2-1

Set in 11/18pt Sabon by DJ Design, Edinburgh

Printed and bound in Great Britain

For my daughters
Aimée and Rose

My hand in yours

Contents

Sainte-Beuve, as he grew older, came to regard all experience as a single great book, in which to study for a few years ere we go hence; and it seemed all one to him whether you should read in Chapter xx., which is the differential calculus, or in Chapter xxxix., which is hearing the band play in the gardens.

RLS

Considering how dangerous everything is nothing is really very frightening.

Gertrude Stein

CASABLANCA

High summer in Marseille, 1959, the streets smelt of human sweat, baking concrete and exhaust fumes. I had come down from the mountains, where I had been working as a shepherd, to find that my girl friend of seven years standing, Rosie Dineen, had left me for, got married to and got pregnant by, a Norwegian lavatory cleaner. That hit me hard, it was a kick in the stomach. But then it was my fault. I had treated her badly, but that didn't help my hurt pride; it was cracked and soiled like an old chamber pot.

I'd found her a job, so that we could be together, in a hotel-cum-holiday-camp, near St Raphael, where I'd been assistant manager for a year. I'd been sacked because I had stood up for one of my colleagues, Jean Renoult; a charming, well-read man with a large family and not much income, who squatted in an abandoned shack in the hills halfway between Fréjus and St Tropez. 'If he goes, I go,' I told the manager, brimming with gallantry, eyes shining. I didn't have a family and I didn't need money.

The manager was a ghastly ex-maître d'hôtel, fat, with streaks of hair combed over his bald head from one ear to the other. His name was Garreau. He hated the world and quarrelled with everybody. He was jealous of the friendship that Jean Renoult and I had. He was envious too of the easy way I had with the women who stayed at the hotel. His wife had a face like a hatchet. Jean and I called her Queenie after her bitch of a dog. Garreau's mistress was a Belgian woman built like a T34 tank, and she moved like one too, and however busy we were I always had to keep a room ready for her.

So, 'If you sack Jean, I will leave at the same moment,' I said.

He was crafty, Garreau. He waited a week or two and then sacked me. He knew, and I knew, that Jean couldn't follow me; I didn't expect him to. He was broke and had three kids and a wife to feed. And then, two or three months later, Rosie Dineen left me for a charming Norwegian student whom I'd engaged to clean lavatories. 'It's a mad world, Masters.'

Inconsolable I returned to the mountains and my work as a shepherd, but my heart was broken. It was then that I went to Marseille and thought about joining the Foreign Legion - but my heart wasn't that broken. I spent a few lonely and self-pitying nights in a cheap hotel opposite the railway station, and wondered.

I thought, shades of Byron, to take off for Greece, but it wasn't that easy in 1959. You couldn't jump on a plane. The shipping office had only one destination on offer that week – Casablanca. I shrugged my shoulders, and Byron was replaced by Humphrey Bogart. I bought a ticket, steerage. If only Rosie Dineen could have seen me then. She'd be sorry when I went down with some incurable tropical disease or was stabbed to death with one of those curved knives that Berbers carried. 'Kismet' would be my dying word.

I was '*right up in the fo'c's'le,*' my journal says, the pages yellow now:

> *I was in a long kind of a hall, low ceiling, hardly lit. Row after row of bunks, each one covered with a threadbare blanket, grey. I was the only European. Black men going to Dakar; Moroccans in jellabas. Bare plank tables for eating, set squat between the bunks. I chose a bed in a corner, smoked a Gauloise and sat cross-legged and listened to the languages, all sounding like a frayed lath being run down an old fence, all sounding of Africa. Steerage stank.*

I knew only one person in Casablanca: Moses Assor, whom I had met briefly in the South of France. I sent him a telegram from the ship and by chance he was back from Marseille on holiday. He came to the quayside, took me home and introduced me to his mother and father and his younger sister. They were extraordinarily trusting. They were going out that evening but nevertheless fed me and left me in charge of their appartment. I was terribly proud of myself. Nobody went to Morocco in those days.

I spent the whole evening on my own, in a long sitting room, half European, half Moroccan in its décor. The windows were open, the air was warm, the darkness friendly, and the sounds from the pavements below were gentle. The only light I had came from the street lamps outside and it made strange silhouettes of the furniture around me.

I searched through the gramophone records and found only one that tempted me – Sheherazade by Rimsky Korsakov – I played it again and again and it has, since that night, retained a special place in my heart. I found a bottle of Martinique rum, chipped some ice-cubes from the fridge, poured a liberal dose and smoked my last cigarette, watching the music leap across the hiding shapes of the room, my feet moving slowly to find new and cooler places on the tiles that covered the floor. I was suddenly a hell of a fellow. Ah, Rosie! You should have stuck with me.

Within a few days the Assors had found me a room on the Boulevard Mohammed V, number 206, in a flat owned by Mme Fortuné Cohen. It was a battered room, octagonal in shape, an odd outpost in a battered building. It smelt of sweaty feet, and several thousand cockroaches had got there before me.

Number 206 was opposite the entrance to the central fruit and vegetable market. Flowers were sold there too and, as I became used to my new life, I began to wander in through the market gates and watch the drivers unload their lorries, picking up any blooms that I found discarded, broken-stemmed, on the ground, taking them back to my ugly room so they could make it beautiful.

On the same street I found a Spanish bar, Las Delicias, a wide square barn of a place with wooden chairs and tables, where old men, mainly Spanish, sat and talked and smoked and played draughts. Behind the long bar, with its brass rail for leaning on, two or three barmen moved in that efficient way that continental waiters have, where the minimum of graceful movement ensured the maximum of speedy service.

Joseph Navarro was one of the barmen. He must have been about fifty-five with a kind but doleful Don Quixote countenance that had been much lived in. He had a questing light in his eyes, and deep lines of experience in his face. He spoke Spanish of course, French, and was trying to learn English on his own.

I had arrived in Casa with no more than forty pounds and could only afford one meal a day. Joseph soon guessed as much and he kept me fed, gratis, at lunchtimes, smuggling plates of tapas across the counter and filling my wine glass whenever it was empty. In return I gave him English lessons while he worked. 'The English language,' he informed me, 'is based on one verb – the verb to get.'

Joseph had a girl-friend called Rosita; a well-built, dark-haired woman, younger that Joseph by about fifteen years. They invited me to their home at least twice a week – another way for Joseph to supply me with food.

They lived in a tiny flat in a side street to the north of the city, and we ate on their narrow balcony, shielded from the eyes of their neighbours by a line of washing. Rosita had a quick temper and lost it frequently; she could hardly be blamed when the cause of her anger was occasionally finding her man in bed with other women on his afternoon off. But they had always resolved the quarrel by the time I got there for dinner, and, as Joseph sat at the table, Rosita would stroke his bare back and kiss his face with a tenderness that swamped him, calling him sweet names in soft Spanish.

But my money was running out and I needed work. After a couple of weeks of searching I found a job as a kind of receptionist in a small hotel. I only lasted three days. It soon became apparent that the hotel was a kind of brothel – not that I minded, but I couldn't keep pace with the owner's whims – who was paying for whom and which women over-nighted without charge. I also found it strange that women who were veiled and begowned should be on the game – all you could see was their eyes. How on earth did you know what you were getting? And if you didn't like what you'd got, once they were unveiled and stripped, would a peeved Touareg appear through the door with a scimitar?

I put that theory to the test one day on the Boulevard Mohammed V. I was walking back to my room when a veiled woman passed me, staring hard. I returned the stare, looking into her huge brown eyes, those deep pools of mystery. I was much taken aback to see one of the deep pools of mystery wink at me – a decided wink, slow and sexy. I stopped to look into a shop window and she came and stood beside me, tilted her head, and I followed her into a grimy hotel around the first corner we came to. The room was 800 francs. The patron hardly looked up from his newspaper. In the room was a spavined iron bedstead furnished with a thin horsehair mattress. It was clean enough.

Under her robe the woman wore a pair of patterned cotton trousers, nothing beneath them. She had a brassiere and a cotton blouse, her breasts were two fried eggs. Bangles clanged as she undressed. Once naked she washed herself on the bidet. I sat and watched; she was as ugly as sin and her bones protruded through her skin like kindling in an old sack. We talked for a while; I told her she needed to eat more, and she told me about her children. The conversation did not last long and after five minutes I gave her all the money I had on me, 1600 francs my notebook says, and then I left. 'Que tu es gentil,' she said.

I saved money overall by eating very little; a period of fasting that lasted for a month or so. I survived on sandwiches that I purchased in the Jewish cafés of the medina, their hot sauces doubling up as saunas. I also discovered the Restaurant Slavia in a dingy arcade where meals cost only 270 dirhams, service and wine included – that is if you paid for them ten at a time by buying vouchers. *In cheap cafés I eat tired meals out of the surly hands of dreamless slaves* – the notebook again. I must have been going through an early romantic period.

Eventually, and longing for a decent meal, I hauled myself up the veined marble steps of the Berlitz Language School and they enrolled me as a teacher: 2.50 francs an hour, not quite enough for a meal at the Slavia. But it was better than nothing; I could eat regularly and pay Fortuné the rent, just as long as Joseph fed me for free at midday.

And then I met Bernadette Devert, a French girl born in Morocco, a *'pied noir'*. She walked into the school in search of an English teacher: 'Of all the classrooms in all the towns in all the world, she walks into mine.' It was manna from heaven. Her father was as rich as Croesus – he was a judge and owned orange groves somewhere down south. I began to eat twice a day.

Bernadette was twenty, had a face full of kindness, a warm laugh, divine ankles, a wry smile and a philosophical sense of humour – she was going to need it. She'd spent most of her life in Casablanca and she'd never seen anything like me. She was languishing for love. And that wasn't all; my self-imposed romantic exile had made me open and tender to all emotion. (Twice a day, at least, I was convinced that I had caught a glimpse of Rosie Dineen in the street, come to look for me). And so I fell in love too, or thought I had and the thought was just as powerful as the reality.

It was very special while it lasted, that time with Bernadette. There was the smell of mint tea on the air, and the palm trees on the boulevards looked skimpy and dishevelled, like mop-headed models. I introduced her to Joseph and she liked him; an important point in her favour. We drove to Marrakech in her father's Mercedes, across the darkness of the desert, with Arab love songs playing on the radio, stopping to look at the stars that had dropped down out of the Arabian Nights.

Often we camped at the beach, just north of Casa, over long indolent weekends, and there would be other tents around us, and singing, with harmonicas and guitars, and the smell of cooking on driftwood fires. Waking at five in the morning we'd find the sea the colour of gun metal, unmoving under an Atlantic mist, and Bernadette and I would break into the surface of it, an ocean that had never been touched before, because it was still undiscovered, and while, in their tents, everyone about us slept, we swam together and kissed of course. Then came the aroma of coffee from the shanty restaurant, further along the beach, where we were the first clients, and the waiter could not stop smiling at us because he could see, as everyone could, that we were in love.

* * *

The lessons marched on at Berlitz. I had been promoted to two or three lessons a day and had met the other teachers, an assortment of travelling misfits. My favourite was Alice, a Canadian girl from Saskatchewan. She was tall, gangly and gauche. She wore her hair in ringlets, and she had a heart of gold.

And Alice found a villa in the diplomatic quarter: four bedrooms and a kitchen, and she and I and two other teachers decided to share. Each of us had a pleasant room and there was a walled garden back and front.

We moved in a borrowed pick-up truck, and Fortuné Cohen watched me disagreeably from her balcony, but I was overjoyed to be saying farewell to her cockroaches. Joseph came to the terrace of Las Delicias and leant against the door, smart as ever in his white apron and black waistcoat, but he was smiling. He knew that I wasn't leaving him.

We zig-zagged across Casablanca, collecting belongings from each of our separate dwellings. Eventually we cut across the centre of town, four of us sitting on a mountain of beds and suitcases, lolling on mattresses, festooned in coats and draped in dresses, with me in my best teaching suit, complete with collar and tie. And startled faces peered at us from bus windows, and drivers hooted their horns, joining us in our joy.

To celebrate the move Bernadette came for dinner, looking new-made, as if the golden evening had just invented her. She wore the lightest of cotton suits, pale brown, and nothing else save a green stone necklace and lacy slippers. We bought a bottle of Gris de Boulaouane from a local grocer's shop and I made an omelette: 'el rey de la tortilla' she called me. Then we sat smoking, dancing occasionally to the radio, talking until past midnight. We made love and just before dawn, with the sky looking like blue serge with stars for silver buttons, we walked to her house, across the top of Casablanca, dancing from time to time, to our own singing. At last we managed to say goodnight, hardly daring to leave each other, not willing to break the spell in case it never returned. I floated back to the villa, brushing the palm leaves with my finger tips, turning in figures of eight around the tree trunks in the park.

The next day, three times I saw her, from the window of my classroom, turning about the school, hesitating on the pavement, me watching unseen. Then I received a letter delivered by hand at the school desk. 'Je t'aime,' was all it said. The most powerful words in the world.

*　*　*

One of my pupils at the school was a Madame Shriqui. I had been obliged on a number of occasions to reprimand her for speaking French in class, something that was not allowed in the Berlitz method.

I can see Madame Shriqui now: slim and attractive, with masses of black hair; a highly strung young woman in her twenties, too beautiful for her own good and, judging by the quality of her wardrobe, spoilt by her husband to perdition. She had taken my reprimands in the worst possible manner, and one day she discovered me sipping a glass of white wine with Bernadette on the terrace of La Tour Hassan, a busy café not far from the school. I was a snappy dresser in those days, and I was wearing a pale blue alpaca jacket and white trousers.

Madame Shriqui stormed her way through the tables and came to a halt in front of us; told me what an abject fellow I was, seized my glass of Boulaouane and flung its contents into my face.

The terrace was crowded and the drama was much appreciated. There were gasps, and then laughter at my expense. Justice had been done, the spectators assumed. The jealous wife had taken revenge on the philandering husband and his blonde mistress. As Madame Shriqui marched away, high heels triumphant, sphincter muscle as tight as an oyster, there was even a ripple of applause.

*   *   *

In November I met an Englishman who was opening a travel agency. When he discovered that I had experience in the travel business he offered me a job taking three busloads of American servicemen, and their women, on a tour of southern Morocco.

'It's a golden opportunity,' the man explained, 'I tell you, tourism is going to explode in this country, if you get in on the ground floor you will make a fortune.' He was right of course but for me the trip was an end in itself: Safi, Essaouira, Agadir, Marrakech, Taroudant, the Atlas mountains and right down to Goulimime on the edge of the Sahara, to see the nomads and the camel market.

In Agadir, I remember, I invited four American girls into my hotel room and we drank a lot of Scotch as I attempted to explain the difference between *Lolita* and *The Rainbow*. I failed miserably, I think, becoming tipsy before I got to the end of my argument, whatever it was, but my notebook remembered the look of the room afterwards:

> *shoes lying oddly on the floor, an articulated reading light throwing a delicious shadow onto the earthenware vase I had bought in Taroudant; five whisky glasses and the ice bucket gleaming, the ashtrays overflowing with the smell of black tobacco, my shirt thrown over a chair, the darkness of the balcony, and the sound of Atlantic rollers washing into the room through the open windows.*

*   *   *

On my return to Casablanca my thoughts turned to London. In less than a year I had been a hotelier, a translator, a teacher, a shepherd and a travel guide. '*If this was what life had to offer*', my notebook reminded me, '*I want more of it*', but I had been away from England for about two years. A broken heart and a sense of adventure had cast me up on this shore, but now it was time to make a decision. It was either settle down in Morocco with Bernadette and become a wealthy ex-pat running a travel business, or move on. An alternative existence was beckoning, and I didn't want it. For the first time in my life I was homesick for London; I wanted street lights shining in wet pavements, the cold of an English winter. I wanted the warmth of a pub, to talk long hours with old friends, the smell of coal fires on the wind and the sounds of the Golden Arrow leaving Victoria on its way to Paris.

I didn't know what to do about Bernadette. It was a tricky decision, so I ducked it – I ran away. I said 'goodbye' to Joseph and Rosita, and even Barq, the Berber street boy who cleaned my shoes in Las Delicias, but I hadn't the courage to face Bernadette. One night I slipped onto the boat for Marseille, in the dark, feelings of guilt flooding my heart, where they still ebb and flow when I conjure up those days. It truly was the end of 'a beautiful friendship'.

*   *   *

At the back of my notebook is a list of what I read in those six months in Casablanca, books borrowed from the American Library:

> *Dr Zhivago, Pasternak*
> *Twenty Stories by Stephen Crane*
> *The Andrews Raiders*
> *The Pocket Faulkner*
> *Collected Poems of W H Auden*
> *The Great Gatsby, Fitzgerald*
> *History of Civilisation*
> *Tender is the Night, Fitzgerald*
> *Further Fables of Our Time, Thurber*
> *The Road to Miltown, Perelman*

Plays by William Inge
Gideon Goes to War. (Wingate by Mosely)
Not As A Stranger, J Jones
Complete Short Stories of E A Poe
Pensées, Pascal
The Life of Henri Brulard, Stendhal
And Quiet Flows the Don, Sholokov
Lolita, Nabakov
La Femme et le Pantin, P.Louys
Aimez-Vous Brahms? Sagan
Maurin des Maures, Jean Aicard
L'Illustre Maurin, Jean Aicard
The Brothers Karamazov, Dostoevsky
Some Came Running, J Jones
The Man Who Lived Backwards

Casablanca Revisited

Thirty-eight years later the guilt still lay heavily upon me and I went back to Casablanca to write a travel article. I was really looking for Bernadette though I would not have admitted it to anyone. I had my old address book and the notebook I'd written in 1959.

I went straight out onto the streets and they were just as I remembered them, noisy and full of people. Under the arcades were the same shoe-shine boys, still banging their little wooden boxes with the backs of their brushes to attract attention. Old men crouched in corners watching the pavements crumble, selling single cigarettes, making it impossible, even for a saint, to give up smoking.

I went hunting for memories along the Boulevard Mohammed V – my patch all those years before; number 206 opposite the central market where I used to buy or steal roses. My favourite bar, Las Delicias, had gone, replaced by a blue-fronted night-club – El Alcazar – and with it had gone Joseph Navarro.

I took breakfast the next morning in the atrium of the Royal Mansour Hotel, a place of ponderous luxury. The early sun filtered through the transparent roof, the handmade wall tiles, in blue, white and green glittered, and the white marble floor shone. At one end of the restaurant there tumbled a waterfall, and finches sang in cages. I thought about my next move, trying to decide whether I was Sam Spade or Philip Marlowe. The Maître d'hôtel whistled by, like the white rabbit in evening dress. 'Bonjoo m'soo,' he chanted to anyone who caught his eye. 'Choyai l'benvenou.'

'Is there a Rick's Bar in Casablanca?' I asked.

The white rabbit skidded to a halt. 'You come for a conference, this is what we do.' He produced a brochure from his pocket.

'Rick's Café, an evening at the hotel,' I read. 'The banquet room will be transformed into a real kasbah, and Rick's Café from the famous Casablanca film will be the décor of the evening. The waiters will be dressed in police costumes of the era and Humphrey Bogart trench coats. A piano player will perform the famous music from the film and every participant will receive a personalized Bogie fedora.' I shouldn't have asked.

I left the hotel, crossed the square, and skirted the terrace of the Café de France, where the smell of coffee rose from a hundred breakfast cups. I crossed the Parc de la Ligue Arabe where there was a cathedral that was no longer a cathedral, built in a special grubby white concrete. In an open door a clutch of women sat cross-legged among their possessions. There was a mattress or two, dark faces and robes of bright cloth.

All around me young men played football in the dust and, under the trees and oleander bushes, students lounged, reading, their lips moving across the verses of the Koran.

In the entrance hall of the apartment block where Bernadette and her parents had lived I was surprised to find her father's brass nameplate, recently polished, still on the wall. André Devert, Avocat. My heart missed a beat. It couldn't be that easy.

I climbed the stairs to the top floor, peering in the gloom at every name on every door – the wrong names. When I got back to the hall, the concierge was waiting for me, her dress loose and flowered, her feet cool and bare. I told her my story and she eyed me like I was trying to open a branch office of the white-slave trade in her kitchen.

'The father is dead,' she said, 'many years. The mother is old, ninety, and she moved to France, I don't know where. There is a friend who might have their number, phone me tomorrow.'

I had another address, on the Place Ahmed el Bidaoui in the medina. There were blocks of flats down one side of the square, mushroomed all over now with white satellite dishes, static against the pale sky like errant moons. Barq, the Berber boy who had cleaned my shoes in Las Delicias had lived in those flats. If I could find him he would know things hidden from me, and discover what I could not.

Barq had gone. The locals shrugged their shoulders. He'd probably left for France. I sat on a bench next to a tramp who was scratching his head like a maniac; perhaps he was a maniac. It was a good time of the day: cool, calm and reflective. A woman strode across the square, straight-backed and stately in an ice-blue gown and a golden headscarf, a baby slung over her shoulder like a novelty knapsack. A skinny man in a jellaba passed by, mumbling. He wore sandals, and on his right foot the word 'pirate' was tattooed.

The mad tramp wandered away from the bench, still scratching his head. Another man sat in his place and smiled at me. He was smartly dressed in a suit of cream linen and carried a brief case. He had black hair and a neat moustache. He was obsessed by Paganini.

'I am writing a book on him,' he said. 'Did you know that Paganini could make an extraordinary sound with his violin, no other violinist in the world could do it. He called it the sound of the '*cannone*'. He was a superstar. Women fainted. They fell in love with him. Men wept.' The man opened his briefcase and showed me his manuscript; a couple of hundred pages of it.

'Paganini played music that was unbelievable. You know, his hands and wrists were not normal. His fingering and bowing were impossible to all but him.' The man's voice became conspiratorial. 'But I have learnt Paganini's secret…it was simple…He was in league with the devil. He must have been. I promise you, there were people in his audience who said they had seen the devil standing next to him on stage.'

When he had finished with me the man in the cream suit closed his briefcase and stood. 'I give you my card,' he said. 'I want you to find a publisher for me in England. They are not interested here.'

'I'll see what I can do,' I said.

At the top of the square was the Hammam Beni Ben Allah. The entrance raised no expectations of comfort or luxury. Why should it? This was a public steam bath for the inhabitants of the medina, six dirhams a throw. In such a place there would be no Sydney Greenstreet with a fez on his head, his voice silky with malice. I didn't mind a bit; after the session with Paganini's biographer I needed some serious repose.

I pushed open the door and went into a tiled corridor that did a left and a right and entered a room about twenty feet by fifteen. There were wooden benches to sit on and a cubby hole behind a wire grille where an old man kept guard. He was so old his first job must have been on a dinosaur farm. He was wearing a felt skullcap, loose shirt and trousers, and about a fortnight of silver beard.

He took my camera from me, my watch, my shirt, trousers and shoes, and placed them carefully on a shelf. I had arrived at the hammam by chance, and so was without sarong or swimming trunks, yet modesty demanded one or the other. The old man reached up to a cupboard and pulled out a pair of Noah's Y fronts, so stiffened by mould that they could have made, with the addition of two brass hinges, a serviceable shutter for a small window. I decided that my own underpants would have to do. Better the devil you know...

I went on through a green painted wooden door and passed into a small ante-room that in turn led into a set of three slightly larger chambers. The air was a warm mist, the tiles were dangerous underfoot.

The third chamber had a reservoir at one end, about eight feet by three, and into it gushed a stream of near boiling water. On the wall was a cold tap. There were plastic buckets handy. I filled one with hot water, adjusted its temperature from the cold supply down to something that wouldn't turn me into a lobster, and then poured its contents over my head and the rest of my body. The heat was deep and penetrating and I lay on the floor for about an hour, melting.

When I went to dress I realized that I hadn't brought a towel with me. The old man lent me one – a scrap of rag worn as thin as a butterfly's wing and as soiled as a stoker's string vest. As I said goodbye, the guardian settled down on a bench for a long nap in the steam, practising for the longest nap of all. I walked back to the hotel, my wet knickers in my pocket, unclad beneath my trousers, dissolute and abandoned.

On my next visit to the concierge, she gave me a scrap of paper with an address in Fes on it. 'This is someone who worked for the Deverts,' she said. 'They may know where the daughters are – there were two of them, you know.'

I had never been to Fes so it seemed like a good idea. I was crossing the Boulevard Mohammed V to get a train ticket when a short, nattily dressed, pop-eyed, middle-aged man glided into my slipstream and came alongside. He looked just like Peter Lorre; the same height, the same build, and he had the same pitch to his voice – poisonous and clammy.

'I saw you at the airport,' he said...'I'm in charge of customs. No, you won't recognize me...I was in uniform.'

I should have ignored him. I could see at a glance that he was a con man, but I was in a benign, off-hand mood. 'That's nice,' I said.

'And guess why I am in Casablanca?' he continued. 'My wife had a daughter today, and I'm going to visit her at the hospital.' His eyes swivelled and showed only the whites for what seemed an age. My stomach lurched – why do people do that? He scuttled a step or two to keep up with me as I quickened my pace.

'We ought to wet the baby's head,' he whined, the whites of his eyes rolling again from behind eyebrows that were untrustworthily mobile. He led me into a dingy café where the dark hung in curtains, gritty like slate dust: one or two drunks peered at me out of the gloom the way deep-sea divers peer out of their helmets. From high in the ceiling Arab music fell and sawed the cigarette smoke into slithers. I ordered two beers and the moment my glass was empty I decided that my curiosity had been satisfied.

'I'm in charge of customs at the airport,' said Peter Lorre again, following me into the sun where the air was luminous. 'I can make things easy for you, very easy.'

'Baksheesh-hasheesh,' I thought. 'Va te faire voir chez les grecs,' I said, an expression that is extremely impolite and implies devious sexual tastes.

'Give me fifty dirhams,' he insisted, 'otherwise you could be delayed at the airport.'

I had visions of a wadge of kif appearing in my suitcase, and extra months of holiday in a Moroccan jail. 'Not a chance,' I said, and dodged into the travel agents.

*　　*　　*

At Fes I booked into the first cheap hotel I came to – working on the theory that proximity to the railway station makes it easy to get out of town on the day, and you don't need a taxi to do so.

The Hotel Royal was in the Rue d'Espagne. It had once been, I suspect, a good two star kip, imported lock, stock and barrel from France. Its exterior walls were painted white and were tightly wrapped in colonial balconies, like a two-tier wedding cake.

My bedroom was large, and the bathroom too, with a massive porcelain bath. There was a rough wooden chair and table, painted in the same fluorescent orange as the benches I'd seen on railway platforms. The reading-light was a brass lamp-holder bolted onto a biscuit-tin lid, which in its turn had been nailed to the wooden shelf that ran behind the bed.

In spite of the size of the bath there was very little water to fill it; the flow was a trickle. 'Any hot water?' I asked the man with the morose face who sat reading a magazine behind the desk in reception.

'Tomorrow morning,' he said, hardly bothering to raise his eyes from the page, but relieving me of a hundred and nine dirhams with a gesture that was both nonchalant and assured. 'Hot, tomorrow morning.'

There was no soap and there was no towel. Never mind; I would dry myself on a dirty shirt. There was no toilet paper either; never mind again. As the proverb says: 'He who travels without toilet paper should stay at home.'

Apart from one friendly cockroach there was nothing to linger in the room for, and I had the address the concierge had given me on a scrap of paper: 43 Place de Florence, which was located in the centre of the new town. I counted the numbers round the square but between 42 and 44 there was an empty house, boarded up over the windows. I wasn't too surprised. Some decades had gone by since anyone had worked for André Devert.

The square lay open to the sun but I liked it. It was unhurried, nothing much moving. A man was mending his car in the heat, and on shady café terraces university students lounged and laughed. Near me an old man in a wheelchair buzzed up and down, hoping to earn a coin or two protecting parked cars on his section of the pavement, clutching at the air for money, and cursing when none was forthcoming. '...'lah I-jeeb,' shouted the defaulting drivers as they made their escape, tyres spinning, '...'lah I-jeeb.' Allah will provide.

I bought a salad sandwich and took a taxi to the tombs of the Merinides, my guidebook having advised me that this was a good spot, and from it I could command a view of the whole of the medina, the largest in the world.

The tombs had been built on the top of a dusty hill, now they were crumbling, disintegrating into the ochre ground. Below me the walled city ran from the Bab el Kuja in the east to the Bab Boujeloud in the west. The medina was an endless jumble of flat roofs, with green tiles and towers here and there where the medersas and mosques stood high above the rest. On the side furthest away from me the houses climbed to the Andalusian quarter and its mosque, a quarter that had been colonized by the refugees who had fled from southern Spain during the Christian conquest.

I sat for a long while enjoying the silence. The medina looked like a huge sprawling animal, replete and somnolent, though I knew that in the anarchy of those winding alleys there was movement and clatter enough for anybody, a confusion of sweat and talk.

Most tourists arrive at the western end of the medina, the Bab Boujeloud, but I entered the souks through a smaller gate –

the Bab el Guissa – where there were no would-be guides waiting to protect me from everyone but themselves. I went forward into half-lit passages too narrow for motor-cars, though the beasts of burden, horses and donkeys, were even more alarming than modern traffic, crushing me to the wall as they passed, swaying under mountains of cargo: planks of wood, hides still dripping from the tanneries, shapeless bales of wool and enormous sides of beef.

But then a wanna-be-guide appeared as if through a trap-door. 'You'll get lost...' he began. I nodded at the sun, well past its meridian. 'If I keep walking towards that,' I said, 'I shall come to the Bab Bajeloud.'

'You'll be hassled,' he threatened, but his enthusiasm had faded.

Before long I was in streets where every inch of space was occupied by a shop or a stall. As I advanced I passed low arches that led into murky dead-ends and mysterious courtyards, where I dared not enter. At every step there was someone to offer their services or their merchandise, following me for a few yards, tugging at my arm until the relay was taken up by someone else. Children were in on it too, their staying power greater than that of the adults, and, when they did abandon their hounding of me, their cousins sprang from the ground in mythological numbers – hosts of dragons' teeth.

I wandered further. There were slices of coconut for sale, tools, tailors cutting suits, tiny open squares where silk merchants planned caftans with women whose faces were hidden. Old men lounged in barbers' shops, and I found a stable yard packed with donkeys and horses, trembling with fatigue, dreading the toil to come, their bodies thin, their faces haunted, their tails too limp to swat the flies.

And everywhere the noise: the hooves of the horses, the warning cries of their riders, the hammers of the metal workers, the saws of the carpenters and the siren songs of the vendors. 'Come look, mister, you don't have to buy, no problem, come look, come look.'

I had dropped into the Middle Ages and they stretched away for ever. It was bedlam and all was bustle and business. The jellabas flowed and floated, the colours clashed and the smells lay over all: wood fires and oil on ancient lathes as they turned; cedar and sandalwood; excrement, animal and human; honey and nougat; dates and coffee; perspiration and freshly baked bread; meat and mint tea and the reek of hot blood from slaughtered chickens.

I stood and watched the butchery for a minute or two. A finger was pointed, the chicken was chosen, and the man with the blood stained apron reached into the open topped cage and seized a victim, never mind its struggles and squawks. In a second the bird's wings were dislocated, terrifying it into a silent immobility. Its eyes bulged as the bright knife was drawn across its throat. Then it was upended and bundled into a metal container, the size of a large flower pot. Its feet quivered and jerked as it tried to right itself, the scuffling pitiful, but the life blood poured away, and soon the body ceased to move.

The whole operation, including the plucking, was completed in the twinkling of an eye, the butcher's hands as deft as a sorcerer's. And sly and skulking, down on the uneven surface of the street, stepping lightly through a dangerous, shifting forest of human legs, the skeleton cats gobbled up the leavings.

Then I turned a corner and saw a young man, half hidden by a latticed barricade of musical instruments, playing a lute, the notes clear and limpid, making the hub-bub from the souks seem distant and unimportant, and not once did the lute-player attempt to sell me anything. The music he made was for himself.

I listened for a good quarter of an hour before hastening on towards the Andalusian quarter. I crossed a walled bridge that spanned a river heaving with rubbish, and then, forcing my way through a throng of people, I came to rest in a haven of calm – an emporium of silk bobbins, glittering on every side, a hundred rainbows, and I sat on the shop-keeper's stool and watched the world go by in the street outside.

A girl in a striped jellaba of black and gold, but with no veil, tilted her head at me and smiled. 'Bonjour,' she said, her French accent perfect. She was twenty-two and earned her living as a washer-upper, imprisoned for a lifetime in the steamy kitchen of some rackety restaurant. Her name was Meriem and she had lived, as a child, with her mother and father in Limoges. Then her mother had died, her father had remarried and now she was stuck in Fes with a step-mother who didn't want her.

Meriem became my guide with no fuss. We looked at embroidered caftans; we stood at the gate of the mosque, and sat on chairs in front of a hole in the wall and drank a couple of sodas. Then we had bread and brochettes grilled on charcoal and dawdled right through the afternoon. We were stared at of course, brashly by the men, covertly by the women: what was she doing with that European? They were curious, very curious, but nothing was said, at least not to me.

Meriem desperately wanted to return to Europe. 'Do you need an au pair?' she asked. 'Are you married, would you like a wife?'

By the time we reached the Bab Boujeloud dusk had fallen, though the edges of the dark were softened by weak pools of light spilling out from shops and cafés. A woman sat on a doorstep and smelt a sprig of mint.

The swallows were wheeling low, twittering across the end of the evening and the roar of men talking was deafening. There were taxis waiting. Meriem refused my offer of money. 'Send me the photos you took,' she said, 'and a husband if you can find me one...'

'I have a pal called Angus,' I said, 'just divorced, he could do with some love in his life. I'll ask him to come and see you.'

She smiled, a sad smile. 'Lah ismak,' she said. 'May Allah hear you.' I kissed her then and got into the taxi and it drove away. I was sad too. No trace of Bernadette, and now another girl disappearing into the rest of her life – traceless also. *Mektoub* – it is written.

* * *

Back in Casa I wandered the gloomy arcades, a Hades of passageways that connect the boulevards, one to the other. The boot-boys live their lives there, stained hands a blur as they cast their brushes from hand to hand over the shoes they polish, the brush hanging in the air waiting for the fingers to come for it. Those with no custom smoke cigarettes and watch the girls go by.

One day I climbed that flight of cracked steps and entered the Berlitz school I had once worked in. I found the same principal's office and the same classrooms leading off the same corridor. There in the staff room I rounded up the usual suspects – the same breed of castaway that I had known in my day, marooned in Casablanca, a little on purpose, a little by accident, the stories similar to mine. Only the names and faces were different. There was Christine, a shipwrecked dancer from a troupe that had toured the Mediterranean; a Swede called Charlie, full of life and the love of it; Stuart, a black Scotsman from Glasgow, escaping from the winters of the north to the sunshine of the south; and Keith, a family man trying not to recognise his homosexuality, and failing.

They reminded me of the old days and they were doing exactly what I had done; scraping a living and putting distance between them and the baggage of the past – laying the ghosts of the Rosie Dineens of their youth.

They were jolly and welcoming. They took me to their house, a beach shack some twelve miles north of the city and they listened with patience as I talked about my Morocco, about trips to Taroudant and Goulimime. Keith cooked and I sat on the porch and watched the Atlantic rollers crashing on the shore. There were a couple of bedrooms, one with a bike in it, paintings and photos on the walls, a yard with a lavatory, a dog called Simon and a cat called Cleopatra, with a new litter of four or five kittens.

There was an attractive Moroccan girl too, called Dounia, a pupil from the school who said she thought she was a lesbian. She was caring for one of the kittens who looked on the edge of death. She wrapped it in a dirty towel and placed it tenderly on an armchair. A little while later Mohammed, Keith's boyfriend, arrived. He was no lightweight, and when he lowered his sixteen stone into the armchair he put the kitten out of its misery; a quick death instead of a lingering one.

On my farewell evening teachers and pupils invited me to the

Seamen's Club, down in the docks, a refuge for the matelots and lorry-drivers of all nations. Before leaving the hotel I telephoned the concierge at the apartment block and reluctantly she gave me a number in the south of France that she thought was Bernadette's, somewhere near Montauban. I rang it immediately. A call from Casa after a gap of thirty-eight years had a certain style to it, I thought.

It didn't work. 'Le numéro que vous demandez est hors de service actuellement...le numéro que vous demandez...'

I took a taxi to the docks, one of those taxis that thinks it's a bus and comes already equipped with passengers – two women on the back seat in jellabas and headscarves. The driver was a scraggy ancient in a black skullcap. He was skinny enough to slip through the grille of a drain and he wore sunglasses as big as dinner plates. Arab love songs stormed out of his radio and came in decibels that shook my teeth loose and had already done for his. I paid him when we arrived at the club and my change was a ten dirham note that was as limp and as soot-laden as a leaf from a bygone autumn. It must have been minted during the Roman occupation and since then had passed through as many hands as a Casablancan concubine.

I had completely forgotten about the Seaman's Club, but I recognized it the moment I walked through the door. Nothing had changed. The pool tables had not moved. This was the place where I had lounged at the bar, being Dashiell Hammett, listening to the tales that sailors told, watching the tarts stride into the building, arm in arm, in twos and threes like bits of a chorus line, legs stepping high, their greetings dripping with provocation. It was the place also where Bernadette would lay her head on my shoulder and we would 'tire the sun with talking and send him down the sky.' And there was a small dance floor in the garden where my love and I could dance under the stars until the dawn crept up over the roofs.

That last night in Casablanca I walked back to the hotel alone, along by the harbour wall. If I hadn't given up smoking ten years previously I would have flicked my cigarette away, into the darkness, and tilted my personalized fedora over my eyes. I had rung Montauban several times but the number was a dud. Well, 'it don't amount to a hill of beans in this crazy world', but whatever happened to you, Bernadette, I'm sorry for my part in it – but then again, wherever you are, remember, we'll always have Casablanca.

LONDON

Casablanca to London in 1959 was a long journey and I took it slowly, boat and train all the way. I spent a week or two back in Provence where I'd left what few possessions I had with Jean Renoult's mother, up in the hills near the village of Grimaud, where my shepherds came from. I stayed briefly in Paris too. I'd been a tour guide there in 1957 and I had friends to see. By the time I arrived in London I was completely broke; it was nearly Christmas and as dark and as cold as I could have wished after the hot summer of Morocco. My mother gave me a roof over my head, but I needed money. She couldn't afford to keep me. She worked as a waitress and earned very little. My father was one of the disappeared.

Straight from school – December 1950 – I had started work at sixteen, in Earlsfield Public Library. I had lasted a year, sacked for having a fight with the janitor. I was ashamed of that episode but it was he who had started it. He called me 'four eyes' all the time, day in, day out. After the library I'd done a stint as a night-watchman in a garage, selling petrol to lone travellers – midnight till eight – at 3s. 6d a gallon, and washing windscreens too.

Then there had been six months slaving in the tropical kitchens of a Joe Lyons tea shop in Bond Street, loading tons of filthy plates and cutlery into a huge belching dragon of a washing-up machine. But being young made everything miraculous. London born and bred I wouldn't have lived anywhere else; it was my playground. London was a fairyland lost in fogs, and I loved it. My free time was spent in pubs with friends, talking, talking and talking, working out how to live, wasting a couple of years. Then chance took a hand, deciding what I was going to do, whom I was going to meet, and by doing so, deciding what kind of person I was to become. I was sitting on the benches of Battersea Labour Exchange in the spring of 1952 when my friend Bernard walked in. He was looking for an assistant projectionist to work a season with him in the Festival Gardens, Battersea Park – The Cinema of the Future – where the audience watched three dimensional films through special glasses.

Suddenly I was cast into a new world and became a new creature: from caterpillar to butterfly, no longer earth bound, I could fly and I was beautiful. The Festival Gardens was a new world; bright and clean and good. I moved from black and white into glorious Technicolor – I had floated over the rainbow and everything snapped into focus. In the Gardens things were lit from the inside, shining; it was a brilliant dream. In the Gardens I was suddenly possessed of many talents, I could dance and I could sing.

There was grass and flowerbeds all around me. There were wide steps leading down to patterned esplanades and marble bridges. Painted kiosks stood by winding paths, and ice cream and hot-dogs were sold in them by young women wearing coloured bonnets. Beautiful girls, dressed as Nell Gwyn in green silk frocks, carried baskets of oranges and wandered to and fro among the crowds. Out of work dancers in the main, they were something I'd never seen before, strolling casually like princesses, poised, full of confidence.

And everyone was friendly – actors waiting for pantomime, artists learning their trade, they laughed as they went through the day. They scorned work yet they did it well. They wore outlandish clothes and didn't worry what others might say. They were travellers from a foreign land, and they told their stories with exaggeration, easily, and their talk was the most wonderful thing. They spoke a new language and I had to learn it. The Riverside Theatre was a treasure house and in the land of the Festival Gardens my feet never touched the ground. It was where I belonged.

The manager of the cinema was 'The Amazing Mr Bungey'. He was the first manifestation of those special people who have come into my life and, for no apparent reason, taken my education on as a duty. Bungey had blond hair, always very carefully groomed. He was not tall, he probably stood about five feet eight inches, but he had great presence. His movements were meticulous. He made others look clumsy. His skin was pale but shone pink by reason of the care he gave it. His cuticles were perfect, his nails polished. The eyes were bright blue, and though his nose was a little too large for his face it was dangerous, an instrument for rooting out lies and affectation and spiking them to death.

Bungey frightened me at first. I was only eighteen when I met him, but he was both good and kind to me, so good that I still find it difficult to understand. Ten years older, he never reminded me of it. He had a mocking smile but he explained things, and, at my request, painstakingly wrote out a book list for me; finger posts to guide me through English literature. He talked to me about the plays he'd seen and the women he'd slept with. He opened doors to bright rooms and shoved me in.

He'd been a conscientious objector during the war and worked with the Friends' Ambulance Service, clearing up at Belsen concentration camp. How had he done it? He always looked so immaculate: stylish, wealthy even, yet he had one suit only, dark grey, and he pressed it two or three times a week. His shirt was white, clean every day with a stiff collar. I discovered eventually that he possessed just two shirts and four collars in the world, often obliged to wear them damp. He wore brightly coloured ties, and suede shoes when they were considered outrageous. He was neat and careful and he astounded me regularly. Bungey was my introduction to the concept of appearance and reality.

But it was with the problem of women that Bungey helped me most. I passed many hours that summer gazing out of the projection box window, moaning in my heart as hundreds of girls strutted by – the hair, the thighs, the breasts, the eyes; so many of them. Not far from the theatre was an ice-cream kiosk set in a diamond of grass and in it worked three or four art students, a type of girl I had never met before; and one of them was Rosie Dineen, delicate and devastatingly pretty. I was smitten, in love for the first time, but she lived in a different world to mine and I didn't know how to speak to her. 'I go over for an ice-cream,' I said to Bungey, 'I buy it, but then I don't know what to say.'

I can see Bungey's eyebrow rising now; it encircled the whole hemisphere in its irony. 'Take a book with you,' he said. 'Read it thoroughly beforehand, or the scheme won't work. Forget to bring it away. Leave it there two or three days and then, when you go back you can start talking about it. You won't believe how soon you'll be talking about things – life, art, sex, bed.' I wasn't convinced. I didn't read a lot at the time.

'You'll just have to try,' said Bungey.

The Bungey Bunk-up Book Plan certainly got me reading. I read the whole of Battersea Public Library that summer and I wondered, as I read, if everybody had started serious reading the way I did, and if those who didn't read got less sex than those who did. Bungey pushed me hard, bringing out his notebook with its endless list of titles. He'd flick over the pages, look at me and say; 'This one next, Michael, and then this one...no man can call himself civilized, you know, until he has read *Scarlet and Black* and *The Charterhouse of Parma*.'

The plan worked of course. I went out with Rosie Dineen for seven years, a passionate and tender affair; that was until she left me for the Norwegian lavatory cleaner.

*   *   *

On my return from Casablanca I tracked Bungey down. He was living in a top floor flat above a harp shop in Old Brompton Road. That year he had been a sock salesman in Harrods, briefly, and written film reviews for the British Film Institute. When I found him he was working on the Bill Book in the accounts department of the Savoy Hotel.

The Bill Book was an instrument of torture, and it was renewed every day, and night. It was perhaps four feet wide by three feet tall. Across the top of its twenty or thirty pages were printed the numbers of some three hundred rooms, each one designated and defined by its own vertical column. And, on the left hand side of those pages were listed all possible purchases. Every tiny square in that book represented money, lots of it. During the day everything bought or provided in the hotel was written in. At night Bungey and three or four others would add up the totals and make a new book for the next day, and all this in pen and ink. 'I'll get you a job at the Savoy,' he said, and he did. I survived three months of it.

It was Dickensian. The office was Dickensian and the people who worked in it were Dickensian. Worn brown lino lay on the floor and the stippled walls were yellow with nicotine that had steamed from rotting lungs. The Bill Book itself, like a revered relic in a temple of Mammon, lay on a tall stand-up desk that was straight from Chancery. We, the votaries – three of us on the day shift – stood by the book in a narrow space. Right behind us, close to our backs, was a regiment of pneumatic tubes, in polished brass and copper, and out of these exploded, all through the day, long cartridges shaped like erect penises. They burst in upon us from all over the hotel bringing messages, and we turned to them, not daring to delay, removing the bills that were scrawled in pencil on crumpled scraps of paper: Room, 146, 'Tea for Two'; 'Valet Service', so much. Then we spun on our feet and wrote the amount into the Bill Book, on and on for the duration of our shift.

From seven to four we worked, or four till eleven at night, and the cashiers, dressed in tails and striped trousers, would run up from front of house and tell us which clients were leaving, and in the space of minutes we would calculate the running total and hand over the bill. When it was busy it was madness. It was the trenches and machine-gun fire. At the end of the day, we were shell-shocked; no one could stand the Bill Book for long, and desertion was frequent.

The Bill Office was peopled by a goodly share of the world's misfits: Mr Beale, a soft little roly-poly man who taught me how to pronounce Frome correctly, he lived there with his life-long friend, and he was gentle and relentlessly good-mannered: Vernon, an outrageous homosexual who taught me what camp really meant, a *prima donna* who flounced and flaunted and used make-up and lived in Holland Road. It was my first friendship with a gay and I came to love and respect him. He was well-informed and full of fun. And Mr Weller, in charge of the credit section, spinning about the office, a clockwork toy, from ledger to ledger, dark-haired, red cheeked, his blue suit shiny enough to see your face in. He had been at the Savoy for years and those ledgers were his life. He rarely talked of anything else, but he taught me something nevertheless – I learnt that office work was not for me, and that this was the first and last time I would work in one however short of money I might become.

Of the three shifts on the Bill Book the four to eleven shift was the least demanding. Not many guests left the hotel in the afternoons so there were no bills to prepare. The pneumatic tubes fell silent and there were always two or three secretaries doing overtime, pretty girls longing for adventure. On my way up to the Bill Office I always crept through the ballroom, or the restaurant, and stole cut flowers from the tables that had been made ready for the evening. The flowers were stolen so that I might alleviate the dullness of the Bill Office, and at the same time present a secretary with a single rose to test her moral fibre. Then I would sit on the corner of her desk and explain the excitement of the only two Latin words I knew: *carpe diem*.

I was caught once, scrumping flowers, by the General Manager, not that I knew who he was. He gave me a dressing down, but I refused to put the flowers back, my argument being that people worked better in beautiful surroundings, and that the Bill Office was a corner of hell, and by brightening it with borrowed blooms and green leaves I was bringing joy to the hearts of men, and the hotel would benefit from such an activity. He shrugged his shoulders and let me go.

And there was more. I had taught two of my London friends the hidden way into the secret corridors of the hotel, beginning at the staff entrance on the embankment – along the scabby carpets, up the back stairs and into the Bill Office. They smuggled wine and glasses under their coats, and I would ring down to the kitchens for sandwiches. Then a suborned waiter would come hot foot to us bearing a huge silver platter, carried shoulder high, loaded down with smoked salmon and tiny triangular sandwiches of scrambled egg, and sometimes caviar.

We feasted in that office, high above London, the dark river outside, Shakespeare's river and Pepys's. And the talk went on until it was eleven o'clock, and sometimes Bungey would come in early and talk with us, always immaculate in his one suit and his beautiful pale brown suede shoes. It was wonderful. It was a cave of stars, that strange nineteenth century space. We were young and full of spirit, and life was so easy, wasn't it? I had travelled, and was going to travel more. I was going to read every book in the world, learning was a physical pleasure. Never mind John Keats, joy was not transitory, you clutched it to your heart and ran with it. The secretaries were soft to the touch, unexplored continents of pleasure lying open to the sky, awaiting their Cortez, their *conquistadores*, and, it was, at last, beyond doubt – I was definitely immortal.

SHEFFIELD

I had three brothers and one of them, Ralph, had drifted into the documentary film business and become a camera operator. He rang me up one day. 'There's a three month location in Sheffield,' he told me, 'in a steel factory. We need a trainee clapper-boy and focus-puller. Do you want it?' Did I want it! It paid three times what I was earning at the Savoy, plus overtime, and I was to stay in a five star hotel, The Grand, instead of working in one.

The offices of the film company, Wallace Productions Ltd, were in Berwick Market, a narrow street that ran parallel to Wardour Street, the heart of the British cinema industry. This part of London had its own magic too. Berwick Market was vulgar with bright colours, awash with noise. The cries of the barrow-boys and the smell of vegetables and fruit drifted up to the little cement lined camera room where my brother taught me how to load film magazines, blind, my hands in a changing bag, and showed me the difference between a fifty millimetre lens and an eighty.

And the pubs: The Fox, The Blue Posts, The French – where we took our lunches – were thronged with 'strangers', and 'steamers' and 'mysteries'; prostitutes, pimps, out of work film technicians, actors resting, the odd star preening, drunks, purveyors of porn, and above our heads floated sapphire swirls of marihuana smoke, shifting solidly when the doors opened and created a draught. It was moustaches, long hair and embroidered denim. It was life full of life, it was Soho edging into the sixties.

My cameraman was Jimmy Ewins, squat and square. His limbs were heavy, his arms and thighs were thick, his fingers stubs of muscle. His neck was a solid column of flesh, his nose an overgrown strawberry and he had the jowls of a basset hound. Jimmy's hair was prematurely grey but that was understandable. He'd had a hell of a war as a cameraman for Movietone News: bomber raids over Berlin; Murmansk and Malta convoys, and speeding to blazes in the London Blitz, clinging to the ladders of fire-engines, his peaked cap turned backwards like the cameraman on a Buster Keaton movie.

Jimmy had a lugubrious air to him, and was not easy to get on with. He was scared of existence. He thought he'd had his share of good fortune. To survive the war had surprised him and he was convinced his luck was due to run out any minute. I liked him. He was a simple man and he hadn't had it easy: taxi-driver, delivery man for the Evening News, bookie's runner, gambler. He taught me to play snooker and poker, he took me to the races – dogs and horses – and he liked me because I had the gift of making him laugh.

The Grand Hotel was an example of a luxury I had never seen before. The silence of the carpets was melodramatic. There was room service, and little hidden bars where we could drink with the musicians who played in the hotel dance-band. The receptionists were the most delightful of women. I beat my brother to the most attractive of them. I had Bungey techniques on my side – books again, candle-lit restaurants – and I stood next to George Formby and Beryl in the lift one evening. But the work was different, that was hard graft.

It was dangerous too and I soon found that the glamour of the film business was strictly imaginary. The steelworks stretched for miles along both sides of the Sheffield-Rotherham road, a road closed in with high sided sheds that were roofed with vast expanses of corrugated iron. Sheffield to Rotherham was a long dark valley and, like the highway to hell, it steamed and smelt of sulphur. There were pools of petrol-blue water lying on the uneven paving stones and they were slippery with dirt. The back to back houses where the steel workers lived were coated in dust. The windows were streaks of grime and the curtains, washed once a week, stayed yellow for ever. Between the sheds ran railway lines, where coal trucks and locos clanked and banged as they were shunted back and forth. The air was sandpaper-rough with grit and smoke from fires that burned day and night. You never saw the sky, and when it rained it rained a soot that fell from a low cloud that you could reach up and touch, and when you coughed you coughed black phlegm.

Inside the darkness of the sheds huge charging chariots ran on grinding rails to feed a long line of furnaces with scrap. And when those furnace doors were open fierce flames came free and leapt out into the gloom, roaring, seeking human flesh and sometimes finding it. And men ducked away from the heat, covering their faces.

At the far end of the works a great steam hammer banged on and on. It shook the floor, the sheds, and the whole of Sheffield even. 'You can hear it as far away as the Rotherham Odeon,' said the steelworkers with pride, 'it rocks you out of your seat.' 'Steelo's', as the firm was called, was a frightening place with the temperature changing from scorching to freezing as you went from one part of a mill to another. What was more, one moment of carelessness and you were dead or maimed.

In the bar-mill great red-hot ingots were passed through a dozen presses until they were reduced to endless rods, maybe only two inches thick. From press to press they curled, first in one direction then in another, guided by metal runners in the main, except in the middle of the shop where one man seized the speeding steel in a huge pair of tongs, curved it over a bollard with the sheer strength of his arms, and guided the steel into the mouth of the next press, back the way it had come. Then he would rest, the red coils deadly around him, rolling a cigarette, waiting until he was next called upon.

Occasionally one of these great lengths of steel would split open at the forward end and jam at the mouth of the next press. That metal travelled fast, forty miles an hour, and there was no way of stopping it, and it would race on, swaying elegantly and lethally, up into the air, twenty or thirty feet high, balancing upright for a long and beautiful moment, and the men working in the mill, some half dozen of them, would yell 'cobble,' for that's what it was called, and they would run for their lives, for if that long serpent of steel were to fall across a human body it would simply carve its way through, taking flesh, muscle, bone and brain with it.

We filmed in the bar-mill one day, from a gantry up above, looking down. 'Cobbles never fall in this direction,' said Albert, who had been assigned to us as our guide and protector. 'You're safe here.' There was a crowd of us on that gantry: Jimmy Ewins, the director, a couple of electricians, and my brother. We had carried up a couple of lamps, the tripod and a silver box with the lenses in it. I was there too, luckily nearer to the one set of stairs than anyone else.

'Cobble!' came the cry, and we stood and watched. Up and up it went, a hideous Indian rope trick with the bite of death in its red steel. It swayed but we knew it couldn't come our way – and then it did, directly towards the gantry.

We leapt and tumbled out of the cobble's path, falling over each other in panic. There were twisted knees and sprained ankles, but luck was with us and we all made it. There could have been a death or two. My brother, being furthest from the stairs, was last down: the spinning metal rod struck him on the shoulder as he took the steps in one leap. 'It felt,' he said, 'like a slap on the back.' We looked. The shoulder pad of his jacket was burnt through, his shirt was scorched, his singlet also, but the flesh was untouched. He had been that close to losing his arm.

The men who earned their living in the foundries were tough, they had to be. But they took us under their wing, and they were good friends. Their faces were black, their hands too and at the end of every day their socks had been welded to the skin of their feet by the heat of the furnaces. They lived with danger every day and called each other 'luv', and they told ghastly stories of men falling alive into molten vats of steel. We drank in the pubs with them, played darts and went to their socials and met their women, and behaved ourselves. At weekends we returned to London and as the three months went by we felt out of place away from the dirt and the grit, away from the accents of Sheffield and Rotherham and the people we had got to know. But I had learnt two new things: I knew now how steel was made, and by whom.

SINGAPORE

I survived the three months in the Sheffield steel works without losing a limb or scarring my body. I was rich too. I had been worked so hard I had not had time to spend much of my pay. I coasted for a while: 1959 had become 1960. I went back to Grimaud for a couple of months to see the Renoult family and spend a week or two with the shepherds, helping them bring the sheep down from the mountains to the coast, and once the flocks were in the lowland pastures I passed a handful of brilliant blue days, lazing in the shade, watching the sheep browse. And I read Stevenson's essays:

> *People connected with literature and philosophy must busy all their days in getting rid of second-hand notions and false standards. It is their profession, in the sweat of their brows, by dogged thinking, to recover their old fresh view of life, and distinguish what they really and originally like from what they have only learned to tolerate perforce.*

I thought a lot too about going to university; that's what writers did, wasn't it? Renaissance Man was in my sights, but there was an enormous obstacle in my way: they hadn't done Latin at my secondary modern school, and there was no going to university, in those days, without it.

I came back to London, full of good intentions. Latin it was. There were only two months until the next round of O-level exams, and I had just enough money to keep me in food and rent while I studied. I was given the confidence to attempt such a thing by an old girl-friend of mine who had read classics. She had actually guided someone through Latin in seven weeks.

'Learn the set books by heart,' she said, 'and I'll give you a lesson a week on the grammar, ten shillings a throw.'

I went into purdah. I stayed at home and sat in Battersea Reference Library for twelve hours a day, nine to nine. I still have the texts, all scrawled over in pencil: Gallic Wars, Book III, and an anthology of Latin verse – and that was how I met the divine Catullus –

> *To long and long, then unexpectedly*
> *To have one's wish is the true crown of*
> *pleasure;*
> *And so I find, now you've returned to me,*
> *My Lesbia, my more than golden treasure –*
> *Brought yourself back of your own sweet*
> *accord,*
> *Hopelessly longed for, beyond hope restored.*
> *Chalk up a white mark for this lucky day!*
> *Does any man alive enjoy such bliss*
> *As I have? Is it possible to say*
> *There's anything in life better than this?*

*   *   *

I sat the exam in November and then I was broke again. I worked as a Christmas postman in Chelsea, and then behind the counter in a grocer's shop in Gloucester Road, Kensington. I did a week of it and then the telephone rang – Jimmy Ewins. He needed a camera assistant, two months in Singapore, the Maldives and Hong Kong, filming RAF aircrew for the Central Office of Information. There was no turning that down.

We flew out in an RAF transport plane, to Singapore first. We were to film in the jungle and in the survival schools. We stayed in the officers' mess in Changi and were frequently informed that we were not dressed properly; it was collar and tie and certainly not shorts in the evening. I loved every minute of it, but then I loved everything. We toiled long hours, seven to seven most days, sometimes working into the night if the script demanded it. The young director, Dudley Birch, and I played as hard as we worked and I was a hospital case by the time I got back to London. We went to nightclubs where the officers socialized, and we lurked in the dives where the other ranks took their pleasures. In the early hours we ate Chinese meals off the food stalls in Bougi Street, wielding chopsticks with skill and chatting to the courtesans of the town.

We were living fast, frightened that the world might end that week so we'd better make the most of it. We went off the map too, often waking up in a village somewhere, in an open sided thatched hut with a naked Chinese or Filipina girl bringing in the coffee: the expense of our pleasures being charged to the production company. The mornings were torture, the hangovers colossal: Force Nine, Ten and Eleven, but that was not all. Somehow we had to find a cab and scramble back to the officers' mess and the day's location. They could film without the camera assistant, but not without the director.

*   *   *

'I could do with that massage,' I said to the hall porter. It had been a particularly hard day and Dudley and Jimmy were out to dinner with the RAF liaison officer, discussing the following week's shooting and our trip to Hong Kong and the Maldives.

For some days I had been asking the porter about traditional massage. At first he had misunderstood me. He'd narrowed his eyes and given a downward cast to his mouth. He was complicit in my sin. 'I know just the place,' he'd said, trying to look trustworthy, and failing. 'You choose the girls as you go in.' I loved the plural.

'No, just massage. I'm too tired for hanky panky. Too shy and retiring.'

'No hanky panky!' His narrowed eyes had flown open with surprise and his mouth had hardened into a sneer. 'No hanky panky...that's tricky!'

But that evening he came up with the goods.

'Traditional massage,' he said, 'really no hanky panky, but not easy to find.'

I gave him a tip. 'No, I mean it is not easy to find the way there...I'll get you a taxi.' He took the tip anyway.

The taxi trip took half an hour, and when I disembarked it was into a pit of gloom. I was far from any main road and there was not a shiny hotel to be seen. Underfoot, as I advanced, I could feel broken earth. I was lost amongst lines of shacks and tented eating houses where naphtha flares and bottle-gas lamps produced a bilious yellow light, weak and watery on the edges of the darkness. Every tent was packed, people squeezed tight together on benches, half-visible and happy behind flaps of swinging canvas. Young boys fanned braziers of charcoal, and in the cool of the evening the motorbike messengers were resting, some of them lying full length, languid on their pillion seats. They waved at me as I passed.

I had a scrap of paper in my hand: 'Massage Place, Blind Masseur, Certificated; Owner – Mrs Tuti Patuti', then the address. I pressed on, asking my way every few yards, until I found myself in an unlit alley where a notice on the side of a small villa bore the same message as the paper I carried. That was about all I could see.

I groped my way along the side of the villa, feeling the wall as I went. Someone heard me. A voice called out, hard and violent. I was suddenly fearful; my cockiness drained away. I stood motionless in the dark, not knowing what to do. I would have escaped at a run but I couldn't see enough. Then a woman, a smudge in a dirty white coat, shuffled out of nowhere, took my hand and pulled me through a door into a lightless corridor. What did she need light for? She was blind.

She touched a switch and in the murk of a lonely 40-watt bulb I saw a couple of rattan armchairs with what appeared to be a cloth-covered bench in between. The woman guided me forward and pushed me hard in the chest, to indicate that I should sit. I did as bidden, falling heavily on to the bench. I had made a serious mistake. The 'bench' was in fact a table with a sheet of glass for its top, and as it took my weight that top shattered and my behind, dropping almost to the floor, became jammed in the wooden oblong of the table's framework, and was pinned in position by long razor-sharp glass splinters. Then came a mighty silence, giving me, immobilized, a long moment in which to wonder if I had castrated myself, or cut an artery in my groin.

There was no pain but that didn't mean I was uninjured. There were lots of important bits and pieces down there, that much I knew. I might be damaged for life, fatally wounded. The probable headlines in the *News of The World* rose before my eyes: '*High-living Government Camera Technician Bleeds to Death in Singapore Massage Parlour*'.

My situation was not enviable. I did not know where I was; I could not speak the language; there was no telephone that I could see, and even if I found one I would be dead before an ambulance could get to me, even if I could tell them where I was.

Gently I pushed myself up out of the wreckage and felt my trousers. No blood as yet! At the same time voices were raised, echoing from two or three distant rooms, only to quieten as the woman, who was still with me, shouted an explanation of what I had done. The voices exploded into laughter – uncontrollable laughter. Here I was, the only sighted person in a house of the blind, and I had smashed to smithereens the first thing I had touched. A middle-aged lady now appeared, probably the mother of the first woman: and she shuffled forward, stooped and felt the smashed glass with her hand. I was amazed that she didn't cut herself, for the shards of glass were like daggers.

I groped for a chair and this time sat very carefully. My eyes were adjusting to what little light there was. The blue paint on the walls flaked in petals to the floor; the ceiling was dirty white, and there were no windows.

Having felt the damage to the table the mother disappeared; then brass rings rattled as the first woman pulled back a brown curtain to reveal a massage bed. With this my reception was accomplished and she went away, shaking her head and giggling. From the far end of the corridor a man appeared, about thirty, dressed in a shirt and trousers. He carried a clean sheet and a pillowcase. He too was blind; he too was laughing.

Slowly he laid out the sheet on the massage bed, feeling his way, taking great pains to fold it square at the corners, making the envelope shape like the best of nurses. He was not a big man, but slight, with slender hands on the end of slim arms. His face was sallow, and his eyes bulged out of his skull, each one gazing sightlessly in a different direction. His jaw was black with stubble and was slung forward like Quasimodo's.

When he was ready he tugged at my clothes and I got out of them and lay down. The evening was warm though not oppressive and in the roof space a pair of pigeons were cooing and courting. Odours came in off the street and I could hear the business of the house going on uninterrupted: somebody chopping vegetables on a board; dishes being washed and an eternal conversation rising and falling in another room.

It was a dry massage, lubricated with talcum powder only. The man began on my feet, slowly, strongly, kneading the muscles, finding out those that were knotted and tired from the day's work, the month's excesses. Gradually the fingers moved up my legs, across the buttocks and on to the back; then the arms and shoulders, even the head. Most of the time it was painful, each muscle suffering, a kind of torture, but I had been through an awful lot to get this far. I would not give up now; I had no intention of asking the man to stop. I gritted my teeth and held on. An hour and half it lasted and by the end of it I was a wreck, a limp flannel. Then without a word the man threw a towel over me and sloped away, disappearing into the dark corridor.

Once the massage was over the relief in my body was extraordinary. A miracle had occurred: blood had been turned into champagne. I ruled an empire – I was as wise as Marcus Aurelius, as all-powerful as Caligula.

I dressed and found the woman waiting for me in the corridor. Twenty dollars, she said, and began laughing at me all over again. I gave her forty, eager to make amends for the broken table. She took the money and made no attempt to count it, not even bothering to wait for a sighted person to do it for her. Back in the dark streets the evening air was soft and humid, the light still black and yellow. From the tented restaurants came the smells and sounds of people eating. Again they shouted greetings to me as I floated slowly by. I was in no hurry.

I ran into Dudley and Jimmy in the hotel bar. They'd had a good meeting; we were to set out in the morning, early. We were going up country on Air Sea Rescue Boats, and then into the jungle to film a survival course. 'It's going to be tough,' they said. Then: 'Did you have a good evening?'

'Quiet,' I said, 'very quiet, just sat about the hotel.' There was no way that I would admit to my misadventure with the glass-topped table.

*   *   *

The letter was sitting on the mantelpiece when I got home. My mother watched me as I opened the envelope. She was pleased; I'd passed Latin with 70 percent. No one in our extended family had been to university; not many people from the working class did in those days. Another letter came along later: Trinity College, Dublin had given me a place to read English and French. I had to be there by October 1961.

I had done no academic work for six years. It would be a good idea, I thought, to save as much money as I could over the following few months and take myself off to Provence where I could live with the Renoult family for virtually nothing, sit in the shade and submerge myself in the first year's reading list.

That was me in sensible mode.

I worked hard that winter, earning as much as possible, right through to the end of May and was just about ready to set off for Provence. I'd been up and down the country – locations in Wales, a documentary in the West Country, a car works in Coventry and some commercials in London, and the money came rolling in. Then, once again, chance took a hand.

After work one day I was in *Les Caves de France*, a drinks club in Dean Street. The rest of the unit was at the bar but, bored with film business gossip, I was sitting on my own in a corner. Beside me, on the bench seat, was a pile of old newspapers. I pulled one out at random from somewhere in the middle of the pile, disdaining the edition that lay on top. It was perhaps a week old – the Evening Standard. I flicked through it and a few pages in began to read: '*Oxford students to follow route of Marco Polo*'. It looked marvellous. I had visions of a long caravan of Land Rovers crossing endless deserts; the old Silk Road, nomad tents, camels, muskets with curved stocks, and bedouin with tanned, lean faces looking slim and handsome. I read the article many times. No, I had not been mistaken, there at the end was the good bit. '*The expedition is on the lookout for a stills and movie cameraman to keep a record of the journey.*'

I wrote immediately to the name and the college that had been mentioned in the article, my good intentions for study that summer screaming at Mach 1 out of the window. In reply to a phone call I went up to Oxford after work a couple of evenings later, and met two young men in their first year, one at Exeter and the other at Keble: Stanley Johnson and Timothy Severin. That was it, that was the expedition, just the two of them. I stayed the night, ate some raw eggs, slept on the floor of someone's study, and was back at work the next morning. Ten days later I was sitting in the sidecar of a BSA Shooting Star motorbike, with cameras packed tightly around me, on the A2 heading for Afghanistan with no idea of the dangers that lay ahead. It would be four months before I saw England again.

THE MARCO POLO ROUTE PROJECT: OXFORD TO AFGHANISTAN AND INDIA

Prologue to the Travels of Marco Polo[*]

Ye emperors, kings, dukes, marquises, earls and knights, and all other people desirous of knowing the diversities of the races of mankind, as well as the diversities of kingdoms, provinces, and regions of all parts of the East, read through this book, and ye will find in it the greatest and most marvellous characteristics of the peoples especially of Armenia, Persia, India and Tartary, as they are severally related in the present work by Marco Polo, a wise and learned citizen of Venice, who states distinctly what things he saw and what things he heard from others. For this book will be a truthful one. It must be known, then, that from the creation of Adam to the present day, no man, whether Pagan, or Saracen, or Christian, or other, of whatever

---

[*] Quotations from *Marco Polo's Travels* are taken from The Everyman's Library edition of 1908, reprinted 1911, edited by John Masefield, published by J.M.Dent & Sons, Ltd. Quotations are also taken from *Tracking Marco Polo*, Tim Severin, Routledge and Kegan Paul, London, 1964.

progeny or generation he may have been, ever saw or inquired into so many and such great things as Marco Polo above mentioned. Who wishing in his secret thoughts that the things he had seen and heard should be made public by the present work, for the benefit of those who could not see them with their own eyes, he himself being in the year of Our Lord 1295 in prison at Genoa, caused the things which are contained in the present work to be written by master Rustigielo, a citizen of Pisa, who was with him in the same prison at Genoa.

* * *

I read *The Travels of Marco Polo the Venetian* before I set out and like my two companions came to feel very close to him. He was the fourth man on the trip and we always called him Marco. We had his book with us and also carried a commentary by a Colonel Henry Yule (1820-1889) who had published a critical work on the *Travels* in 1871…and we loved proving him wrong. But the Colonel, as we called him, didn't make too many mistakes.

My preparations were a rush: I managed to borrow three still cameras, and I had one of my own as well as a couple of light meters. I was also lent two Bell and Howell 16mm movie cameras and promised unlimited film stock by Editorial Films, where my friend Dudley Birch was a director. I went up to Oxford on the evening of Exeter College's May Ball, and camped in Stan's rooms. There was music, jollity and drink, and hosts of pretty girls in ball gowns trotting up and down the staircases.

There wasn't much of a send-off when we left Oxford. None of my family came to wave goodbye; I'd said my farewells in Battersea. I discovered later that most of my relatives thought I would never return – alive that is. The next morning, in the college quadrangle, amongst the debris of the previous night's merry-making, we raised a glass of bubbly. Pictures were taken for the Oxford Times, and a handful of hungover revellers raised a cheer as we drove the bikes down Turl Street to someone's garage to finish our packing. There were two bikes, brand new, BSA Shooting Stars, huge 500s, far too heavy for us. One bike had a sidecar for me to sit in, with the cameras and tripods stowed all round me. The second bike had a huge coffin-like box bolted to it, carrying our provisions: iron rations, plastic jerrycans for petrol and water, a petrol stove, a tent, tools and sleeping bags. Space was at a premium and the rules for each of us were simple: two shirts, two pairs of socks, three pairs of underpants, one pair of trousers, a Barbour jacket, knee length boots and a pale blue crash helmet with the letters MPRP on it – Marco Polo Route Project. We took no guns. In the wilder parts of Turkey, Persia, and especially Afghanistan, firearms would have been a temptation for tribesmen to rob us, sell the bikes and dispose of our bodies in a dusty grave.

Stan and Tim had put months of effort into organizing the trip, and they had been very thorough. Tim was studying geography, and Stan, classics. Both were from public schools, backgrounds totally different from mine, though it made no difference. We got on famously – we had to, we were going to spend a lot of time together. Stan looked like a rugby player, stocky, with a mop of blond hair that stuck out every which way, like straw. He was full of life and fun. Tim was slim and intense, a scholar, eager to get on with things. There was only one thing wrong with them: neither of them had a licence to ride a motor bike. It was not a problem, they explained, they each had an international permit which allowed them to drive once they were abroad. As soon as they were over the Channel, they said, they would be legal. Well, they would, I had no licence at all, I would never be legal.

*   *   *

We wouldn't pick up Marco's trail until we got to Venice, so the trip across France and Switzerland was a jaunt. We flew the

Channel, Silver City, for free – Stan and Tim were past masters at getting things for free. We camped that first night in the dunes on the beach at Le Touquet, and got sand in absolutely everything (except the cameras). So much for the desert explorers.

Stan and Tim had not thought to put the sidecars on the right hand side of the bikes, so once on the continent I sat exposed and unprotected in the middle of the road. The power of the machines, and perhaps the sudden legality of his situation, had gone to Stan's head. There was no doubt that he was the best driver of the three of us but he drove with a dangerous combination of speed and insouciance. My vision of oncoming traffic was better than his, especially overtaking lorries, but, what with the rush of wind and the noise of the engine, he was unable to hear my shouted directions at moments of danger. If the road wasn't clear I had only one recourse; I would belabour him about the crash helmet, as hard as I could, with a rolled up newspaper until he had retreated to a safer position.

As I was in the sidecar I was given the job of navigator and took the expedition over the wrong pass from Switzerland to Italy, over the Furka instead of the Saint Gotthard. It was the beginning of June but at 8000 feet it was still winter with ice and snow rutted deep on the road. Officially the pass was closed and it was a gruelling drive, dangerous too. That day, as we came down below the snow line, we had our first accident, the first of many. Stan took one of the bends too fast and we crashed into a low stone wall.

The passenger sidecar parted company with the bike and skidded and spun across the road I stepped out without a scratch, and I never complained again about the sidecar being on the wrong side of the bike. Had it been on the correct side I would have been shot over the wall and down into Italy a little sooner than I desired, a victim of my own navigation. A village blacksmith welded the sidecar back to the bike the very next day, but it was never the same; it wobbled badly along the rough roads that were to come, and I wobbled just as badly with it.

Venice

Spick and span in bright white overalls, showered and shaved, we were taken by police launch to visit the Mayor of Venice. We were toasted in champagne and given a presentation copy of Marco's book. We were interviewed by local radio stations. Stan and Tim wangled our hotel for free – The Hotel Marco Polo – and the city of Venice presented us with a voucher for 100 litres of petrol. The whole world was smiling.

I filmed the courtyard where Marco Polo's house had stood; the Corte del Milione. There was a plaque on the wall: '*Here stood the house of Marco Polo who travelled through the farthest countries of Asia and described them.*' Marco's nickname, *Il Milione*, had been well-earned. When Marco told his stories of Cathay he described what he had seen in terms of thousands and hundreds of thousands. His contemporaries found it difficult to believe him – he was a spinner of lies – *Il Milione*. And, of course, where Marco's house once stood is buried a fabulous treasure, a great coffer filled with diamonds and gold that he had brought back from his travels. On his deathbed, the legend goes, he was asked to retract at least some of the tales he had told. 'Ah,' he replied, 'I have not told the half of it, not the half of it.'

We would have tales to tell, too: We were about to motor across Yugoslavia and Bulgaria, Iron Curtain countries, not visited by many. We were apprehensive to begin with, but we met with nothing but kindness and interest on our way. '*In Belgrade,*' writes Tim in his book, '*we became the centre of huge interested crowds. Whenever we stopped the motor cycles two or three hundred people would gather around…On these occasions Mike enjoyed himself hugely for he would chatter away at a rate of knots accompanying himself with wild gesticulations and finish triumphantly with his pockets full of cigarettes and his eyes sparkling from glass after glass of slivovitz which his fascinated audience had thrust upon him.*'

In southern Yugoslavia we left tarmac roads behind us and entered a land of dusty tracks, deep mud when it rained. The passenger sidecar took a hell of a pounding and began to fall apart, and I took to riding pillion on the stores' motor cycle. By the time we arrived in Istanbul we were dirty and dishevelled, a ragged crew, gaunt and exhausted.

Istanbul

In each country we visited we had sought to change American dollars on the black market and, on arrival in Istanbul, we parked in a side street off Taksim Square and waited for a dealer to appear. Instead we got Arghun, a round faced man in his mid twenties, who was wearing a bright shirt of clashing colours. He appeared suddenly behind us, coming up the steep steps of a basement shop.

He listened to what we had to say and then told us to go to a bank. There were, it seemed, heavy penalties for changing money illegally, and the banks gave as good a rate as anyone else. 'But,' he said, 'we would like you to come home and stay with us'

We were understandably wary to begin with, but all along our route, from the first day until the last, from Oxford to Bombay, no matter what the religion – Muslim, Christian or Hindu – we met amazing hospitality, and Arghun's family was yet another example of it. They radiated an extraordinary openness and generosity of spirit. It was a beautiful innocence that was everywhere in the days before flower power had beaten a path to the East, and before the Beatles had sought some kind of philosophical understanding in India. During the long four months of our trip we came across only two other travellers covering the same ground: a French duo in a Deux Chevaux, driving to Kabul. As it happened our paths crossed half a dozen times and we were always pleased to see them. They were good men.

So we stood with Arghun on the pavement, wondering what to do. Then his father appeared, a portly figure in a bright clean shirt, and wearing trousers whose creases were so sharp you could have sliced carrots with them. Then two or three daughters came out of the shop, their dresses crisp; they smiled. One of them spoke English as well as Arghun: 'You must stay with us,' she said.

*   *   *

We stayed a week. They weren't rich, their shop was nothing more than a water-seller's shop, selling the sweeter waters that came from the city's deep wells and preferred by many to the piped water that was supplied by the municipality. They lived in a tall narrow house in one of the poorest quarters of Istanbul. They cleared the bottom room of furniture and children, and we carted our gear in and slept on the floor in our sleeping bags.

We ate every evening with the family and they fed us royally: bread, cheese, sausages, hot peppers, tomatoes, beans and rice, peaches, apricots, grapes, plums and nuts; and glass after glass of Turkish tea. During those days Arghun became our guide, interpreter and adviser. We went everywhere – the Blue Mosque, the Aya Sophia, the Yerebatan Cistern, the Mosaic museum, Byzantine frescoes, the Egyptian Bazaar and the Grand Bazaar where we had leather bags made to replace our fibreglass panniers which had split open and fallen apart. We saw the tourist's Istanbul certainly, but, thanks to Arghun, we saw much that tourists don't see. When it was time to leave not one member of the family would even consider the possibility of being reimbursed for any expense they might have incurred, and when at last we boarded the ferry for Asia, Arghun and his sisters stood on the dock to say goodbye, tears in their eyes. I asked Arghun if there was a particular reason for them being so upset.

'Yes,' he said, 'we are worried about your safety. Where you are going is full of danger; we want you to come back, you know.' As the ferry left the shore we stood at the rail, silent in sadness: Arghun and his sisters were not the only ones with tears in their eyes.

Istanbul to Mount Ararat

To the east of Ankara we entered rough country, Marco's Lesser Armenia, the Anatolian plateau. It was a landscape that was savage and empty, hardly changed since Marco's day or even since 'Xenophon's Ten Thousand' had wandered and suffered there in the fourth century BC. The roads were powdered gravel, dangerous with drifts of dust. Every day we were smothered in a fine white grit. Goatherds threw stones at our bikes, and their huge mastiffs pursued us, leaping up at our legs as we rode by, their teeth bared; and we yelled at them and beat them back with tyre levers.

In this way we came to Kayseri and at last picked up Marco's route. He had sailed up from Acre in The Holy Land, had landed on the southern coast of Turkey, at the port of Ayas, and had headed inland to pick up the Old Silk Road. This part of Anatolia was a forsaken place, a wild plateau, desolate and lonely, though the distant mountains were stunningly beautiful, streaked with lines of bright colour; greens and crimsons, browns and purples. There was little movement on the roads, nothing but the occasional lorry transporting goods between the larger towns and tankers carrying petrol and oil; huge vehicles, six and eight wheelers, every one of them bearing a dozen or so passengers on top of their loads – the only way for the locals to travel, and for drivers to earn money on the side.

We went on towards Erzinjan, reading Marco's words as we went:

'*Greater Armenia is an extensive province, at the entrance of which is a city named Arzingan, where there is a manufacture of very fine cotton cloth…It also possesses the handsomest and most excellent baths of warm water, issuing from the earth, that are anywhere to be found.*' We wanted very much to find those baths but a footnote to the entry, in my edition of 'The Travels', cast doubt on their very existence: '*…of their existence at Arzengan I have not been able to find notice in the works of the Eastern geographers.*' Colonel Yule was a sceptic too, but that was enough to put the three of us on our mettle. Marco had no need to lie, and we believed in him and not in *Il Milione*, the teller of tall tales. We followed Polo the explorer, and we would prove him right.

We asked everywhere along our way, as well as we could, but it was impossible to communicate with anybody until we found some French-speaking schoolmasters sipping tea in the empty school at Erzinjan. Their pupils were on holiday, the days were long, and they were delighted to see us. If nothing else we relieved the boredom. Sadly, though they were very helpful with the problem of 'the fine cotton cloth', they were certain that there were no hot springs in or near that area. Marco must have meant the next town, they suggested – Erzurum – that was it.

At last, after a couple of hours' discussion, and very disappointed, we left the teachers and continued our journey eastwards towards Erzurum. We had not gone many miles when we came to a wide patch of marshy ground which stretched into the distance to the south of the road. We stopped, dismounted, and sniffed; a cold smell of sulphur lay thick around us. It was late evening, the sinking sun poised on the horizon. We advanced into the marsh and found the ground treacherous, the consistency soggy and spongy. Clouds of midges surrounded us, visible, like pale grey chiffon scarves about our heads. We went on, the sky became darker and the smell of sulphur became stronger, tiny streams wound silently into shallow pools. We knelt frequently and thrust our hands into the water: always the water was cold.

Then out of the gloom came a lonely silhouette, a peasant, behind him three water-buffalo. 'Sejak Su?' we asked. 'Hot water?' He turned and pointed, and there, a hundred yards or so away, disappearing into the dark, was the outline of a broken down mud building.

We went back to our machines and found a track that brought us round to the building. It was totally dark now, but we could hear springs splashing out of the ground and running off into the marshes. The building was small, say seven yards by seven, there was no roof to speak of and a weak moonlight fell onto a rectangle of water that was contained in blocks of stone. We lay down on the ancient paving and plunged our arms into the bath; it was warm, and bubbles caressed our hands. It was a moment of sheer delight; we had discovered Polo's '*handsomest and most excellent baths of warm water*'.

There was something very special about the next morning. We lingered at the springs, lounging like Roman senators, proud to be bathing where Marco had bathed seven hundred years earlier. We had reached the end of the world – what centurion needed to go further? But late in the afternoon, and loath to leave, our moral fibre undermined by the luxury of the caressing waters, we loaded up the bikes and set out once more, along the road to Erzurum.

It wasn't long before we were back in the bleakness of the wild plateau, and high on a mountainside, at dusk, we finally lost the passenger side car. It fell apart. We unbolted the bent and twisted struts and threw the thing over a cliff. Within minutes it had been borne away by some small figures below us. Perhaps it was flattened out to become part of a roof, a chicken shed, or even carted off to Istanbul to begin a new life as a children's ride on a fairground roundabout, speeding round and round for ever.

A bitter wind got up that night, scouring across the cliffs and cutting into us. In the dark we hunted for large rocks to hold down the tent, to stop it blowing away. They were miserable hours, perhaps the lowest point of the Marco Polo Route Project, certainly up to that point. Chilled to the bone we crowded close to keep warm and ate handfuls of cold rice, bought earlier that morning in a '*battered caravanserai*'.

As soon as the dawn came up we were back on the road; but there was a new problem. None of us had ridden a motorbike without the support of a sidecar, and on the loose road surface it was a tricky deal. Stan was admirable and mastered the technique in fairly short order; skidding and falling off the bike a mere dozen times that first morning. I didn't like it very much – I was on the pillion – but I managed to learn a technique myself: how to roll over backwards as the bike slid away from the vertical, and to keep my legs from being crushed by the bike as it went over in the dust. Stan persisted. 'We've got to press on,' he would say at each fall, 'we've got to press on.' It would have been hell if either of us had broken a leg out there, but

Stan was just the chap to have in the trenches with you. He would always have always been the first over the top with his swagger-stick and whistle, impervious to bullets, and the bulk of his body would have protected whoever was right behind him, and that of course would have been me.

* * *

In the central part of Armenia stands an exceedingly large and high mountain, upon which it is said, the ark of Noah rested, and for this reason it is termed the mountain of the ark. The circuit of its base cannot be compassed in less than two days. The ascent is impracticable on account of the snow towards the summit, which never melts. In the lower region, however, near the plain, the melting of the snow fertilizes the ground and occasions such an abundant vegetation, that all the cattle which collect there in summer from the neighbouring country, meet with a never-failing supply.

We came to those pastures below Mount Ararat that day and sat among the biblical black tents of a tribe of Kurdish nomads; a scene unchanged since Noah's time. We had stepped into the Old Testament and we were well met. We made billycans of tea on our petrol stove and the nomads provided us with warm milk and bread and grapes. The men of the tribe sat with us, colourful and handsome in velvet waistcoats that glittered with intricate designs of golden embroidery. Their magnificent horses roamed free, without hobbles or halters. The children stared at us, and the handsome women – they wore no veils – were tall and stately in bright robes of red, orange, purple and yellow: silks and shawls flowed from their shoulders, and their riches were shown in the beads and headdresses of heavy silver they wore, and which glinted in the sun.

Into Persia: Tabriz

Marco described Tabriz as being *'surrounded by delightful orchards producing the finest fruits'*, but the Marco Polo Route Project could find nothing of that sort, or anything that looked remotely like it. All we could discover was dust and dirt, and silent villages with high adobe walls on either side of the tracks we followed; not a person to be seen.

Not far beyond Tabriz the silencer fell off one of the bikes and Tim and Stan set about patching it up and bolting it back on. There was nothing much I could do and so I left them to their work and began to explore the village we had just entered. I continued a little way along the road, and then turned right into a narrow track that was no wider than an alley. Again, there were high mud walls on either side.

I had not gone far before I came to a place where a wall had fallen, spilling out its mud bricks and leaving a gap large enough to pass through. I stepped over the bricks and was astonished to find myself in a garden, an orchard in fact, where a stream ran, making a sound that was the next best thing to drinking. Two young men lay beneath an apricot tree that was heavy with fruit; the grass was, after the bleak colours of the world beyond the wall, brilliant.

The two men should have been dumbfounded by the sight of a European, dressed in boots and dust-stained Barbour jacket, dropping from the sky into their painting of a garden, but not a bit of it. It might have happened every day. I was welcomed with warmth, and invited to join their feast, food that was traditional in that part of the world: yoghurt and small cucumbers, delicate and refreshing, and unleavened bread dipped into a honeyed syrup.

Somehow, without sharing a language, we entered into a long conversation. Once again my moral fibre took a battering and I stretched out and eased my limbs without a thought for my companions as they slaved over a hot exhaust system. Eventually, after an hour or so, they tracked me down, luxuriating in Paradise and still eating.

I didn't deserve it but they were forgiving. After all, I had discovered the orchards and gardens for which Tabriz had been famous in Marco's day, which fact seemed to prove that he was more likely to have journeyed by the route we were following than by any of the others cited and discussed by various learned commentators. We were pleased with ourselves. We had made yet another discovery when we could so easily have driven by, seeing nothing beyond the high mud walls. It deserved a celebration and so we lingered long in the shade of the garden and raised a glass of the coolest Tabriz water to Marco. Once again he had proved himself right.

But the day had not finished with me, and I went from a 'spot of time' to a brush with death. Stan and Tim had gone ahead on the solo bike to find a refuge for the night. I came behind on the stores' bike. We had been struggling for some hours through a range of mountains, grinding and climbing through the hairpins of the Tehran road which lay inches thick in white dust. I was covered in the stuff, looking more like a ghost than anything else. At last the road escaped from the hills and ran straight before me, on a high embankment, descending into a vast salt plain. I increased my speed. I wanted to catch up with the others who were no doubt lying back in some caravanserai, getting their revenge for the 'orchard incident', sipping glass after glass of tea, and stuffing their faces with fresh eggs and rice, one of our favourite meals.

Halfway down the embankment, with the salt plain still some hundred yards or so below me on either side, I lost control of the bike. I didn't know it then, but one of the front forks had sheared in half and there was no way now that I could steer. All I could do was to go down through the gears and brake very gently. So down I went, losing speed. Right behind me, pushing me close and half-hidden in its own vast cloud of dust, was an eight wheeler with its trailer swaying behind. The driver, seriously demented, crazed by the endless kilometres he drove, kept his hand on the horn just in case I didn't know he was there. I made no hand signals to him, friendly or otherwise; I was hanging on to the useless handlebars for dear life.

At last the embankment came level with the plain, and the bike came to rest, just off the road. The pursuing lorry raced on, still honking, but now in derision, with as many vulgar hand-signals coming from its driver and passengers as a man could wish for. Its cloud of dust settled over me, my teeth were coated in grit, but I was grateful – I had survived. I got off the bike and reached for a cigarette. It was some while before I managed to light it. My hands shook and the matches broke against the box.

The Valley of the Assassins and the Old Man of the Mountains

The following account of this chief, Marco Polo testifies to having heard from sundry persons. His religion was that of Mahomet. In a beautiful valley enclosed between two lofty mountains, he had formed a luxurious garden, stored with every delicious fruit and every fragrant shrub that could be procured. Palaces of various sizes and forms were erected in different parts of the grounds, ornamented with works in gold, with paintings, and with furniture of rich silks. By means of small conduits contrived in these buildings, streams of wine, milk, honey, and some of pure water, were seen to flow in every direction. The inhabitants of these palaces were elegant and beautiful damsels, accomplished in the arts of singing, playing upon all sorts of musical instruments, dancing, and especially those of dalliance and amorous allurement. Clothed in rich dresses they were seen continually sporting and amusing themselves in the garden and pavilions, their female guardians being confined within doors and never suffered to appear. The object which the chief had in view in forming a garden of this fascinating

*kind was this: that Mahomet having
promised to those who should obey his will
the enjoyments of Paradise, where every
species of sensual gratification would be
found, in the society of beautiful nymphs, he
was desirous of its being understood by his
followers that he also was a prophet and the
compeer of Mahomet, and had the power of
admitting to Paradise such as he should
choose to favour. In order that none without
his licence might find their way into this
delicious valley, he caused a strong and
inexpugnable castle to be erected at the
opening of it, through which the entry was
by a secret passage. At his court, likewise,
this chief entertained a number of youths,
from the age of twelve and twenty years,
selected from the inhabitants of the
surrounding mountains, who showed a
disposition for martial exercises, and
appeared to possess the quality of daring
courage. To them he was in the daily practice
of discoursing on the subject of the paradise
announced by the prophet, and of his own
power of granting admission; and at certain
times he caused opium to be administered to
ten or a dozen of the youths; and when half
dead with sleep he had them conveyed to the
several apartments of the palaces in the
garden. Upon awakening from the state of
lethargy, their senses were struck with all the
delightful objects that have been described
and each perceived himself surrounded by
lovely damsels, singing, playing, and
attracting his regards by the most fascinating
caresses, serving him also with delicate
viands and exquisite wines; until intoxicated
with excess of enjoyment amidst actual*

*rivulets of milk and wine, he believed himself
assuredly in Paradise, and felt an
unwillingness to relinquish its delights.*

*When four or five days had thus been
passed, they were thrown once more into a
state of somnolency, and carried out of the
garden. Upon their being introduced to his
presence, and questioned by him as to where
they had been, their answer was, "In Paradise,
through the favour of your highness": and
then before the whole court, who listened to
them with eager curiosity and astonishment,
they gave a circumstantial account of the
scenes to which they had been witnesses. The
chief thereupon addressing them, said: "We
have the assurances of our prophet that he
who defends his lord shall inherit Paradise,
and if you show yourselves devoted to the
obedience of my orders, that happy lot awaits
you." Animated to enthusiasm by words of
this nature, all deemed themselves happy to
receive the commands of their master, and
were forward to die in his service. The
consequences of this system was, that when
any of the neighbouring princes, or others,
gave umbrage to this chief, they were put to
death by these his disciplined assassins; none
of whom felt terror at the risk of losing their
own lives, which they held in little estimation,
provided they could execute the master's will.
On this account his tyranny became the
subject of dread in all the surrounding
countries.*

* * *

It wasn't long before Tim and Stan returned to find me sitting
by the damaged motor bike. We waited for the next Tehran-

bound lorry to appear, and with the help of the driver and about a dozen passengers we managed to get the broken bike and the stores' sidecar up on top of the lorry's high cargo, pulling with ropes from above, and pushing with hands and arms from below. It was a desperate struggle.

We decided that Stan would go straight on to Tehran, where we had back-up and a place to stay. There he could telephone London for replacement parts for the broken bike, and plan the next part of the journey. Once he had gone Tim and I searched for a caravanserai – chay-khaneh being the modern name – at last finding one, at dusk, near the town of Kazvin. Chay-khanehs were the only hostelries on the road to the east; set many miles apart they were '*les cafés routiers*' of Turkey and Persia. They were rough and ready places but we came to appreciate the food and drink they provided, and the social mix they offered. We never knew what we were going to get in the way of sustenance, hospitality or local villain.

Built from mud bricks, and always close to water – a stream or a well – it was at the chay-khanehs that the lorry-drivers and their passengers bivouacked, sleeping on the ground, as we did, for our tent had long since been disposed of, and we slept under the stars more often than not.

The design of these buildings was simple. At the front was a room or two for travellers to eat and sleep in, unfurnished save for carpets on the floor, as distinct from on the wall. At the rear was the kitchen and, though by now we had a few words of Persian – bread, water, eggs, meat, good day, thank you – we generally went into the back, stood by the stove and pointed to what we wanted. The staple beverage was tea and we drank gallons of it.

Tim and I studied the maps that night and, given that we were certain to be delayed in Tehran for at least a few days, we decided to visit the Valley of the Assassins – the Alimut, the locals called it (a contraction of *Mulihadet-ul-Maut,* meaning Heretics of Death.) It was pretty certain that Marco had not visited the valley, but his account of the Old Man of The Mountains, Hassan Sabbah, is so evocative, romantic even, that the idea was irresistible. Even if that had not been the case the name would have been enough to entice us – it has such a ring to it – The Valley of the Assassins!

The Alimut was not, according to the travellers in the chay-khaneh, far from the main Tehran road. Good news, we thought. We didn't have much money on us, having given most of it to Stan, but that didn't matter; we'd be there and back in an afternoon. We left the following morning and ran into difficulties immediately. There was a confusion of mountains in the direction we needed to go, the Elburz Range, and dirt tracks every hundred yards or so led towards them. It was impossible to know, and stupid to guess, which was the correct route; there were no signposts, and passers-by had no idea what led where. For hours we rode back and forth along the Tehran highway until, in another chay-khaneh, we found a nonchalant lorry-driver who had no doubt in his mind which was the correct route. We took his advice; it was the best bet we had.

The track narrowed as we went forward, Tim driving solo for the first time. The bike was unwieldy with our over-loaded camel bags on the back, making it so unstable that it reared up like a frightened horse at every opportunity. We came off a great deal, especially when the track became little more than a path for mules. We were past masters at rolling off the bike but, as we climbed higher into the mountains, we also had to make sure that we rolled away from the precipices that appeared from time to time on either side of us. These were real grown-up precipices: no trees or shrubs to hang on to, and sheer enough to make sure that once over the edge there was no coming back. So much for our afternoon jaunt.

There was desolation all around us and silence, apart from the labouring of the bike's engine. We wobbled on, up and up, the track twisting this way and that; but beyond every ridge we discovered another, and never the descent we longed for – the road that would lead us down to the valley. Before long a cold clamminess of cloud settled upon us and we were cut off from the world entirely, alone in a secret and dangerous place, the shale beneath the wheels bright and treacherous with moisture, the precipices invisible, but nonetheless menacing for that.

Well into the afternoon we emerged from the cloud and the

track began to descend. Now we could see, and what we saw was beyond our words. We dismounted to stare: *'stout Cortez...silent upon a peak in Darien'*. Below us and shining in the Persian sunlight lay a river gorge, the river itself intermittently visible as it meandered deep down, glittering silver. On the far side of the river rose a sharp escarpment, as vertical as a castle wall though a thousand times higher, the colours of it magnificent: crimson, verdigris, a dark purple that was almost black and copper blue. And beyond the escarpment was more cloud, lying like golden lakes over the vast depression of the Valley of the Assassins, cloud from which seeped the rains that made the valley green and gorgeous, and simple for the Old Man of the Mountain to transform into Paradise.

We remounted and went on. The track dropped rapidly to the river until at last we were level with it. We were on the edge of a wide bank of rich grass and further along, a caravanserai, the most wonderful I was ever to see: no dust, no sand. It was surrounded by pasture and shaded by a huge tree; it was in fact that quatrain from Omar Khayyam:

> *Here with a loaf of bread, beneath the bough,*
> *A flask of wine, a book of verse, and thou*
> *Beside me singing in the wilderness, and*
> *Wilderness is Paradise, enow.*

There were mules too, maybe a dozen of them, grazing, and on the bank, under the branches of the tree, reclined the muleteers; not small men, but strong and tall. They welcomed us with a self-confident ease and smiled at the way we looked I suppose, dishevelled and woebegone. We ate and drank and refreshed ourselves. I could have stayed there for a month; but we didn't. We asked the way to The Eagle's Nest, the castle of the Old Man of The Mountain. They shook their heads at us, sadly. Our bike was of no use to us now, but we could leave it there, the only way into the valley was through the gorge that stood opposite to us, where a tributary flowed into the main river. It was deep and fast. We would need mules. They clicked their teeth, surprised that we had brought no equipment with us

– tents, sleeping bags, food. We shrugged as if we were young gods who lived on ambrosia plucked from the sky – young gods with hardly any money on them. We would walk.

They smiled again. 'Yes, of course.'

The gorge was narrow, forcing the river to hasten through it. It looked dangerous, but we convinced ourselves that where a mule could go, so could we. We stepped into the main river and crossed it easily enough, though as we approached the mouth of the tributary the thrust of the current became stronger, and we were hard put to it to keep our footing. The waters surged around us, waist high. At one point I was lifted off my feet and, pirouetting like a ballet dancer, holding the bag of cameras above my head, I was borne back a good ten yards. But we were determined and waded on, swept this way and that, our world reduced to that stretch of white water and those coloured cliffs. And then we were through and the walls of the gorge fell away and we were into a valley so wide and long that the end of it was not visible, nor was there any sign of the castle of Hassan Sabbah.

The valley was another country. It was a green Paradise, with shallow ditches irrigating a criss-cross of rice paddies; stands of willow and clumps of rushes completed the landscape, though there was not a house to be seen, nor was there an obvious trail to follow. Tim and I were in a sorry state. We were exhausted and the mud underfoot sucked at our boots. The previous three or four days had been hard and we had not rested properly since Istanbul. Our spirits drooped.

At that point we came across a muleteer, with three mules, who was returning to the gorge without passengers or burden. We sat on the ground and negotiated a fee for him to take us to the castle of Hassan Sabbah at the end of the valley. The muleteer was short of work and we agreed on three tuman each for the trip. It was a bargain, heaven sent; Tim and I could not have walked much further, and we still had to find somewhere to spend the night.

We rode for some time and our morale rose with every minute. '*Mike was regaining his normal high spirits,*' says Tim's book, '*the comparison between the Assassins' Valley and the*

more spectacular Hollywood westerns was too much for him,
and soon the sierras rang with the time-worn film phrases about
"a place big enough for a man to breathe in, fit to build schools,
churches and bring up families."'

We journeyed on and the clouds settled on the valley and
brought darkness with them. The damps of the night settled too
and it would have been dismal, as well as injurious to our
health, had we been obliged to spend the night in the open. At
last the muleteer, as surly as any of his animals, and demanding
more money every step of the way, led us over to the valley wall
and up to a small hamlet.

There was not one light in the narrow alleys of the village
when we arrived, and we went from door to door, searching for
a household that would give us shelter. At last we were
accepted in one of the houses, the mules went to a stable and we
were shown into a crowded room, warm from the number of
people in it. They made a space for us on the floor, squeezing
up tightly together; food was prepared, and two hurricane
lamps cast a yellow light over the men that stared at us, a frieze
of faces from a holy painting. We were gently questioned.

What was our destination. 'Tehran?'

'No, China.'

'China, eh? China,' they said to each other. Heads nodded
sagely. China was certainly further off than Tehran.

The talk went on but our eyes were heavy, our muscles
aching. It would be good to sleep. A couple of very old blankets
were passed to us and Tim and I, with twenty or so others,
stretched out on the dirt floor. Then the lamps were
extinguished. I yearned for sleep, that dirt floor looked as soft
as a mattress, but sleep was hard to come by. Bed bugs, fleas,
lice and mosquitoes, snores and many other noises saw to that.
I itched and scratched and turned and burned in the dark, and
where before I had longed for the night now I longed for the
day.

Yet in the morning we had other troubles. We paid our hosts
what they demanded of us, but found that we had no money
left to pay the surly muleteer who for his part no longer wanted
anything to do with us. Things turned nasty and the muleteer

snatched one of my cameras from me. How could Europeans be without funds? There was a scuffle and I snatched the camera back. It wasn't looking good for the Marco Polo Route Project, surrounded as we were by dozens of angry villagers, all talking at once in a language we could not understand. Suddenly the words 'Valley of the Assassins' took on a threatening resonance; the romance had drained from our adventure. Would Stan ever find our bodies?

Fortunately, there was a doctor in the village, on his monthly visit from the capital, and he spoke excellent English. He was sent for and at last we could explain why we had no money with us but, we promised, once in Tehran we would send whatever was owed to the muleteer. The muleteer was hard to convince, his countenance as dark as a sudden squall, but at last he accepted the situation and we agreed to post the money to the doctor's address, and he, in turn, would deliver it to the muleteer on his next visit to the valley, together with a bonus. Now we were all friends. There was a drinking of tea all round, an endless shaking of hands, and the sun rose above the horizon in the muleteer's face.

It might have been wise to have abandoned our visit to the Alimut there and then, but we had come so far and suffered so much that we both felt it would have been cowardly to retreat. We determined to go on. The villagers provided us with enough food for the day, and also a guide to show us the best route to the end of the valley. We still had some way to go but towards dusk – we had set out late – we came, at long last, to the huge rock, rearing high and sheer-sided, on which had stood the stronghold of Hassan Sabbah. There was nothing left of it save a few stumps of stone, but it was easy to see why it had taken the Mongols four years to capture it.

In the village below the rock we found an American adventurer, dressed in a kind of safari suit, who had come over the mountains with half a dozen mules, a guide and an armed interpreter. 'There are still wolves and bandits in these mountains,' he told us. His words were stern but we could see the puzzlement on his face as he looked behind us, his eyes searching for our escort and equipment. It was difficult for Tim and me to resist the obvious temptation – so we didn't: 'Oh, we just walked up here,' we said, resorting to that understatement for which the English are supposed to be renowned, 'we're glad we came, though.'

The Village of the Magi

On the way out of the Valley, climbing high into the cloudy ridges, and on the same treacherous track that had brought us down to the Alimut, we came off the bike once too often. I escaped without injury but Tim's right foot was caught and crushed beneath the full weight of the bike. I managed to lift the machine off him in one huge adrenalin heave but he was in great pain. I dumped the bike with the owner of a small farm that I found down a side track, and our luck improved when a party of prospectors came by in a jeep. They took us to Tehran and Tim was installed in hospital, his foot X-rayed and then encased in plaster. When I next saw him he was on crutches: no more motorbike for him.

Marco's journey had taken him to the port of Bandar Abbas on the Persian Gulf, where he had hoped to continue his journey by ship but, deciding that the craft on offer were not seaworthy, he had returned up country and continued overland into northern Afghanistan by way of Meshed and Herat. Tim decided to follow the same route, crutches and all, by bus and lorry, doing his research as he went. Stan and I were to follow the road south, doubling up on one motorbike, down to Kerman, crossing north-western Pakistan and into Afghanistan via Quetta, and then on to Kabul where the three of us would rendezvous at some future and unspecified date. It was bound to work out, wasn't it? Probably. Whoever got to Kabul first would spend their time and energies in attempting to obtain visas for China and permission to travel into the Wakhan Corridor, a particularly sensitive area to the east of northern Afghanistan. On our way Stan and I were to visit the village of Aveh, situated in a lost corner of the Great Salt Steppe, somewhere south of Tehran – a village that according to Marco had been the home of one of the Three Wise Men, and also the starting point of their journey to Bethlehem:

> *In Persia there is a city which is called Saveh, from whence were the three magi who came to adore Christ in Bethlehem; and the three are buried in that city in a fair sepulchre, and they are all three entire with their beards and hair. One was called Baldasar, the second Gaspar, and the third Melcior. Marco inquired often in that city concerning the three magi and nobody could tell him anything about them, except that the three magi were buried there in ancient times. After three days' journey you come to a castle which is called Kala Atishparastan, which means castle of the fire-worshippers; and it is true that the inhabitants of that castle worship fire, and this is given as the reason. The men of that castle say that anciently three kings of that country went to adore a certain king who was newly born, and carried with them three offerings, namely, gold, frankincense, and myrrh: gold, that they might know if he were God; and myrrh, that they might know if he were a mortal man. When these magi were presented to Christ, the youngest of the three adored him first, and it appeared to him that Christ was of his stature and age. The middle one came next, and then the eldest, and to each he seemed to be of their own stature and age.*
>
> *Having compared their observations together, they agreed to go all to worship at once, and then he appeared to them all of his true age. When they went away, the infant gave them a closed box, which they carried with them for several days, and then*

becoming curious to see what he had given
them, they opened the box and found in it a
stone, which was intended for a sign that they
should remain as firm as a stone, in the faith
they had received from him.

When, however, they saw the stone, they
marvelled, and thinking themselves deluded,
they threw the stone in a certain pit, and
instantly fire burst forth in the pit. When they
saw this, they repented bitterly of what they
had done, and taking some of the fire with
them they carried it home. And having placed
it in one of their churches, they keep it
continually burning, and adore that fire as a
god and make all their sacrifices with it; and
if it happen to be extinguished, they go for
more of the original fire in the pit where they
threw the stone, which is never extinguished,
and they take of none other fire...let me tell
you finally that one of the three Magi came
from Saveh, one from Aveh, and one from
Kala Atishparastan.

Stan and I headed south towards the holy city of Qum. At
Baquilabad we intended to bear west, into a featureless desert.
We had no sidecar now and no luxuries like a change of clothes
or iron rations: just sleeping bags, a box of tools, motor oil,
jerrycans of water and petrol, cameras, film stock and medical
supplies, mainly salts and pills for dysentery and diarrhoea.
Nevertheless we were loaded down with three enormous camel
bags, attached to the bike just behind the pillion passenger, one
each side and one at the rear. So heavy was our load that we
had paid an ingenious Tehran mechanic to design and install
extra metal supports for the carrier. It was a wise precaution.

At Baquilabad, in a caravanserai, we left as much of the
luggage as we could and prepared for a dash into the desert,
and a quick return. I should have learnt my lesson in the Valley
of the Assassins, but I hadn't. Our excursion was to take longer

than we thought.

The surface of the desert was a kind of salty crust and we made good time. Stan had taken to motorbikes like a natural and enjoyed driving them, leaning forward like a cartoon character – Tintin I thought – a smile of pleasure fixed to his face but the small tracks we followed, such as they were, gave no indication of where they led. Once more there were no signposts to be seen, and no inhabitants to question. The desert was empty to the horizon, except, eventually, for a dust-devil, moving away from us, like a plume of smoke, small in the distance. So for want of the Magi's star, and with Marco's story of the burning well of the Zoroastrians in our minds, we followed it, and of course it led us directly to Aveh. But there was no great town here, no kingly residence, just an adobe village like thousands of others. In the main square, around the well, the women were drawing water and washing their linen. There was a pile of water melons in the shade of a wall, and storks had made clumsy, unkempt nests on the roof-tops. The children straggled in groups, staring at us with wide and beautiful eyes, saying nothing, surprised into silence.

It was not long before we were invited into the headman's house and refreshed with tea and melons. Villagers crowded in to gaze and listen to us talk and find out where we had come from. We made long and involved attempts to ask about the Magi but it was difficult for us to make them understand what we were after; our Persian was still very small. We were not even sure they knew the biblical story anyway; in all probability we had made our journey for nothing.

We slept on the roof of the headman's house, and were provided with cushions and carpets. In the morning our host walked us around the village, and I took photos. At the end of our stroll, on the edge of the village, he showed us a pentagonal mound, with a flat top, the only thing in the village that was out of the ordinary: 'Zartusti, Zartusti,' he said, pointing, and at last we understood that he was pointing at the remains of a Zoroastrian temple. Stan and I were content. Aveh might well have been the site of the pit where the fire of Zoroastrianism had begun: a religion dating back to Marco's time, and beyond, a religion older than Islam. Our friend Marco was right again; the three places he mentions obviously have a connection with fire-worship and – who knows – with the Magi themselves.

Satisfied with the result of our research, if it could be called that, Stan and I said our farewells to the villagers and went to leave. But we were in trouble again. Guarding our bike when we returned to it were the four armed soldiers of the Aveh police force. The sergeant had seen me filming and taking stills and, though we didn't know it, we were in a military zone without written permission.

'Show me your passports.'

Stan and I looked very stupid indeed. In our haste we had left all our travel documents – passports, visas, and letters from various embassies – with our luggage at the caravanserai on the main road, half a day's drive away.

We were taken into custody, and the sergeant became very irate. We were spies. He would make a report, which would take hours to write, and it would then have to go to his superior officer, some forty miles distant. Meanwhile we would be locked up in the police station and we would wait until due process had occurred. In our cell Stan looked at me in despair. This could take days if not weeks.

After a while Stan managed to convince our captor that it would be a good idea if he, Stan, delivered the report on the motorbike, thereby speeding up the process of the law. I would remain behind as surety of Stan's return – a hostage. Stan grinned. He had an idea.

We had been let out of the cell during these negotiations, and Stan's plan was that I should leap on the pillion as he set off and we would make a dash for freedom. I was not too keen on this stratagem, pointing out that our four soldiers were all armed, and escaping prisoners, in all the films I'd seen, were likely to be shot, quite legally, and sitting on the pillion I was the one who would be in the direct line of fire. In any event the sergeant wasn't daft. He was sending one of his soldiers with Stan to make sure that he went to the right village, and also that he returned.

He had assumed, perhaps correctly, that Stan didn't hold me

in enough esteem to be sure of coming back to see that I was released. The chosen soldier, his face rigid with fear, got astride the bike and Stan let out the clutch and roared away in a cloud of dust. I settled down to wait. This could take a long time but, since setting out to follow Marco, I had learnt the deep secret of the east – don't be in a hurry and don't get impatient. But how I longed for a book.

Now that Stan and the bike had disappeared from the village there was nowhere I could go. I wouldn't get far in the desert on my own so I was released from the lock-up and allowed the freedom of the pleasant little courtyard that lay at the centre of the police station. I was fed and watered: bread, cucumber and yoghurt appeared, brought by my friends of the previous evening, and gradually the sergeant's heart melted and the children of the village were allowed in to visit me. I taught them to play 'Fivestones', the game I had played as a child in the streets of south London. It was a huge success. I pulled faces and I sang silly songs. I was a hit. Things got better. I was allowed to wander the village, an armed guard by my side, but we were soon on excellent terms and the village children skipped along with us. My imprisonment was a delight.

An hour or two later that afternoon the soldier who had set off with Stan, reappeared but on foot. I couldn't understand what was said but I guessed that Stan had turned the bike over for the umpteenth time and the soldier had decided that he'd rather walk than ride. Where Stan had gone I couldn't fathom. I spent a pleasant night in jail, once again fed by the villagers and, just as I was waking and thinking about breakfast, Stan drove into the village: dusty, tired and with a huge grin of triumph stuck on his face.

Before the sergeant could get angry again Stan produced our passports, our visas and some very impressive looking letters which gave us permission to do almost anything and go almost anywhere. I don't know if the sergeant could read them or understand them but the stamps and seals must have convinced him of our *bona fides* because we were suddenly free. A small feast was prepared and a thousand and one cups of tea were made and consumed. We shook hands all round, everyone smiled. We mounted the bike and headed out into the desert, leaving for ever the village of the Three Wise Men.

I don't know how many millions of tourists have been to Bethlehem, the destination of the Magi, but it's certain that none of them has enjoyed tea and yoghurt in the jail at Aveh, where the Magi set out from – but I know which of the two places I prefer.

Afghanistan

We headed south. We saw the exquisite mosque in Isfahan, found silk looms in Yazd, just as Marco had said, and wandered the bazaar at Kerman. The summer heat was mortal and we went south-east into the burning heart of it, into a frightening emptiness somewhere between the Dasht e Lut and the Baluchistan desert, a 'sun-smashed' upturned cauldron of hell that smelt and tasted of a bitter iron. We drove as fast as we could, obliged to keep the bike up to speed lest the petrol vaporize in the engine – 'Come on, Stan, we can do it, only a thousand miles to Kabul!'

Our last stop in Persia was at the outpost of Zahidan, a square-built fort where ragged conscripts examined our exit visas. We bivouacked out on the plain by the side of the road to Pakistan, revelling in the fresh chill of the night. Stan was soon asleep, the sleep of the innocent but, even after the long hours of the day, I remained awake, a strong desire for solitude invading me. Tim, Stan and I had been living in close company for many weeks; eating together, sleeping together, washing together. Now I wanted a taste of loneliness, above all I wanted it in that wild and boundless terrain.

I slipped out of my sleeping bag and wandered into the vastness for half a mile, maybe further. I stopped when I thought I would and lay on my back, staring into the dark, letting the emptiness work on me. It was frightening, it dissolved my flesh and made it nothing, liberating my spirit. And I saw into the minds of those lovers of the desert who have described the endless beauty to be found in those spaces. The upturned bitter cauldron of iron became a nomad's tent of soft shining cloth: and the stars had come down to earth to be touched, and had given the 'night a thousand eyes'. Suddenly, *'To see a World in a Grain of Sand And a Heaven in a Wild Flower, Hold Infinity in the palm of your hand, And Eternity in an hour'* – was a simple exercise.

'Why,' I said, stretching out on the rocky ground and embracing the sky, 'it's a piece of cake.'

*   *   *

At dawn we were into Pakistan and once over the border the old British Raj gave us a tarmac road, a small village, and a military man sitting in an office, straight as starch. He had regimental tags on his shoulder straps, khaki shorts – perfectly ironed – long socks and boots polished with so much spit that the depths of blackness in them were beyond measure; and on the wall was a notice-board that could have come from Aldershot barracks. It was uncanny and, for an instant or two, made me weak with homesickness. But best of all, further into the village, was a government guest house with proper beds, clean sheets and showers, and a meal cooked and served by an amah and a bearer.

Alas, it was just a brief sight of bliss, for we had no time to linger. The next day we were winding into the hills, towards Quetta, desert all the way, and over another border, into Afghanistan and on to Kandahar. We had done it: hard miles of heat, dust, flies, punctures and dysentery, until finally we came to Kabul, and The Hindu Kush – the roof of the world.

*   *   *

We camped in the grounds of the Turkish Embassy and eventually Tim arrived from Herat in an old and battle-scarred Dakota. It was a joyful reunion. We applied for visas for China; no luck, there was no question of it, nobody travelled across the Western Provinces in those days. And the Afghans weren't helpful, either. There was not even a possibility of visiting the

Wakhan Corridor, that narrow panhandle that sticks out of the north-eastern corner of Afghanistan and runs through to China; there was Russia to the north and Pakistan to the south. Too many borders, too many warlords, and carefree travellers were not wanted. We were undesirables.

Nevertheless Tim determined to spend a week or so trying to change minds in embassies and government departments. During that week Stan and I set out again: north to Charikar, and then west into the Chardeh valley. A whirlwind excursion to the lakes of Band-i-Amir, going by the giant Buddhas at Bamian on the way: two massive statues, the largest 170 feet high, later blown to smithereens by the Taliban. The idea behind our trip to the north was to get some movie footage of the Old Silk Road, a portion of Marco's route that we hadn't seen; an opportunity for us to explore a little more of the mighty Hindu Kush:

> *The mountains are exceedingly lofty, insomuch that it employs a man from morning till night to ascend to the top of them. Between them there are wide plains clothed with grass and with trees, and large streams of the purest water precipitating themselves through the fissures of the rocks. In these streams are trout and many other delicate sorts of fish. On the summits of the mountains the air is so pure and so salubrious, that when those who dwell in the towns, and in the plains and valleys below, find themselves attacked with fevers or other inflammatory complaints, they immediately remove thither and remaining for three or four days in that situation recover their health.*

On our return to Kabul, Stan and I found that our journey with Marco was over. We had no wish to abandon *Il Milione* at this stage – in fact, the three of us had a compelling desire to follow him along the Wakhan and into China, and I for one have always regretted that we didn't; but it was impossible. Tim had tried everything but the embassies had been stone-faced. It was time to leave: we were no longer travellers, but tourists.

There was one problem to overcome, and we did it in the usual spirit of the Marco Polo Route Project. Problems were our meat and drink, and we were, by that time, as tough as old boots and as resilient and devious as Jesuits. There was only one bike for the three of us! Well, never mind, we had the extra luggage supports that had been welded on in Persia; we had courage, élan and humour on our side, and a half-inflated inner tube on the carrier for comfort. Stan drove, Tim came next and de Larrabeiti rode behind. We looked wonderful, a twelve limbed Hindu God with three crash helmet heads. We had left Oxford looking clean and efficient with an excess of equipment. Now we were three bedraggled tramps suddenly on holiday, astride a wreck, our clothes torn and worn. What superfluous baggage we still possessed we threw away. What need had we of baggage? We were hard men; we could live off the land, eat anything and sleep anywhere.

We had three weeks to get to Bombay where a liner with a full cargo of women would be waiting, and we would start by motoring carefree down the Khyber Pass, my duties as expedition photographer finally at an end. In that first settlement in Pakistan, just beyond the border, where the sloping street was crowded with Pathan tribesmen, quiet in dark robes, their faces astonishingly handsome, their black hair bobbed, their brown eyes full of suspicion, their rifles polished and ready, I left my cameras stowed. A German journalist – I had been told the tale in Kabul – had photographed the women of that very village too long and too often some months previously, and a shot had rung out, echoing clear. It had been a good shot; through the lens, through the camera, through the eye, and despite the brain, I suppose, being small, through that too. The tribesmen, crouched motionless and silent on their haunches, had not even bothered to shift their gaze. Anyone of them might have pulled the trigger; after all, they were all excellent marksmen. What was a dead German to them?

Our ruin of a motorbike bore us forward into Pakistan and on to India: Peshawar, Rawalpindi, Lahore, and the Golden Temple at Amritsar – we were joyful, grateful to be alive. Stan drove like a master, bearing us through an adventure, across the top of India, along the Grand Trunk Road: Delhi, Agra and the Taj Mahal, to the holy river at Varanasi, and the smell of burning bodies on the ghats, and at last – Calcutta. And always the road was a moving throng, it teemed with life: women, children, porters, cows, pigs and goats, decorated lorries and brightly painted buses. 'See,' says Kipling, '*the Great Road which is the backbone of all Hind...grain and cotton and timber, fodder, lime and hides...All castes and kinds of men move here. Look. Brahmins and chumars, bankers and tinkers, barbers and bunnias, pilgrims and potters – all the world going and coming...such a river of life as nowhere exists in the world.*'

After a train journey of three days we reached Bombay. We had clothes made there: trousers and shirts, that was all. We still had the motor bike. It was such a mess that it hardly seemed worthwhile taking it home, but we watched with a great deal of reverence, affection even, as it was lifted on board the ship, oil dripping from the gear casing.

There were hundreds of women leaning over the rails as we came aboard, returning immigrants from Australia mainly. They had done a month of a six week voyage and were bored out of their minds. We were lean, tanned, hard-looking young men with a host of travellers' tales to tell, and we hadn't seen a woman close to for more than four months. It is fair to say that we went berserk. We attended all the dances, chose partners, and changed them too, and walked hand in hand along the moonlit decks with Patricia, Rosemary and Daphne. We sat up late drinking and talking – oh! what fine and amazing chaps we were. We had been everywhere and done everything.

During frequent visits to the bar I made the acquaintance of a mad French professor who threw chairs overboard when they stopped serving drinks at one in the morning. He maintained that his mind had been destroyed by two years of trying to teach Australians the literature of his country. Another theory of his was that more women were seduced on board ship as they entered and sailed up the Red Sea than anywhere else in the world. 'Symbolism,' he said, wagging his finger in my face, 'symbolism! Women go crazy in the Red Sea. They'll be all over you, you won't be able to keep them out of your cabin. They'll want you to fill them with children. They'll promise you their father's fortune. I tell you, beware the Red Sea.'

I laughed at him, derided him even, but it was strange – mad as he was, his theory was spot on.

LAVENDER HILL

I liked being a traveller, and later in my life became used to changing places, never mind how abruptly – Vancouver to Mexico; Madagascar to New York; it didn't matter. But returning to South London after Marco Polo was very strange. Disembarking at Marseille, we came from Paris to Victoria and parted company there, the three of us, just like that. One of my three brothers came to pick me up but driving back to Battersea, still dressed in Barbour jacket and boots, and carrying a camel bag, I felt troubled. The magnificent journey was over and I felt lonely, cut off from what I had known for four months on the trail.

I asked my brother to let me out at the east end of Lavender Hill. 'I'll walk the rest,' I said.

'You have to come down to the shop,' he said. 'They're having a few drinks for you.'

I got out of the car, and the first thing I noticed was the house that had been the last port of call on my evening paper-round, at the age of fourteen. I'd done a morning round as well: six o'clock, getting up in the dark. That's when I'd started travelling, street to street; more than the other kids did. I'd been aware even then that Lavender Hill wasn't King's Road, Chelsea. So Battersea was a dump, but at least it was my dump. I'd been lord of the roads then: a second-hand Raleigh bicycle, a different girl to talk to in every street, just like a sailor in every port; pigtails and pink ribbons, pleated skirts, broad-brimmed school hats in navy blue felt, long bloomers the same colour, blouses that bulged, white ankle socks, and striped ties.

The grey light of Lavender Hill was strong about me as I crossed the bottom of Cedars' Road, where a 34 tram had once crashed into Hemmings the bakers. That light knew me, knew my past. My mother had lived in a mews flat there; three kids to bring up, and no help from my father, the 'disappearing Basque'. I knew every paving stone; every shop, every pub; waiting outside for my brothers. "'Ere, Mick, here's a tanner, take this note down to Joan Stucky, Broughton Street, you know, the one with the big Bristols.' Wordsmiths, my brothers, wordsmiths who could deliver a punch, and frequently did.

I hesitated outside The Craven public house, where, in 1917, my grandfather had been given a white feather by some toffee-nosed girl from over the river. She hadn't noticed that his leg had been shot to pieces and his hair was prematurely grey from the three days he'd lain wounded in No Man's Land. Well, the pubs were still pubs, that hadn't changed. Why should they? I'd only been away four months, though it felt years. The same stale beer smell, a solid curtain of it. The windows etched with fern-leaf designs, and wooden doors concealing a yeasty mystery.

A sharp flurry of wind blew a dusty newspaper against my knees. I went to primary school here, off the tram and up that steep alley, Wix's Lane. I hated the dirt and dust when I was young, and the memory of that hate rose in me, new born, as I walked. I felt, as a child, that I had been condemned to a lifetime in those concrete streets where my mother was born, her life an impotent struggle to escape. And perhaps there was no escape for me, either – I was destined to be for ever banished from the world of romance, where the sky was always blue, the breeze a caress and money grew on trees.

I came up the slope of Lavender Hill, where there had once been dozens of market barrows, naphtha flares at night, up past the three rising kerb stones where my grandmother had pushed a woman down and into the road, breaking her ankle, a woman who had been making eyes at her husband, Ned Leary. On past Rush Hill Road where Aunt Norah lived, married to Uncle Harry who was always borrowing a quid off my mother so he could go to Wimbledon Dog Track and lose it. Then to the corner of Stormont Road where the paper shop I worked for had been and where the lovely Julia lived. I used to follow her home from school, cycling, that posh school across the Common, Clapham County: her with her full skirt, her homework in the basket on her handlebars, the ruby mouth, the perfect teeth.

And then her house came on my paper-round. *The Star,* every evening; *The Express* every morning. We talked, walked on Clapham Common. And one winter's night, in the freezing cold, I held her close in the front garden of a house in Fontarabia Road, and kissed those sweet lips and caressed her small breasts, resilient and yielding, ice and fire mixed, her thighs as slippery as the flesh of fish. And then I walked home because my bike had a puncture, but it was only six streets to my street – Altenburg Gardens – my patch, and nobody ever asked where I'd been. And the grey light kept silent even though it had crept like fog into every secret room I'd ever kissed a girl in. Maureen Pringle, Margaret Walsh and Sheila Moore.

I pushed on, past Sugden Road – Auntie Bec and Uncle Frank and cousin Terry at number 19. Frank drove a van for the *Evening Standard.* Terry was a waiter at the Trocadero. Past Belasco's, my mother's favourite removals' firm for her many changes of address: moonlight flits sometimes, only just ahead of the bailiffs or the landlord.

As a 77 bus passed I leapt on to the platform, just to travel one stop, skipping off at the traffic lights, to stare down the beetling hill of Latchmere Road which leads to the Public Wash-house. Every Saturday I went – we had no bath at home – again on my bike. Buy a slab of soap, and plunge into one of those deep Victorian tubs with the lions' feet, luxuriating as long as possible in clouds of steam. There were wooden slats on the floor and grey scum rode on the surface of the water, cracking when I put my knee up through it. Grey again; that colour pervaded the whole of life then, but I can ignore it now. I have travelled further than the streets of my paper rounds since and seen the blue sky.

Sheila Moore. My brother had a greengrocer's shop in Battersea Park Road for a while, and sometimes I'd go with him to Covent Garden, at three in the morning, to help him load. I could shift a hundredweight of spuds at age fifteen. On Saturdays we drove an old Commer lorry up and down the streets of Lavender Hill, and the housewives and their daughters came running from their houses at the sound of our klaxon, to buy bright vegetables and fruit; greens, yellows and reds. How summery it seemed. Sheila Moore. Eighteen to my fifteen. Short blond hair, a triangle of a face, and a brilliant blue jumper; another blue sky to touch. And inside that jumper – shifting hillsides of dreams, mountains of pleasure.

She took to hanging round my brother's yard, waiting for me to finish work. It was snowing I remember, not white snow, but the grey snow of Battersea. So in the grey snow Sheila took me to the first field on Clapham Common, behind the silent air-raid shelters that only a few years before had been alive every night with beer and parties, sex and laughter. Now it was my turn. She raised the blue jumper and placed my hand in paradise. She seemed so much older than me – a courtesan from ancient Alexandria, and all was warm and we melted the snow for a radius of five hundred yards, and flowers sprang out of the winter's earth. I'll always remember you, Sheila Moore.

In a way Clapham Common informed our lives; a secret meadow where we could have sex at night, a promenade for walks on Sundays, a bandstand, girls showing their bloomers at netball, old men playing chess on collapsible tables, twenty-two yards for cricket and a football field, piled coats for goalposts. And, as if built in the wrong part of London, there were huge mansions along North Side. I hated those mansions, and envied them. Adults, rarely in my family, sometimes explained that envy was an unproductive emotion and should be avoided, and yet it was the basis of everything I ever did or ever thought. I wanted that mansion, that girl, that knowledge, that wisdom. I was in love with everything, feeling and fact, that I did not possess. I was a gluttonous and underhand lover too, planning and scheming to satisfy my desires, though at the beginning, none of my schemes worked. I had nothing and, worst of all, I knew I had nothing.

But I was a traveller. The other kids stuck in their own streets but I went on voyages delivering papers. I knew multitudes, I knew those mansions with their gravel drives and their châtelaines in fur coats, driving Humber Super Snipes as big as hearses. And through my pores I soaked up the determination that lived on the North Side of Clapham Common, and I knew what it was – it was the determination of the inhabitants of those grand houses not to deny themselves a single one of life's pleasures. Nor would I.

I halted at the bottom of Elspeth Road, not far past the Town Hall where I had sung a comic song on stage for St Vincent's annual charity show, and where my brother Ted had beaten up a bloke who had tried to steal his girl. The old fish and chip shop was still there, and I stepped through an unchanged door and bought myself a bag of Proustian chips soaked in vinegar. The smell caught me by the throat, no madeleines or lilac for me, and carried me back to certain Sunday afternoons – vinegar to mint sauce. Brothers and uncles and cousins back from the pub; leg of lamb and two veg, all provided and cooked by my mother and rapidly consumed, and then the endless games of cards: Nap, Rummy, Poker, Whist, and one I never mastered called Tu'penny-ha'penny.

At tea time a barrow would rumble down the street with a man shouting something that sounded like 'Kidnee-wayeer.' What it meant was me sent down to the dull desert of a Sunday afternoon to buy cockles, mussels, winkles and whelks. My brothers, still wordsmiths, had a generic name they'd invented – ''Ere, go an' get us some wockles, Mick.' And go I did.

And bottles of sable Guinness would appear from beneath the table. I can remember the grace of the men leaning forward, the grins as if they were smuggling secrets, and the beer fizzing and foaming as the bottle-openers were levered against the metal capsules. And my mother, thin and tired, but smiling and laughing at the vulgarities that were bandied about through the long, lazy forever of the afternoon. 'That Joan Stucky, she's got a pair, ain't she Ralph?' A smirk, the knowing wink, the grown-ups with their mysteries. 'I ain't telling, but she 'as, all right...poke yer bleedin' eyes out...suffocate yer, they could.'

On the other corner of Latchmere Road, away from the fish

and chip shop lies the South-Western Magistrates' Court, where my grandmother, Rebecca, was summonsed to appear on the second of May, 1928, for keeping a betting house (fined thirty shillings). Her husband had died a couple of years previously, the wounds in his leg turning gangrenous and killing him at last. Influenza, said the doctor, so there was no army pension, and Rebecca was left with ten children to bring up. And, also at the top of the Latchmere, my uncle Dennis ran round the corner to catch the eternal 77 bus one day and found himself in the middle of an affray. He was struck on the head by a legally wielded truncheon and carted off to the cells (fined five pounds).

On the opposite corner stood a department store once, Bon Marché. My mother took me in there one Saturday, third floor, to buy a new pair of shoes. The old ones weren't worth mending, and the cardboard that we inserted as a temporary sole kept wearing through. A couple of days later a V1 fell on the roof and the bottom of Elspeth Road disappeared, all the way up to number 34 where my grandmother lived. My mother heard about it on the wireless at work; she was a waitress in a pub in Holborn, The Princess Louise. She rushed into the street straight away and jumped on a tram, without taking time to change out of her apron or the mob cap that waitresses were obliged to wear. She often told the story: climbing over a mountain of debris to find her mother knocking out what was left of her front windows with a broom handle.

'Look at the fucking dust,' said Gran, 'just look at the fucking dust...fucking Germans...killed my effin' husband, now they're trying to kill me...'

The evening was coming on as I came level with the bottom of Altenburg Gardens. That was my street, and we lived at number 48, a first floor flat. Twenty years of my life spent there, three to a bedroom more often than not. Daisy Bunce lived opposite: ah! 'the green light at the end of Daisy's dock'. She was wise and experienced beyond her years. Already at sixteen she had made a bee-line for my brother Ralph, then maybe twenty-two. Envy came again, refreshing and simple. I wanted Daisy Bunce. I listened at doors and spied through keyholes. Luckily for me the affair didn't last. Ralph was too good-looking, too busy with life. Then she reeled me in and, for her own amusement, folded me in her knowing embrace. Daisy Bunce was a shop-girl who was free on Wednesday afternoons when her house was empty, and she would lie on her parents' bed like a flitch of bacon, with big brown eyes staring at me, and say, 'Take my clothes off.' And I did, and James Elroy Flecker, the man who wrote about the artist's journey to Samarkand, wrote me a poem for south of the river:

> Evening falls on the smoky walls,
>   And the railings drip with rain,
> And I will cross the old river
>   To see my girl again.
>
> The great and solemn-gliding tram,
>   Love's still-mysterious car,
> Has many a light of gold and white,
>   And a single dark red star.
>
> I know a garden in a street
>   Which no one ever knew;
> I know a rose beyond the Thames,
>   Where flowers are pale and few.

I passed Altenburg Gardens and went to the top of the slope that leads down to Clapham Junction. I would normally have gone home, but had been instructed to go to my brother's cleaning shop, so I continued. This was the heart of my territory, though my paper-round had not come this way. The trams used to grind up this hill: numbers, 26, 28 and 34. Great towering machines, magnificent like pharaohs; red painted outside, hard seats of wooden slats inside, controls that were all shiny brass and a bell in the floor that you could stamp on 'by accident' as you disembarked.

Another V1 fell here on the Pavilion Cinema, killing hundreds, and turning a bus over as it took on passengers, a number 77 of course, killing everybody inside it. They found the conductress's headless body on what was left of the roof of the post-office nearby. That's what the kids in the street said. We lost all our windows that day too. I remember scraping the dust off the margarine so I could make a Marmite sandwich.

The ruins of the cinema were still there, boarded up. Suddenly, against my will, I decided I shouldn't fight against Clapham Junction. I was softened by the familiarity of it all, the history of it; every brick was saturated in my past. Even though there had been changes since the war; the bombed shops had been rebuilt, and the cafés were a bit smarter. And gone was the eel-pie and mash restaurant where big booted workmen used to walk down the centre of the table so the other customers weren't obliged to shuffle along the benches to get out of the way. Now there were dinky little plastic beefburger joints everywhere, all tomato ketchup and espresso coffee.

Outside Arding and Hobbs, the department store of my childhood and youth, scene of my first forays into minor shoplifting, I took a deep breath. I was back. In the middle of the Junction were the underground public lavatories, all wrought iron and green paint. And beyond that The Falcon, Uncle Jack's favourite pub, where my brothers – all three of them – and a couple of cousins, had a fight with another family, one distant mythological and epic Christmas. I can see them now at the yuletide table, full of drink; silly paper hats, swollen lips, black eyes, laughing and drinking away the pain, recounting the battle and making my mother smile in spite of herself, and me with my heart swelling with pride.

I crossed the road and jumped onto a passing bus, number 19, as far as The Prince's Head. My family would be waiting for me at my brother's shop in the High Street. There were empty rooms above it and the family had given parties there before; parties that could last a couple of days, with people sent out for supplies. We would sing songs and drink too much.

The passengers on the bus stared at me. I was still in my jack-boots and Barbour jacket, looking lean and tanned, odd for October. I would not be able to stay more than two days in London, however good the party. I had to pack and get my books together. I was already a week late for my first term at

Trinity. I took another deep breath and admitted to myself that I was scared at the thought of my next adventure. What was waiting for me in Dublin? My heart skipped a beat with the fear of it, but then in that same heart grew a conviction that Lavender Hill had worked an ineluctable spell on me. The grey grit of South London had got into my blood, formed it even, and that blood was strong, and would see me through no matter what: whatever I did, whatever I became. Whatever happened to me, nothing would turn that blood to water...*nothing.*

Trinity College, Dublin

You're bound to fall in love when you go to college, at least once. That's what I was told. Well it was six times with me. I fell in love with Dublin, with Trinity College, a corrugated iron cottage, a 1926 Fiat, Harry Bovenizer and of course the woman I was to marry.

The first sight of Front Square, walking through Front Gate – that was something. Those amazing proportions: the proportions that RBD French, my tutor of English, used as a example of eighteenth century politeness and decorum. And the rain gleaming on the cobbles – that captivated me too – every stone representing a broken heart, decades of broken hearts.

It had taken me long years to get to Dublin and I was proud of the journey. I was to live there four years; 1961-1965 – and I was proud of that too. I had wanted so much to get to Ireland. Something to do with my mother's name being Rose Leary, I suppose, her father being Ned Leary, one of those Irishmen who had volunteered for the trenches of Flanders and had been mortally wounded in them.

So there I was with a room in Brighton Square – where Joyce was born for Pete's sake – and I drank in Slattery's, O'Neils, The Old Stand, Jammet's, Rice's and a place called Sean Murphy's in the Liberties.

Harry Bovenizer worked in the Reading Room and he didn't look a bit like a librarian. He was tall, at least six feet, broad-shouldered, strong looking, big practical hands, red-cheeked with black hair; handsome like a pirate is handsome, only he had a shiny old suit on him. He must have started in the library straight from school and just stuck at it. He had good work mates and it wasn't a tiring job, so that left him plenty of energy for getting up to larks, evenings and weekends. And he took me under his wing.

His father, Barney, was the gate man at Mount Jerome cemetery, and the whole family – mother, brother, sister – lived in the gate lodge, a solid square Victorian pile that sank down into the ground. Barney stood in a nook of the lodge at a stand-up desk and counted the corpses as they floated by in their hearses, entering their names into a ledger. He was the Charon of Dublin with a battered old cap set straight on his head with the letters MJ at the front of it. But if you went beyond him and down a steep flight of stairs, you would reappear a different person in a different dimension, welcomed into the warmest sitting room in Christendom, a room smelling of brewed tea, freshly baked bread and home made jam. And there stood the mother in her wrap around apron, and we'd sit there, all of us, and yarn away – never mind the studies, never mind the books.

And then out through the back door into yet another dimension, another world. It was the magic that only occurs in children's books – you were through the looking glass. You had stepped into a living wilderness that was twice as extensive as the dead world of the cemetery up above. Had that territory been on a parchment map, there would have been a legend saying 'Here be dragons.' There were high trees and impenetrable bushes, an Amazonian undergrowth. Half-hidden in the greenery were a couple of wooden sheds where car engines could be winched off their mountings, swung high on chains that glinted with oil. There were old tyres, car seats to sit on, and guns everywhere.

This was Harry's playground, this is where he left Trinity College library behind him, where he changed costume, where he sat with a rifle on his knee and waited for a rat or a pigeon to appear. There was no noise; Harry's guns had silencers on them. 'Very good for poaching,' he explained. For early in the mornings, before work, he would set off out of the city, with his chums Brendan and Liam, in a Volkswagen van, the property of a Chinese doctor, the mystery of whose identity I never solved.

They would park out in the woods somewhere, or by a canal or river, and take aim at a line of early morning rabbits, or a swim of ducks.

'Them rabbits never hear a thing,' Harry often said, they just look at each other, surprised you know, as one by one they fall over, even the ducks never know what hits 'em.'

Then he was back home and into the shiny suit and on the bus to the library, red face smiling, shouting a cheery 'hello!' to the porters at the gate, the best bit of the day already done and only a bit of work between him and an evening that was full of promise.

I was never up early enough to go on those dawn expeditions but many an evening I sat with Harry and his 'da' when the cemetery closed. It was a corner of heaven on the Rathgar Road; rare moments, and the rarest thing about them was that I knew they were rare, and I knew also that I'd better buckle those moments to my heart because I wouldn't get them a second time. Nor should I tell my secret; the world would be jealous of me and come to steal that time away.

And there were some mornings, as I dragged myself from bed in Brighton Square, when I'd hear a thump on the door of my basement flat, and with a mug of tea in my hand I'd open up on the day to find, lying on the steps, the dew and the blood still wet on them, a brace of ducks or a pair of rabbits, thrown from the Chinese doctor's Volkswagen. It made me jubilant to remember, once again, that life was just full of life.

At the end of my first term Barney sold me his old Ford Prefect. He called it Sputnik. Ten pounds, cash. It was black and it had a fuselage like a Spitfire. It had leather seats, a long gear stick and its own peculiar smell, a smell from the early days of machines, a smell of character and substance. It was from a time when cars had their own personality. I felt rich and proud. I had never had a car, I couldn't even drive.

I had dropped from a large rambling apple tree of a family: three brothers and a sister; uncles and aunts and cousins. None of us had a car in the early days, though there was one uncle who drove for a living – Frank – he careered in a yellow newspaper van at speed all over London. He had one of those cowboy jobs, racing past news stands at fifty miles an hour, throwing out bundles of newspapers without stopping. 'Star, News, Standard' he used to shout, his voice sounding as rough as a bucketful of tin-tacks from the smoking he did.

'I can't drive,' I said to Harry. 'Only a motor bike and that very badly.'

I got short shrift from him. 'Jesus,' he said, 'don't you worry about a little thing like that...I'll teach you in an afternoon.'

I went into the post-office and put a quid on the counter and they gave me a driving licence. I have it still, a fine green harp embossed on it: Dublin C.B.C., 4 Kildare Street; 7th December 1961.

Harry took me into Phoenix Park one Saturday afternoon and let me drive round and round for an hour, then he took me into the madness of Dublin traffic itself; O'Connell Street, College Green, Pearce Street, Grafton Street, St Stephen's Green.

'Ah, Michael,' he crooned at me from time to time, 'you're a natural.'

I may have been a natural but my hands shook and my stomach was water. It is more than likely that the standard of driving in Dublin at the present time is better than it was in 1961, I have no idea. All I could think of on the day was that in all those cars, buses and lorries and vans, there was not one driver who had taken a test. It was not a thought to be easy with.

By the end of the year I was stepping out with Celia, a tall slim good-looking girl from Devon. She had a graceful upright stance, a low pitched voice, golden hair and a figure to die for. Eighteen she was, that's all. I saw her that first time striding through the arched portal of Front Gate, the skirt swinging the way skirts swing, tense with life. '*She walked unaware of her own increasing beauty*', unaware of her own elegance and the effect it had, '*a flower of good breeding.*' She was as bright as a blue sky too, and I saw the talent, the resilience, the softness and all the love that made her what she was, and I was flooded by that love and knew that this was the girl I wanted to tie my life to, and I felt that love that only comes once and I took it into my heart and held it there. So this was why I had come to Dublin.

Heads high in the Ford Prefect we drove south out of the city, down to Bray, a million miles 'them days' from the sophistication of the capital. We went to Greystones and walked along the beach; into Delgany and took stout in the pub. I can remember the drinkers looking at us, the way people look at the lucky ones who still have the bloom of youth on them and are so obviously in love. We made everyone smile.

Driving on we crossed the main road and found a small track heading up a hill, a couple of bungalows, a flock of ducks wandering. The hill became steeper and the Ford only just made it, bumping and jolting from left to right, the wheels spinning in the dust. Halfway up, on a little flat space, we stopped, braked, and placed a stone behind the rear wheel.

We leant against the car to look at the view. There was nothing to say in such beauty; we simply held hands, happy to be together. The hill dropped away towards to the east. Then a spread of country till the eye came up against the spire of Delgany church, clean and clear in the June sunshine, the trees still, and on the horizon, the sea golden and too bright to look at.

There was a five-barred gate to our left. We went through it, along a cow track, overgrown, the grass knee high maybe. It led to another plateau where there stood an ugly little cottage built of corrugated iron and painted in a faded grey, a paint that would have come out of the tin faded. The roof was painted in a rusty red, the rust also being a constituent of the paint. And again the view, the view we had seen earlier, beyond Delgany to the sea at Greystones; the sun lower over the water now and the waves of it waiting for the moon.

And so the following autumn, back for my second year, I rented the corrugated cottage, thirty shillings a week. I also shared a set of college rooms with Laurie and Sebastian: number 10, Front Square, one pound. Celia had a room in Hatch Place, one pound, sharing with some girls from UCD. We were lordlings, rich on our tiny grants; nobody lived as well as we did, not even the wealthiest of students with the wealthiest of fathers. Not even Gloria 'Double-Back-Action-Breech-Loading-Gore', nor the Bailey boys who spent money on her.

The corrugated cottage was lined with asbestos sheeting. It was furnished with the throw-outs of abandoned bedsits on the north side of Dublin. There was a double bed, an old Victorian dining table, some chairs with rexine seat covers, cracked crockery and ancient lino on the floor, worn and torn. There was no heating, no water and no lavatory.

But there was a pump at the bottom of the hill, close to the bungalows. I bought a couple of plastic jerry cans and each time we drove by I filled up with water. We had bowls for the washing up and we bathed in college. Harry found me two or three second-hand paraffin stoves and we put new wicks in them. Things were looking good – but there was no lavatory.

I decided on the long drop solution. I borrowed a pick and shovel from Barney at Mount Jerome, cemetery tools, and went out to the back of our cottage, and in the overgrown, head-high weeds that closed us in behind, I dug a square hole about six feet deep. I scrounged or stole timber, four by twos, from a building site in Bray, and shoved long lengths down into each corner, bracing them with struts at strategic points – a hammer and nails job, Harry called it.

These uprights rose about six feet above the ground and odds and sods of planks, from various places and painted in many colours, were sawn to length and nailed to the sides. For the roof there was a square of marine ply, painted yellow. The rainbow carsey we called it. There was a door of sorts, swinging awkwardly on strap hinges, but the seat was the difficult bit.

I only had an old builder's saw. How could I cut a circular hole in a couple of planks of wood and fix them together? Not easy! So I made the hole in our lavatory seat a diamond shape, just four straight lines large enough to accommodate the largest of buttocks. We had proper bog-tosh too, discarding the idea of squares of newspaper hanging on a piece of string, although they might have been more picturesque and more in keeping with the architecture. Finally I purchased one large container of Jeyes fluid and the rainbow carsey was ready for its christening.

The attractions of Delgany were irresistible and, as time went by, we began to spend more and more time there, our friends too. Extravagant meals we had, twenty or more of us, up on that hill, gazing at the view, medieval feasts that lasted from midday till dawn, with our messengers bringing up gallons of Guinness from the village in buckets. And the villagers in their generosity took Celia and me to their hearts, and rather than think unkind thoughts always spoke of us as 'Mr Beatty and his sister'.

So the village pub became a haunt and walks on Greystones beach a frequent pleasure. But not all was perfect in Delgany. It was unfortunate that the grass that grew right up to the cottage door was infested with sheep ticks, which burrowed with delight into the skin behind our knees, sucking blood: there was only one remedy – we burnt them off with the bright tips of Sweet Afton cigarettes.

*　　*　　*

The Rabelaisian Society had been founded by Sebastian Balfour. It had about half a dozen members, myself amongst them. The movement had been founded with the sole aim of countering the primness of those young ladies who came from the English Home Counties. Rabelaisians were to promote vulgarity on all possible occasions, especially in the presence of those ladies. Sebastian wanted to make sure the English colony at Trinity did not sink into complacency – the English disease. He, together with Laurie, had purchased an old Austin Hampshire saloon, which he called Panurge. Panurge gave Sebastian mobility, and he was a frequent visitor to Delgany.

Perhaps he thought I was too happy, or even complacent, in the country. One night, after some hours in the pubs of Dublin, he and Laurie leapt into Panurge and headed south to where Celia and I lay fast asleep in each other's arms, warm and tender in the corrugated cottage. Sebastian and Laurie had already been responsible for getting me evicted from a room in Mount Street by writing 'Balls to the Landlady' on the front door in green paint, a graffito for which I got the blame.

Celia and I were woken by stones and clumps of grass clattering heavily on the thin sheets of metal that formed our roof. The noise went on and on. Celia was scared but I was terrified. After all, I was the man and supposed to do something. Still the noise continued. I could only think that the local Opus Dei and the Sisters of Mary in league with the Jesuits had discovered that Celia was not my sister after all, but something much more sinful. What else could it be?

I still had the pickaxe from the building of the lavatory. I knocked the head of it free and with its handle in my hand I switched on all the lights and went out onto the front step, waving the weapon above my head, my terror making me appear brave.

'You bastards!' I yelled. 'Come up here where I can see you. You'll get this lump of wood round the back of your head. I'll kill the lot of you. I'll get a few boys out here from Dublin will see to the likes of you.'

Now it was time for Sebastian and Laurie to feel fear. They could see that I was roused enough to crack their skulls open. Slowly they rose from the grass, helpless in a colossal mirth, clutching tightly to one another in their glee. I was mightily relieved, but I could have killed them in all truth. My whole body was shaking. I had seen myself tarred and feathered and ridden out of town on a rail – another godless sinner returned to the Sodom and Gomorrah that was Trinity College.

But then, it was midsummer's eve. Sebastian and Laurie had brought wine and prawns, cheese and brown bread and grapes and cake; and above all they had brought a record of Mendelssohn's music for *A Midsummer Night's Dream*. We sat outside, the moon was up (surely it must have been), and we played the music a hundred times and raised our glasses to the light on the sea. And gradually I forgave them, but it took a couple of hours and many a glass of wine.

*   *   *

In my last term I took a walk up the hill behind the cottage and, lost and forlorn, overgrown in a copse, I found a 1926 Fiat: an open tourer, long, solid and sexy with huge wheels and an aluminium body. It was a wreck but I fell in love with it, and here it was, rotting gently in Silver Springs. I found the owner, who had almost forgotten about it, and I bought it for twenty pounds. I must have been crazy; I *was* crazy. What could I do with it? I was never a mechanic.

I got it towed to Rathgar and found a lock-up garage. When it was time to leave Dublin, Harry got it to the docks for me and it was swung onto the Liverpool boat, handsome in the sky like that, then down majestically into the hold in a rope net.

At Liverpool I was faced with the problem of getting it off the boat and transporting it to London. The crane driver was easy – ten shillings did the trick. The customs' officer was a gift from God. I can see him now, slightly built and stooped in his uniform, buttons of brass, bald, a gentle man with a gentle voice, glasses.

'What a lovely car,' he said. 'So you've been studying at Trinity. Ah, how I wish I could have done that. I would have read English Literature, like you, I think. I love Wordsworth.'

Wordsworth wasn't my favourite but I had a complete works with me. I opened my trunk, crammed to the top with books, and dug and scrabbled and came up with the Oxford edition in its blue cover.

'Here,' I said, 'something to read in the evenings.'

His eyes shone with gratitude. 'Wonderful,' he said, waiving the duty on the car. 'Now, how are you going to ship it to London?'

There was a whole Hades of lorry drivers in Liverpool and my customs' officer knew every denizen of its dark spaces. He stood guard over my Fiat while I went, under his direction and bearing his recommendation like the Golden Bough, to a broken down little office on a street corner. It was painted dirty green, the windows were opaque with dried mud, and on the pavement before it stood a brazier of coke, glowing red. By the brazier stood a shifty looking fellow whose eyes were so close together he looked like a Cyclops. A captain of skulduggery, his mackintosh was tattered and a racing pink stuck out of its pocket. A grease stained pork-pie hat was jammed to his head.

He was a dealer in contraband. Empty lorries that had off-loaded at the docks drove by him before they went anywhere else, the drivers touting for unofficial cargo. My Fiat was unofficial cargo.

Cyclops's soft lips folded in and out over his broken brown teeth as I told him what I wanted. 'Not easy, a big car like that,' he said. 'Might cost a bit.' I slipped him a couple of quid and stood by the fire, warming my hands. Lorry after lorry came by; the drivers, leaning out of their cab windows, shouted their destinations.

'Newcastle, Sheffield, Carlisle, Southampton, Glasgow.'

'Nah,' Cyclops would yell back. 'Nah.' Or he would give them the good news. 'Pier ten...a load of cement, or timber, or steel girders.' He wrote these loads and destinations down in a grimy red notebook and waited for the drivers to return, lorries loaded now, again leaning out of their cab windows, this time with money in their fists.

Then my lorry came and a highwayman leant out of it.

'Car for London,' said Cyclops.

'What car?' he asked and I explained, and the driver smiled; he liked vintage cars. 'A tenner.' We closed the deal.

He was a good man, Val. Back at the docks he talked the crane driver into loading the Fiat for nothing, and that night we slept in a medieval doss-house, a room so full of beds that you had to climb over them to find your own. There must have been ten sweating men in there, snoring and farting.

I was worried about how to unload the Fiat in London. I had phoned a friend, Angus, and he was to meet me in Blackheath.

'Find a garage with a hydraulic ramp,' I told him, and he did.

The garage foreman was not too happy about the deal but I paid him and he became happy. At last the car was on the ground and in London. I had arranged with another friend to leave the Fiat in his garden; trouble was that his house was on the far side of Shooter's Hill, the deep and dangerous side which is about two miles long and nearly as steep as Beachy Head.

The garage breakdown truck was to haul me there, a fixed tow I thought, an iron bar or something. Not a bit of it. The tow was a length of rope, a soft tow. I don't know what came over me. I agreed.

There were of course no brakes on the Fiat. I wasn't even sure if the steering worked. The tyres were ancient, the canvas visible through the worn rubber. They could have ripped themselves off the rims at any moment. There were no seats either and I was obliged to stand on the girders of the chassis, like a charioteer in Ben Hur, hanging on to the steering wheel to keep upright.

We started off sedately enough, but it was rush hour. There was traffic all around me, drivers hooting, shaking their fists and cursing. Angus drove his Peugeot 403 behind the Fiat and to the side, preventing the outside lane from overtaking, protecting me. We breasted the hill, went slowly over the brow, and then down we went, down and down.

As the two tons of Fiat picked up speed the breakdown truck picked up speed also, the driver saving himself. There was no way we could slow down, it was dark and car lights were gleaming and flashing on all sides. Faster and faster we went. Terror made me mindless. I waved at Angus to come alongside, I wanted to get off, I wanted to leap onto his car, never mind the danger.

I was going to be killed. Somebody would pull in front of us, the breakdown truck would brake and I would crash into it at full speed and be thrown out under the wheels of a double-decker, squashed on the black tarmac. Was this how my brilliant career was to end? It would be typical of my life, a symbol – speeding downhill with no brakes and out of control. Well, I had learnt something at Trinity; only poetry could sum it up: Catullus again – *'frater, ave atque vale,'* – *'Hail and farewell, brother.'*

THE PELOPONNESE

'Nauplion is named after Nauplius,' said Macgregor. 'He was the father of Palamedes, who invented everything from dice to the Greek alphabet, and lighthouses. Odysseus had him stoned to death at Troy...on a trumped up charge, I might add. Crafty chap, that Odysseus.'

I had hitch-hiked into Nauplion that afternoon, spending the long vacation from Trinity in the Peloponnese, no particular destination in mind – though Nauplion immediately became a favourite place. The streets were shady and inviting, calm and unhurried, and they lay under a hill on the top of which stood a magnificent Venetian fort. From the streets climbed sets of steps, steep and narrow, passing under balconies of wrought iron that were supported by hefty beams of wood; balconies draped in jasmine and blood bright with geraniums. Down in the harbour the heat lay heavy and nothing moved; not even the boats drifted at their moorings. In the distance lay the bare mountains that hid the cities of Argos and Mycenae in a haze of shimmering purple.

I had got talking to Macgregor at aperitif time on the terrace of a café in Sindagma Square. Boys were kicking a ball around; a few men sat on benches reading newspapers, and a score or two of young girls, each as lovely as a legend, were promenading in pairs.

A few years over sixty Macgregor was still a handsome man with an upper-class drawl and a diffident manner that made him seem, in spite of his name, very English. He wore a crumpled seersucker suit of blue and white stripe; a suit that he must have purchased, well worn, from a Somerset Maugham philanderer. When he talked he was embroidering a conversation that he had maintained for many years; from friend to friend and from woman to woman.

'I was a purser as a young man, White Star Line. They don't have so much fun on ships these days, we were always up to something. We used to send down to the infirmary for a gross of condoms, and play the Madrasi Boat Race – fill champagne flutes with bubbly, put a condom on each glass and bet huge amounts of money on which one would come off first. I won a fortune, I used to put an Alka-Seltzer in mine. The others were always too scuppered to notice.'

'I've come to rest in Nauplion now,' he said in answer to my question. 'Divorced...my wife committed adultery with a shop, back in England. Funny things shops, they take people over, rather than the reverse, I mean. Incidentally, do not miss the museum here, it's superb, there's a suit of armour that's 3,000 years old, not to mention another in Argos, with a crested helmet.'

The armour was indeed astounding; above all, because it was old enough to have gone to battle on the windy plains of Troy, and it took only a smidgen of imagination to see a Hector or an Achilles in it. It was a verdigris colour, skinny in the chest, with shoulder plates and, covering the lower abdomen and reaching to the knee, three skirts of metal, one over the other.

'In Greece,' insisted Macgregor, 'you should always have a classical dictionary in your pocket – a Lempriere preferably.' He was right, of course, and was kind enough to lend me his well-loved copy of 1809 ('I tell myself it's the one Keats used,' he declared, 'and all the s's are printed as f's.').

I took the Lempriere to Mycenae with me, arriving in the full blaze of noon. I was convinced, at first, that my timing left much to be desired but, as I sat in a scrap of shade, the site emptied and the last American tour guide called in his coachload of high-school students and they went away in their long Bermuda shorts. In half an hour Mycenae, cursed of the gods, was deserted.

The Lion's Gate impresses by reason of its sheer size and

weight; huge uprights and a lintel so massive that only Cyclopean builders could have raised it. To the right was the circle of tombs, named for Agamemnon and his companions, and in front of me, at the very top, the emplacement where the palace had stood.

I sat and read the Lempriere, and the ground, dusty with myth, creaked under the deadly blows of the sun. Here Clytemnestra and her lover Aegisthus murdered Agamemnon on his return from Troy, and here also Orestes put the adulterers to the sword in the temple. 'They were buried,' said Lempriere, 'beyond the ramparts of Mycaenae, as their remains were deemed too unworthy to be laid in the sepulchre of the king.'

The lunchtime respite from tourists did not last long, and down by the entrance I found a running tap and, straw hat and all, plunged my steaming head under it and listened to yet another group leader as she told her story.

'Heinrich Schliemann located this site in 1876, guided by a remark in Pausanias, which indicated where Agamemnon had been buried. Schliemann unearthed 19 tombs which he decided were those of the king and his companions – the men wore golden face masks and golden armour, the women golden headbands, necklaces and bracelets, all now in the Mycenean room at the Athens Museum.'

A day later I found myself in Macgregor's car, Lempriere on my knee, being driven down to Monemvasia. 'I'm on the *qui vive* for a rich widow,' he said. 'My ex-wife has got money, of course, but she has no idea how to use it. Napoleon must have met her on the retreat from Moscow...I tell you, she's a nation of shopkeepers all on her own.'

I rented a simple room in the new town, on the beach, opposite the great rock that surges up out of the bay and makes Monemvasia famous; a huge, natural fortress that was occupied in turn by the Byzantines, the Franks, the Venetians and the Turks. Every morning of my stay the sun rose behind it and threw slatted shadows through my shutters and across my counterpane. Every morning, too, the rock was black against the light, the waves all glittering silver, the fishing boats silhouettes from a fairy tale.

'Monemvasia gave its name to Malmsey wine, you know,' said Macgregor. 'Very good for drowning Dukes of Clarence in...now that's what I call a skinful...'

The next morning I rose with the sun and went to visit the old town. It lies on the rock's southern flank, across a causeway, round and up to the main gate; a vaulted chicane too narrow for motor vehicles. Beyond the chicane I found myself in an alley some ten feet wide, paved with slabs of stone. A man went by me leading two horses, their panniers heavy with sacks of cement.

I followed the horses past the Church of Christ in Chains. Beyond the church square the road became rougher, lined with empty houses, half restored, half ruin. Further on the road became a track and led from deepest shade to blinding sunlight, until at the end there was only grass and grit, another gate and stepped fortifications climbing a precipitous cliff.

At first sight this cliff appeared unscalable, but near a small chapel I discovered a path leading to the top and followed it, surprised to find the ascent gentle although the footing was treacherous. The path worked its way between boulders and brought me to the church of St Sophia, which stood on the very rim of a precipice.

Behind St Sophia, the path rose again, rougher and craggier, up into a wilderness of thistle and briar and thorn, dark green and grey, waist high, and across this wilderness there rose ruin after ruin making an already desolate landscape seem threatening – '*Childe Roland to the Dark Tower came...*'.

I pushed on through the ruins until I reached the summit of the rock. All around me was the same harsh emptiness, forbidding, lending itself to despair. At the rock's edge I came to a gathering of crumbling walls, stepped under an arch, and looked steeply down to the modern settlement; the causeway and the harbour. I could see the taverna awnings, the fishing caiques, indolently moored, the white houses and the pitiless mountains that formed the horizon.

But the ruins of Monemvasia, where I stood, were in a different age, and in their silence revealed a supreme gift – a total separation from the rest of the world. The present did not exist; time and its concomitant rules did not work up here; Monemvasia enveloped the passer-by in its own mythology. I could have been standing on this cliff edge at any time during the previous two thousand years and, as if to prove it, that was when she came through the archway behind me.

I thought immediately of a dryad rising from the pages of Lempriere and me as Pan, the goat-legged randy shepherd, a mythological encounter on a mountain top. Why should the ancient Greeks have all the fun? But she was modern all right; she wore a white cotton skirt, full; a white blouse, undone, her breasts loose, and a white sunhat. Her legs were brown and bare and on her feet were sturdy sandals, unbuckled, of an ancient design. Her features were regular, deeply tanned – her eyes all the more blue for that – and she had that sun-burnt, honey-blond hair that I have always found impossible to resist. She looked as fit as a fiddle, cool as a cucumber and about 35 years old. She came from Vancouver. She smiled, she knew everything, and liked the fact that I was so young.

She took my hand and drew me back through the arch and into a corner formed by two broken walls. There was a rug on the ground where she had been sunbathing, naked.

'It's the perfect place,' she said, 'Greece,' and her arms went around my neck.

*   *   *

Macgregor was waiting for me, sitting at a table on the edge of the main street, eating souvlakia and salad and drinking a draught wine of an indeterminate colour, somewhere between pink and amber. He continued our conversation as soon as he saw me, as if there had been no hiatus.

'My wife's chief complaint was that I never had a proper job,' he said. 'But, you know, as I potter round the Peloponnese, leafing through Lempriere, the Retsina ice cold, every zephyr a caress…well ultimately, I think I've got it right. In any event, I'd rather be an Odysseus of the islands than a Sisyphus of the shops – wouldn't you?'

On the other side of the restaurant I saw the woman from Vancouver, the buttons of her shirt now fastened, sitting with her two children and her husband, a burly fellow looking as heavy as she looked slight. The children were about ten and twelve. At a table close to us was a man with a moustache and a girl with a body full of contours and comfort. They entered our conversation and our tables came together. She, Catherine, was Greek-American, he was from Athens.

'I was on holiday a year ago,' she said, 'you know, Delphi, Parthenon, all that stuff. I went into this bank, just to change money, that's all, and this guy was there.'

Adonis, for that was his name, gave a bashful smile.

'You know what this mad fool did?' Catherine threw back her head and laughed. 'He got up from his desk, walked round the counter, told his boss he was out for an hour or two, and took me straight to an ice cream parlour...a married man...and now we're going to get married, only we're having the honeymoon before the wedding. It only happens in Greece.'

'It happens in Greece, all right,' moaned Macgregor, 'just like Helen and Paris...and you know the trouble that caused.'

I bought another jug of wine. Adonis bought another and Macgregor another. Even Dimitri, the restaurant owner donated a jug. 'Aspro pato,' he yelled. 'Bottoms up.'

The meal went on, the evening became night, the lights gleamed yellow. Moths fluttered into flame and the impregnable bulk of the rock of Monemvassia vanished into a black sky.

'You know,' said Adonis, 'the Ancient Greeks said there were three terrible dangers in life: fire, ocean and women.'

'Oh, not women,' said Magcregor, 'wives.'

'But it doesn't matter,' Adonis went on, 'because Monemvasia is a paradise – here the dogs don't chase the cats, and the cats don't chase the rats. My friends, life is too brief to take seriously.'

'Tell my ex about it,' said Macgregor. He stared at me. 'Beware of marriage, whatever you do.' And another jug of wine landed on the table, Dimitri's face leering behind it.

Travels in Greece, I thought, brought nothing but joy and knowledge to a young man.

ASKERN

'Phone me urgently,' the telegram said. It was waiting for me in my pigeon-hole at Trinity; my second year, during the Easter holidays. It was from brother Ralph.

Ralph was on the point of shooting a training film for the National Coal Board, as lighting cameraman. He needed an assistant, someone he could trust not to cut up rough about the hard conditions, a someone who would bring a sense of humour with him. It was a two-month job and the money would be good, lots of overtime; 'Double Bubble' to the trade. If I could wangle a disappearance from Dublin, I would soon put together enough money to finance a long summer in the south of France. The Renoult family had Breton friends who owned a converted *bergerie* halfway between Fréjus and St Tropez, standing on its own, lonely, up a hill about two miles in from the beaches. It stood empty from June to September, and it was mine and Celia's for the asking.

I didn't even think of refusing Ralph's offer. I would do more reading in the *bergerie* than I would in Dublin. The Trinity term, all six weeks of it, was a tipsy whirlwind of receptions and dances leading to The Elizabethan Society's garden party and culminating in the all night shindig of the Trinity Ball. I went to see my tutor. 'I've got a place at Aix-en-Provence university,' I lied. We were encouraged to spend at least one term in the country of the language we were studying. There were no questions, no confirmations needed. My absence was ratified. 'Yes, Michael, enjoy yourself, but try to do some work.' I was on my way.

I was excited by the idea of spending time in a coal mine. It was in Nottinghamshire, not far from Newstead Abbey, Byron's stately home. I dragged the whole film unit there one day. 'We have to see it,' I insisted, 'the great hall, the cloisters...'. The film crew, apart from my brother, must have found me slightly odd. I didn't tell them I was at Trinity, and not many focus-pullers they knew spent their spare time reading Balzac and Stendhal in French, especially in the car on their way to work every morning.

This was not my first venture into a mining community, nor my first dealings with miners and their families. I had been evacuated twice during the war. In 1939, when I was five, I had been sent to Arundel, Sussex; marooned in a detached house that reeked of furniture polish, where neither sofa nor settee carried a stain. It was misery. I still remember the nightmares – a huge green dragon on a yellow plain, pursuing me relentlessly over mountains and dark valleys. I wet the bed every night. I learnt hate and despair in Arundel. It wasn't their fault, but I disliked Mr and Mrs Basil Simpkins with all the intensity of a maniac. They had no children of their own and they had no experience of a snotty urchin from Battersea. I was to be reformed: I had table manners to learn, and no 'afters' unless I finished my first course. I yearned for the shapeless rough and tumble of life with my brothers in Eaton House, on the council estate at the bottom of Battersea High Street, with the smell of the River Thames and Price's Candle Factory pungent in the nostrils. How could my family do this to me? There was no warmth in Arundel, and I needed warmth. Never mind the war – take me back to London.

It must have been hell for my mother. There was no money from the disappearing Basque and she was working as a skivvy for the Red Cross ladies at 13 Carlton House Terrace, facing St James's Park, Central London, a palace of tall elegant rooms full of Horlicks tablets and bars of chocolate. There was a difficulty, though: it was a condition of her employment that my mother be single and without children. In spite of this, on a visit to the Simpkins household, she discovered me weepy and neurasthenic, a bone-cage of a wreck, and swept me up into her arms and bore me away to the railway station. I can feel it now – my heart bursting with joy unconfined, and – more joy – we arrived in London just in time for the Blitz: bombs dropping, the sky aflame, and shrapnel in the streets.

During the air raids, and they came every night, my mother was obliged to put on a tin helmet and climb to the roof. There were all sorts dropping on London: high-explosives, 250 pounders and land-mines weighing a thousand pounds; but there were also incendiaries, small, but they burned fiercely on impact, and my mother's job was to get to any that fell on the roof of number 13 and extinguish them with bucket-loads of sand.

She had four sons by then, though two were out at work. The two youngest, Ralph and I, were obliged to hide in the cellars during the day, emerging into a proper life only at night, like Fagin's thieves. We soon became street-wise, street-wise enough to collect the shrapnel that littered the roads and gardens of the city. Beautiful, it came in all colours and shapes, bright wild flowers of steel, blooms of death. We had a drawer full of it, too heavy to open.

Sometime in September that year, when the raids were at their heaviest, my mother was up on the roof and Ralph and I were sheltering in one of the lowest cellar rooms, a handful of servicemen with us. The 'All-Clear' sounded and she reappeared. Her face was pale, dirty, strained too. 'Come up on the roof,' she said. She'd never said that before. We followed her up the stairs and out into the night, the servicemen in our wake; there might have been a dozen of us. We went slowly to the front parapet of the house, the sand crunching under our boots, reverently, as if approaching an altar in a church.

What I saw that evening marked me for life. The sky, from horizon to horizon, was crimson, lined black with smoke. The air was scorched, bitter like hate, and the bells of hell were ringing on the fire-engines. London was burning like it hadn't burnt since 1666. I looked up at my mother, Rose Leary from Battersea: her face, under the tin-helmet, was wet with weeping; her town was burning. Some of the men were weeping too, and one of them swore. 'We'll get the fucking bastards, just you wait, we'll get 'em.'

The life at Carlton House Terrace didn't last. My father began to reappear, sometimes drunk, sometimes not. He could be heavy-handed; I saw him hit my mother, and my brother Ted when he tried to intervene. My mother's secret was discovered; she lost her job and I lost my supply of Horlicks tablets and chocolate. My mother had to find work in a hurry and somewhere to live; that meant back to Battersea. The Blitz intensified. In a manoeuvre that served several purposes at once my brother and I were evacuated to Askern, a mining village in South Yorkshire.

It was winter in the north. There was no Christmas. I remember the cold; there was ice on the lake where we skated and slid, without supervision. 'If that ice snaps you won't never come out, there's parts o' that lake that have no bottom,' the locals told us.

I liked Askern. In spite of the cold, it was warm and welcoming, full of miners. Big men with solid practical wives. And it was reassuring to have my brother Ralph there too, though he lived with a different family. Askern had been a spa once, rivalling Harrogate in the purity of its waters. A railway line had been built to it to encourage tourism. I used to ride on the level crossing gates as they opened and closed and watch the steam engines go by. Then in 1911 it was discovered that the Doncaster seam came that way and Askern became a mining village and the spas were forgotten; coal dust settled in the streets and on the curtains.

I liked the school also. It was a wooden structure built in a square, like a cloister with grass in the middle. The teachers were like the rest of the town; straightforward, reliable and commonsensical. They liked people, me included. It wasn't the Arundel of Mr and Mrs Simpkins, and I wasn't wetting the bed any more; the green dragon had gone.

I lived in a two down, two up end of terrace house not far from the railway line, and within spitting distance of the mine. Mr and Mrs Woods had taken me in and they had a son, Eric, whose bedroom I shared. It was small but then all the rooms were small. We spent most of our time in the kitchen. There was a black range, always clean and polished, a red glow of coals behind the bars, ashes underneath, and round covers on top that Mrs Woods could lift up and out of the way with a poker, revealing bright embers. When Mrs Woods baked, the smell of bread filled the house and even the street, saliva flooded the mouth. The whole village smelt of bread, but then we all knew it would – the women of Askern all baked on the same day.

The lavatory was in the yard, and there was no bathroom. Mr Woods worked at the pit-head but he still came home black and Eric and I were sent upstairs while he scrubbed himself down in a galvanised bathtub in front of the fire. Eric and I washed in the same bath every Friday, sharing the hot water, boiled in kettles. Eric always got to wash first.

But I was the one who was sent to do the shopping. Eric was nowhere near as cunning as a street orphan whose wits had been sharpened on the Battersea grindstone. 'I could get my foot on a dropped pound note before anyone else had decided if it was an autumn leaf or a bus ticket.' So I was the chosen messenger of Mrs Woods. 'Cheek of the devil,' I overheard her say one day, 'he always comes back with a bit more rations that he should, and a bit more change too. He's certainly fly all right. They 'ave ter be in London.'

And there was a cinema where, on certain evenings, Mr and Mrs Woods took me to Band of Hope meetings, setting me a good example, setting me on the right road, my back firmly turned on perdition. For the ministers of the Band of Hope harangued miners at length on the evils of drink and made them swear to be teetotal, and their wives were content and insisted their men sign the pledge and repudiate alcohol for ever.

I didn't mind; on Saturday mornings I was given two copper coins so that I could speed off to that same cinema. Saturday was the day of the 'Tuppenny Rush', the cinema show for the kids of Askern, and we all ran there, some in clogs, the wood hitting the tarmac hard, the clatter pitiless, just to remind the poor they were still poor. Every seven days we sat, mouths open, staring at the screen, gawping at the serial, an episode every week, an improbable sea story, all to do with speed boats and villainous plots, each episode ending with a cliff-hanger, the hero with waves rising up to his chin, death certain, for the heroine too. My God! How could anyone so beautiful be allowed to die?

The serial began and ended with the Scherzo by Litolff – my introduction to classical music – and after the excitement of the cinema came my first encounter with the female buttock, when a girl of nine, Carol, led me from the cinema and down to the riverside and there, hidden in a secret marshland of whispering rushes, she took my hand and slid it into her bloomers. I have never forgotten the cool voluptuousness of her flesh, the touch of it as smooth as sin, as tempting as ice-cream. I rarely hear Litolff's Scherzo these days. Just as well, for when I do that tiny buttock fills my hand and Carol's face smiles at me, enticing and mysterious, all-knowing.

At lunchtimes I would race home from school to eat, but before I did I was sent to the pit-head with Mr Woods's 'snap' tin to deliver at the wheel-house, where the cage went down. I ran like a steam engine up that hill, on a gritty underfoot of coal dust. All Askern tasted of coal, and smelt of coal fires; and a coal-coloured cloud lay heavy on the roof tops. If the wheels of the cage were turning I would stand and watch for a moment, hungry as I was, till they had spun to a stop. I wanted so much to go to the bottom of the shaft and along the pit road to the face. Mrs Woods just laughed at me. 'You wouldn't want to be a miner, son, stay out of it. Anyway, there ain't no mines in London.'

Forty-three years later, in 1984 and 1985, there was a national miners' strike and the men were out too long, badly led by their union. I read about the miners of Askern and my heart felt for them – the whole village out of work, no wages, little food. I had money at the time: I'd been working as a sound assistant on a film, and I sent a couple of cheques to the Askern soup kitchen, explaining that I had lived there once, and loved it. I received a letter of thanks, of course – it reduced me to tears.

1.3.85

Dear Mr Larrabeiti,

I am the N.U.M. secretary of the Askern Miners' Welfare Club. I am also the current Mayor of Askern, so please accept our many thanks from the people of Askern.

Askern pit employs over 1100 miners of which today only 16 are crossing picket lines...I've enclosed the Town Journal which the Council issued at Christmas to the people of Askern. My message is on the back page, as well as a poem I wrote after a conversation with my young son.

I am 35 years old and through the Club I've raised £30,000 for various charities over the last 6 years. I have never been in trouble in my life, yet in this dispute I have been put behind bars, had my house attacked with 9 building bricks by working miners from Nottingham which missed killing my daughter by inches. I've seen London police overrun this town and treat its people with a violence you will not believe – they asked our children if their mothers were prostitutes – I could go on and on, these are just some of the things ordinary people have had to endure, and yet we are still on strike because all we want is to work, our community, our proud way of life.

People like you have helped us survive,

*God bless you and your family for helping
to keep our soup kitchen going.*

*Yours sincerely,
M J Porter.*

And then a week later –

Dear Michael,

*You were right, the last few days have been
hectic. We marched back all together last
Tuesday, it was the emotional experience of
my life...the street where you lived in
Askern is still there but the cinema as you
guessed, is gone. The centre of Askern has
changed quite a bit but Moss Road etc. is
still just the same.*

*It would be a great pleasure to meet you
and take you for a drink at the miners'
club...Many thanks for your further
donation which I think is now too much for
one individual so please don't send any
more. I will give you a guided tour of the
area as well...you would be welcome to
spend the weekend with us...Once again,
Michael, thank you very much.*

*Yours sincerely,
Michael.*

And how did I leave Askern when my time as an evacuee was
over? With no farewells, no ceremony. Galloping off to the
Tuppenny Rush one Saturday morning, the shopping done,
bubbling with energy, a skinny body full of life, I hared round
the corner and as I came towards the level crossing a voice
called out my name in a London accent. 'Hey, Mick!' Only my
family called me Mick. I hardly recognised the person talking to

me: my brother Ted, all smartly dressed in a new gabardine mac, his face scrubbed clean for the journey. He'd come to take me home. Just like that.

I was never to know if the hero and heroine of the serial were to escape the rising waters and the machinations of the villain. But, child or adult, you took life as it came in those days; it was soft and silly even to dream of an alternative. Life was a no-man's-land pitted with shell holes full of mud – I was used to it. I'd had seven years, off and on, of being left with Aunts, and eighteen months of it in Arundel with Mr and Mrs Simpkins. Now, without a moment's notice, without even a letter of warning, I was plucked from the warmth of a miner's kitchen and hauled off south, back to the war where I belonged, complete with a thick Yorkshire accent that drove my mother mad. I remember no emotion; it was simply time to go. I didn't even know where my family lived now. It would be a new rented flat and a new school – somewhere would be good, even anywhere. Above all it would be London and more shrapnel.

*   *   *

Twenty-two years after Askern I went down the Nottinghamshire pit, a deep one – and there was a two mile walk to the coal face, into a three foot seam; no standing up, crawling all day, pulling safety film lamps into position, trying hard to keep the camera lenses clean and dirt out of the camera boxes. We were filming the use of automatic pit props: two roads driven into the coal face, some eighty yards apart, and the metal hydraulic props advancing mechanically in between. There were miners to drill the holes for the explosive charges, a machine to cut the coal, and tough navvies in singlets to load it onto a conveyor belt, wielding shovels as broad as barges. The backs of these men were ropes of muscle, tattooed with indigo scars where the sharp edged rock of the low roof had cut into their shoulders, and the skin had healed over, the blood mixing with coal dust. That colour was in there till they died and took it to the grave.

As it was cut away the coal face advanced and left behind it an emptiness with nothing to support the earth above; a void the miners called the 'gob', and the gob creaked and groaned continually, scaring me witless. I was aware, every minute, of those millions of tons of rock that lay between me and the open air. I thought of them as a great sapient section of the planet, shifting always and possessed of an evil and downward intent, biding its time, ready to fill that three foot corridor where I spent my days; eager to crush my skull into powder and mash my brain into the dust. And large lumps of the gob came crashing down regularly, in a hurry to fill the unnatural gap where the seam had been, and each time I heard a fall I imagined an avalanche and leapt from my skin, making the miners chuckle. 'You'll get used to it,' they said.

I never did, but I got used to a lot of other things: to eating sandwiches that were gritty with coal dust and smudged with black fingerprints; drinking whole flasks of sugary tea; peeing where I could; taking a pocketful of toilet paper down with me every day so I could creep into the awful gob to crouch and shit when I had to; and getting used to working longer than the miners, across two shifts to finish the filming in time; saying goodbye to one band of men, welcoming another.

We got to know them well, a score of them, good men, protecting us, knowing that by the end of the day we were worn to a thread, happy to ride out the two miles to the shaft and the cage, lying on the conveyor belt, relaxed on a bed of coal, our bodies caressed as they rose and fell over the rollers that drove us along. 'Don't fall asleep,' the men said. 'You fall asleep and you'll end up in the machine, cut and sorted into anthracite nuts.'

After that the showers – a host of naked miners with their blue scarred backs, and then the drive into Nottingham: a five star hotel with a quiet restaurant and bottles of wine. But the more we worked, the more we got to know the men, and the more the feeling of fear came and grew. Not the fear of being in the pit, crawling in that three foot space, but the fear of the outside – crossing the road, a limitless universe, fast moving cars and hordes of people we didn't know. Away from the pit there was just too much of everything. I came to miss the dark, the closeness, that bond men make when working or fighting together. I was in the trenches, and I came to need that feeling every day.

Going to the pit was like going home every morning, trudging through the stone dust to the coal face; it made me want to sing as I marched. The smells, the warmth, the sweat. It was two months well spent, not a moment wasted. I had come full circle and was proud of it. Askern had let me live with the miners as a child – Nottingham had allowed me to work with them as a man. As an education it was as good as Trinity College, even though it gave me not a single letter after my name.

PRAGUE

The money I'd earned in the Nottinghamshire pit kept Celia and me for months, idle and intellectual, in the South of France. Our house, the Bergerie, had pine woods all around and a view of the Mediterranean through the trees. There were no neighbours within sight or hearing. Only Aimé Blaye visited from time to time; a farmer who owned peach trees and vineyards in a nearby valley and picnicked with us occasionally. When harvest time arrived we spent marvellous hours with him and his sons, picking the fruit, lazing in the shade when the work, or some of it, was done. The world was somewhere else, we were mythological.

Jean Renoult brought us provisions once a week, ate with us frequently and kept us supplied with demijohns of red wine at 30 centimes a litre from the Roquebrune co-operative. We read books and ate by the light of oil lamps and candles. There were hordes of tourists on the beaches but we rarely saw them. It was far too hot for city folk to walk into the hillside. Their regime was night-clubs, restaurants and a kind of dazed recuperation on the sands of Les Issambres and La Gaillarde.

We swam, at seven in the morning, skittering down the hillside paths on two old bikes that came with the Bergerie, the air cool about us, the beaches empty, cold wisps of mist rising from the still surface of the sea; no noise, just waves breaking, effortless, lazy, a listening quiet, two or three hours of private pleasure before 'les estivans' crawled from their tents and hotels and came out to clutter the sands.

And, in the quiet and the stillness of those early mornings, we would watch as the sunlight crept up the sky, turning the 'wine dark' sea into a golden blue. The chill would go and, across the wide bay of Fréjus, the roofs of St Raphael emerged sharp and clear. At nine or so, when the world became crowded, we walked slowly up the hillside, pushing our bikes, back to that other world, found the deep shade of the woods and read and talked. It was a far cry from the three foot seam.

I read a lot of poetry that summer – a lot of anthologies. Poems that sang the world into existence: the past, love and dreams, giving me words as gifts, telling me everything, giving me men and women. 'People is Poems' – someone must have said it. Donne, Keats, Marvell, Clare, Pope, Shelley, Browning, Hopkins, Hardy, Yeats, Owen; so many, *too* many – '*ars longa, vita brevis*', dammit.

I had the run of Jean's books too; Montaigne to Pascal, Racine to Baudelaire, Laforgue to Vian: I discovered Prévert as well, and I stole one of his verses for Celia:

> *Une orange sur la table*
> *Ta robe sur le tapis*
> *Et toi dans mon lit.*
> *Doux présent du présent*
> *Fraîcheur de la nuit*
> *Chaleur de ma vie.*

It was easy wasn't it? – travel and poetry taught you most things: the people you met and the great minds you read formed you, but there must be contemplation when you returned home; you must allow your soul to reap its harvest, to catch up with you. Activity for the sake of killing time was an evil, the sign of an empty mind; even the idea of 'killing time' was a perverse conception. '*Extreme business,*' says RLS, '*is a symptom of deficient vitality; and a faculty for idleness implies a catholic appetite and a strong sense of personal identity.*' It got you through life, activity, but you owed it to yourself to think about the quality of your existence. You were given only one crack at it, and you had to do your best to get it right.

It had been through Jean and his mother, whom everyone

knew as 'Bonne Maman', that I had become friends with the shepherds of Grimaud and Cogolin and later begged them to take me to the mountains with them - the transhumance: more than a hundred and fifty miles on foot, with three thousand sheep, from Cogolin to the pastures beyond St André des Alpes. The pastoral life - where the three great religions had come from, not that I converted to any of them, but walking that road I had felt the earth and its rhythms beneath my feet. I became a pagan instead.

When Garreau had sacked me from the hotel and my position as assistant manager I had no idea what to do or where to go. Jean had come to see me as I was packing. 'Provence,' he said, 'is all round you. It is full of sun and waiting to be explored, a complete contrast to the life you have been living here.'

It was a contrast all right. Jean called a taxi and sent me and my trunk along the coast to his mother's place. An hour later I was standing, exquisitely overdressed in white trousers and an alpaca blazer, at the end of a stony track in the middle of a vineyard, halfway up a rugged hill some several kilometres behind the town of Grimaud. I removed my jacket, hooked it to a branch and, as nonchalantly as possible, climbed through the blazing heat of the afternoon and the noise of the cicadas, up to Bonne Maman's house. I was entering a different world.

Bonne Maman was as remarkable as her son. Her husband, an artist turned engineer, had died only a couple of years previously. All she had to live on was the minutest of pensions and, after moving from one rented shack to another, had come to rest in a two-thirds derelict farmhouse called Rascas.

Like most Provençal farmhouses Rascas was tucked into a hillside in order to protect it from the mistral. Extensions had been added to each end of it at various times, but they were now in ruins. Bonne Maman lived in three rooms in the middle of the house: one down and two up. There was no electricity and water came from a well a hundred metres away. Brambles grew up to the door and in through the windows. There was no lavatory and the track from the valley was a vertical path by the time it reached the little plateau on which the house stood.

Bonne Maman must have been about seventy when I met her, and I fell in love with her and her house within seconds - but then so did everyone. Her living-room-cum-kitchen was a treasure trove. On the walls there were at least a score of her husband's paintings, showing, as far as I could tell, undeniable talent. There were several fine pieces of furniture from her great days in Paris, books, silver oil lamps, and above the fireplace there hung a portrait of her husband painted by his cousin Raoul Dufy, done in dark browns and yellows - worth a fortune that she was determined never to realize.

Rascas was a castle on the top of a hill and Bonne Maman was the châtelaine, just waiting for troubadours to come by. She held court there and I was a fortunate onlooker. I threw off my gigolo shoes and my sea-island cotton shirts, and began to cut back the brambles. I found a broken bike in a nearby ruin and mended it. Now I could cycle down to St Pons les Mûres, on the coast road between St Maxime and St Tropez, climb a gate, cross a vineyard and come to a deserted beach and picnic alone; there where now the holiday apartments of Port Grimaud stand with their security gates, their breeze-block 'Provençal' towers and their fibre glass power-boats at the door.

Our social life, or rather Bonne Maman's social life, was a busy one. Although she lived on her own there were often a dozen people at her table. Visitors of all sorts appeared from everywhere: there was Edmond the sculptor, dressed always in a rough red shirt, who came from across the valley to lounge on the grass, his beautiful woman with him; and Émile Pélissier, a peasant farmer, a confirmed bachelor under the thumb of his mother, who used to escape to Rascas for dinner bringing bottles of wine from his own vineyard; the Abbé Persat too, an Avignon priest who brought under-privileged kids from high-rise flats and camped with them behind Rascas in the summer months. And there were sisters and cousins from Paris who couldn't understand why Bonne Maman stayed in such a slum, and once a week Jean would arrive with his wife, Licette, and their three children. We were a crowd at table, outside in the dying day, in front of the house, eating like kings, the wine of

Provence a glittering red, the conversation never-ending, the songs and laughter coming as the sun went down. I was a world away from the falseness of life in Monsieur Garreau's hotel.

Every three or four days I would trek into Grimaud for provisions, a knapsack on my back, learning the hillside paths, cutting across the vineyards. Often I saw a shepherd or two, Marius or Joseph, Lucien and Jules, unmoving, hardly visible in the shade beneath the trees, their flocks standing like statues, exhausted by the sun. The shepherds were strangers to me then, but that didn't stop them shouting out to me: 'Get me a packet of Gauloises,' and I'd wave a 'yes', then I was across the footbridge and up the steep track into Grimaud itself, the ruins of the chateau perched high above me. And on to the baker's, the grocer's, the post office, and the butcher's, until I rounded off the expedition with a pastis in the café on the square, watching the old men play pétanque, with my eyes tempted away across the plain to the view of Cogolin and the village of Gassin, a silhouette on its hill, and beyond it the blue glint of the sea.

When there were no guests bedtimes were early and I spent hours lying on my counterpane, reading by the golden light of an oil lamp; reading Jean de Florette - the scents of Provence bursting out of the pages; and the essays of Montaigne - my hoots of laughter keeping Bonne Maman awake late into the night. And our breakfasts - just two friends together in that cluttered living-room, the Dufy on the wall, the early morning sun slanting through the half-closed shutters, the murmur of flies and bees outside. That sojourn at Rascas was a rare privilege, and I knew it was. I lived every busy and lazy second of it.

Living with the shepherds was an early encounter with love, the love of people and the lives they led, but there had been other encounters with that love: the Festival Gardens; the steel works, the coal mine; the film industry; the travel business; four years at Trinity. It was magic; we were all under a spell, the miracle of being alive – we were all stardust. Jean was profoundly jealous of my experience with the shepherds, but for all the right reasons; he was a pagan too.

'Just go, Michel,' he said one night in a bar at St Raphael; waiting to put me on the night sleeper to Barcelona. 'Travel for the joy of it. It gives your life back to you, all new, like you've never seen it before.' Jean was an angel, leaning over the world, helping people to become content with the hazard of their existence, making sure they enjoyed their minute of eternity.

About three weeks before our tenure of the Bergerie was to come to an end, and Celia and I were due to catch the train for Dublin, Jean brought me a message that had been 'phoned through to him at his place of work. I was to contact a friend of mine in Manchester. The nearest phone was in the bar tabac at St Aygulf and I cycled there the next day. Did I want to take a group of people to Prague, via East Berlin, for a firm called Yorkshire Tours? In those days anything behind the Iron Curtain was mysterious and outlandish, dangerous even – that was where the communists lived: Bulgaria, Hungary, Czechoslovakia, Poland, Yugoslavia, Albania, and you didn't go to any of them for holidays.

It was a black and white spy film over there: shadows on walls, meetings with Mata Hari in every bar, and secret service men followed you everywhere, their raincoat pockets bulging with automatic pistols; your hotel room was bugged and you were thrown into prison if you were suspected of espionage, for ever. Did I want to go? Not half.

*　　*　　*

There never was a tour operator like Yorkshire Tours. It was not a large organisation, quite the opposite, but it was special. It sent out maybe a dozen trips a year and was run by Laurie Shaw, and his wife Ida, from a small kitchen at the back of a terraced house in Huddersfield, where the walls and windows dripped with a condensation that steamed from the kettle that always stood on the hob of the black range. Tea was always being mashed; dark solid tea that could hold a teaspoon upright and stain your teeth as black as chewing-tobacco.

Laurie was a life-long card carrying member of the Communist Party, and had been taking people behind the Iron

Curtain since the days when only Kruschev thought it was a good idea. Laurie was a legend and a man with a mission. He wanted to show the English that there was nothing wrong with communism or the Eastern Bloc; even commies were people. But he was preaching to the converted for the most part. His clients were left wing, dedicated, and tough. Laurie led them into adventure at the cheapest prices possible. He sent his clients by coach to the state subsidized railway networks of the east. They slept in schools, and tramped over snow-bound passes carrying their luggage; they brewed tea, to Laurie's recipe, on primus stoves in wind-swept lay-bys, and made it an even more vicious mixture by the addition of evaporated milk. Laurie's clients were the SAS of tourism – they dared and, ultimately, they won. They laughed at misfortune and they stood shoulder to shoulder in adversity.

I wasn't obliged to go to Huddersfield but, having heard so much about Laurie and Ida, I decided that I had to see them. I had to sit in the kitchen where the tours were masterminded, and perhaps receive some instructions, though that wasn't Laurie's style. So, a couple of days before I was to make the trip, I took the train north. One thing I did know: there was no pay nor any hope of tips. This was socialism at work; but for the group leader at least all expenses were paid.

Opposite Laurie's house stood The Khyber Pass General Stores. Out of the rear window, across the tiny back-yard, the soft green moors rose perpendicular to the sky. In the kitchen itself Laurie sat at an ancient three-leaved dining table that was covered in school exercise books, each one full of close, crabbed writing, two lines of writing to each ruled line, to save space and money. These were the plans and records of voyages past, present and future. Laurie was a bony little man with not much flesh on him, roughly shaven. He wore, even indoors, an old raincoat, and under it a grey flannel shirt with a crinkly collar and black and red check felt slippers. Ida wore a wrap around floral apron and made tea the moment it was called for.

I asked for instructions and information about the trip and was told hardly anything. 'It always works out,' Laurie said, his voice, warmly clothed in its Yorkshire accent, reassuring and full of spirit. Nothing could go wrong. Not even freezing to death when the heating systems broke down on the Trans Siberian, 20 below.

'Don't worry, lad,' I heard him say to a group leader, who happened to phone when I was present. 'Any road, all get together in the same compartment, put yer cap on and close t'winder.'

'Nice to meet you lad,' said Laurie as Ida poured the tea into my cup. It had the consistency of toffee. 'Now you'll meet up with the bus from Huddersfield at King's Cross Station. It'll only be half full, when it arrives, the others get on in London.'

'Visas?' I asked. You couldn't cross the Iron Curtain without visas.

'Yes, all taken care of,' said Laurie. 'One of my operators will meet you at the side of the station. She'll have done all the passports and visas. She'll be carrying 'em in a plastic bag, no one ever steals a plastic bag, do they? There's two groups, yours going to Prague, and another going to Leningrad. There's a German-speaking Russian, Ivan, he'll be with the Leningrad group. He hasn't done it before either and you'll travel together as far as East Berlin, then you get different trains at different stations. He'll show you t'ropes. You'll pick up the tickets for Prague at Friedrichestrasse...Ivan'll have the money...and he'll give you some for expenses. When you get to Prague there'll be someone waiting for you at the end of the platform. He'll be Czech of course, but he should speak English. They generally do.'

Waiting for the bus at King's Cross I was very much on edge. It was an hour late arriving from Huddersfield, and when it came it brought with it the snottiest of coach drivers. Short, red-faced, with smarmed down hair, his face wore a sneer of disgust that only fleetingly became a smile when he saw suffering in others. I was nice to him; I needed him on my side to get me through, but I wanted to kick him from the word go. Ivan was there too, a double dealer of the first water. He was a runaway Russian whose English wasn't very good, and, contrary to what Laurie had said, neither was his German.

Laurie's operator arrived as promised, just as time was

getting short and it began to look as if we might miss the next three ferries at Dover. She was well beyond sixty, wearing a long brown coat which reached to her ankles, and a hat with a narrow brim held onto her grey hair with a hatpin of the kind my granny used to use. Her plastic bag was full of visas and passports and I distributed them down the bus, calling out the names as I did so. It didn't work out too well for one of the clients; I was dismayed to discover that his passport was incomplete – no visa. I expected an argument, an out-and-out row. No such thing. He accepted his destiny like a martyr who knew he was going to heaven. He shrugged his shoulders and left the bus without a murmur of complaint. He knew about Yorkshire Tours and had travelled with them before. Yorkshire Tours was a religion which you accepted with complete faith, and he was a votary.

It was just as well he left us because we were three seats short on the bus. We did what we could. One client sat on the floor, and Ivan and I stood all the way to East Berlin, a journey of twenty-four hours. It was good training for what was to come.

The clients took it in their stride, all of them veterans of Yorkshire Tours; librarians, union officials, social workers, retired teachers and a hit squad of half a dozen pioneer feminists, licensed to kill. They took against me immediately, due to my film business habit of calling both men and women 'darling' or 'cherub'. I wasn't allowed to call them 'girls' either, let alone 'lover'. It was no good my explaining that steel workers and miners often called each other 'luv', so I curbed my tongue, especially as their leader was as tall as a Douglas Fir and with thighs that would have crushed any male to death had he been foolish enough to sail his vessel close to them. I named her legs Scylla and Charybdis without deciding which was which. But she had a smiling round face and cropped blond hair. I thought she was smashing but didn't dare say so. Her name was Oona.

There were twenty-seven clients in my group and amongst them was a man dressed like a vicar. I took him at face value to begin with: He wore a dog collar, a black beret and a black raincoat, all set off with silver hair and a beard that would have graced the countenance of an Elizabethan courtier. Gradually though, he gave himself away. It didn't matter what subject was raised in conversation: he could better it. It didn't matter who had been where, he had been further, higher, deeper. He had climbed Mont Blanc, had herded yaks from Tibet to Nepal and had ridden a horse from Patagonia to New York. He was a marvel of derring-do and knew everything.

We motored across Belgium and Germany and some dozen lay-bys and brew-ups later – everyone providing their own enamel mug – we arrived in West Berlin. Snotty, the driver, couldn't off-load us quick enough – a twenty-four hour porn-club might well have been his destination. I followed Ivan and his Leningrad group into a railway station, and my group followed me, trusting and happy. I don't know why; I spoke no German and had never been to Germany before. It was that Yorkshire Tours thing again, 'Che sera, sera'.

We boarded a suburban train and soared across the Iron Curtain, disembarking after a short journey, into a kind of holding enclosure somewhere in East Berlin. We lined up, as instructed by Ivan, in strict alphabetical order of surname, to coincide with the names on my list, which was like a bill of lading. Being forewarned, I slid some West German marks to a border guard, and we shuffled through a row of Orwellian doors. Our passports were examined by a man in a glass cage and so, one by one, we arrived in a different country. It was eerie. The customs' hall was full of stereotypes in dull uniforms and all carrying guns. Surely, they must be actors.

Then it went wrong. As group leader I came through the doors last, and in that other land I found my group waiting for me, dazed but smiling; but of Ivan there was no sign. He had forgotten that he was supposed to buy my tickets out of the enormous amount of money he was carrying. He had simply pushed me from his mind and had disappeared with his group to the station that served Leningrad. I was meant to cross East Berlin to another station, the one for Prague.

My guts turned to water. I had 28 tickets to buy and nothing to buy them with. My twenty-seven milled about me, expecting firm leadership. I had none available.

I employed democratic socialism and told them all what had happened. 'Oh that's all right, you look after the luggage, and we'll go and explore for a couple of hours.' Marooned in a pool of suitcases I stood there, bereft, with no idea what to do.

Out of the blue a German student smiled at me and I grabbed him with hands of steel. He wanted to practise his English and he'd come to the right person. I sent him off to the Leningrad terminus with instructions to look for Ivan and his group. 'Bring him back,' I pleaded, nearly in tears, my voice wobbling on the edge of hysteria, 'or at least his wallet.'

We just made it. Ivan returned with a wad of West German marks. 'Sorry,' he said, 'I forgot.' I could have wrung his neck – an open-air Siberian lunatic gulag would have been too good for him. He bought me 28 tickets and sleepers for the trip, and gave me my float in dollars. With only minutes to spare we boarded the night express to Prague. The night express to Prague! The words rolled romantically off my tongue. Everything had fallen into place and I could relax.

Not quite. There was no restaurant car, but Yorkshirites always travelled prepared for a siege. Cheese and lettuce sandwiches no more than a day old appeared; nuts and raisins; apples and bananas. We sat around or paid visits, from compartment to compartment, the trip developing into a kind of rolling dorm-feast with duty-free vodka to make us festive. And then, when we might have thought of rest, we were made to stand in the corridor while East German border guards inspected our passports and searched for seditious books. An hour or two later the Czech soldiers marched in and went over the same ground and I watched as Oona and her feminists became totally demoralized by those slim bodies and smart uniforms, those long coats and military buttons. They were jolly, the Czech border guards; they were eager to join the party and dawn came long before sleep.

Our train was at least eighteen carriages long and when it clanked into Prague the next morning we looked from the windows, a frieze of yellow faces, to discover that we had come to a halt a good hundred yards from the platform. I had a wide selection of octogenarians with me: a man with a gammy leg, a polio victim in a wheel-chair, and a desiccated Jewish woman. She had a tongue as dangerous as a circular saw, and it made the same sound – rusty teeth ripping into tough timber; words flew from her mouth like tin-tacks from a nail-bomb.

Luckily, Oona was big and tall and strong, and far more decided than I was. We leapt the four or five feet to the track and lifted the oldies from the carriage steps, one by one, stiff as corpses, their faces bloodless with fear. The luggage came out with the able-bodied Yorkshire troops.

I drew breath and looked towards the station. There was no one to be seen, apart from my straggle of tourists, their feet slipping on the ballast as they progressed towards the sloping end of the platform. My guts liquefied yet again. The next few minutes would put Laurie Shaw's alchemy to the test – would base metal turn into gold? Would there be someone waiting for us, someone who knew we were coming and knew where we were going? Where would we sleep that night, where would we eat? Nuts and raisins don't last for ever. I had been given no address to go to, in fact I had been given no instructions at all. I could hear Laurie's Yorkshire voice echoing across Europe: 'Don't worry, lad. There'll be someone at t'station t' meet yer.'

I lingered at the back of the group, putting off the moment of truth. I fussed over the woman in the wheel-chair. Slowly I pushed her up the ramp of the platform. In the distance I could see the group milling again, their faces turned in my direction, a black cloud hovering just above their heads. My heart shrank. I had visions of us camping on Wenceslas Square; taken into custody as vagrants. And then he appeared, and the world became a proper place, the sun shone – Zdenek Lustig, a young man in his mid-twenties with an open face and a ready smile.

'Yorkshire Tours?' he asked, and I could have kissed him, indeed would have done if I'd known how the feminists would have taken it. I was desperate to be accepted by them and had not used the word 'cherub' all night.

A bus was waiting for us but it was only for the transfer. All our visits were to be made by public transport as befitted true socialist orthodoxy. We came to rest finally in a student hostel on the outskirts of Prague, sharing rooms and a kitchen. The group wasted no time; they made beds and breakfasts and unpacked their belongings into plain wooden cupboards. They were undaunted, they were pioneers; they could have captured the Winter Palace. Later that morning they were given a guided tour and then they were on their own. And so was I.

On the second day I checked through my documents and discovered two things. One: Ivan had not thought to buy return tickets for my group, not to mention sleepers. Two: our accommodation voucher was valid for four nights only – we were supposed to be staying seven – a shortfall of three.

On the telephone Laurie Shaw was a rock, unperturbed. In my mind's eye I could see that kitchen steaming; the nerve-centre of a vast network. 'Now, don't worry, Mr. de Larrabeiti, I'm sure you'll work it out somehow.'

It was Zdenek who saved the day. We went to the State Tourism Office and they issued tickets and sleeper reservations against my Yorkshire Tours reputation. Finding a place to sleep was trickier but eventually we were squeezed into a proper hotel, doubling up in rooms with Georgians and Bulgarians. The twenty-seven saw this as a bonus.

'We're really meeting the people now,' said Oona, and that night she and I gate-crashed a Ukranian knees-up. 'We'll show'em,' she cried as she propelled me round the dance floor like I was some kind of industrial floor-polisher, her muscles rippling with pleasure. 'We'll show 'em what Brahms and Liszt really means.'

Getting the luggage across town was the main difficulty.

'I can't get a bus,' explained Zdenek. We were having a council of war and changing money in a hotel room, and he turned the radio up full blast, pointing to the ceiling. The secret police were listening. 'You have to order buses weeks in advance. Taxis are not an option, too expensive for Yorkshire Tours. But I do have a cousin with access to a good socialist van. Dollars will do it?'

It was great fun really. The twenty-seven went off to do their own thing with instructions to meet us in a certain restaurant for dinner that evening, while Zdenek and I shifted all the bags out of the hostel, and loaded them into the cousin's van. It took three journeys but I came to know that route across Prague well enough to walk it blindfold, and, in adversity, Zdenek and I became blood brothers.

Things were smooth for a while after that; we went to concerts, museums and took excursions to the country. On the last night the twenty-seven elected to eat together in the poshest restaurant Zdenek could find, paid for him, drank lots of pilsner and sang music-hall songs. The return journey to Berlin went swimmingly, with a night long raucous picnic and complaisant border guards. But the moment I walked out of the station in West Berlin and saw Snotty's face I knew the honeymoon was over. I made the sign of the cross with my fingers but to no avail. It may work with vampires but stronger magic was needed to ward off that evil eye of Snotty's.

At least he had come with a bigger bus; we all had seats, and that looked like a good omen. It certainly fooled me for a while. The group from Leningrad arrived on time, cheerful, but without Ivan. He had vanished the moment he'd got them to Leningrad, they said, never to be seen again. It was of little consequence, they were used to looking after themselves. Perhaps he'd been picked up by the KGB and was in the Lubianka. Sadly no one cared enough to speculate.

The bus seemed fine, though mechanically it wasn't in the peak of condition. Snotty had to hold the gear lever down when he was in second – otherwise it flew out and the motor over-revved until he got his foot off the accelerator. In this fashion we left Berlin, on the autobahn, with Snotty surly at the wheel, heading into the dullness of an East German countryside where the grass was grey.

About a dozen miles short of the West German frontier the bus began to fill with diesel fumes. 'It's just a hole in the exhaust,' said Snotty. In the absence of Ivan I was commanding officer, and I didn't relish the idea of the bus breaking down and us stopping in East Germany; indeed, we were strictly forbidden to do so. But panic was spreading. The air we were breathing was foul and some of the clients were confusing diesel with petrol, convinced we were going to burst into flames at any second. This panic conveyed itself to me – I believe in cowardice, it's a sensible emotion – and I stationed myself near the door. Women and feminists last.

We were still a mile or two from the frontier when there was a mutiny, led by the Jewish woman. Snotty gave in and stopped the bus; after all, the fumes were now thick and black and poisonous. The moment the bus halted the passengers disembarked in a hurry, coughing their way out on to the tarmac, and began walking towards the frontier post which was now visible on the horizon. Smoke poured upwards across the sky in a massive plume of burning oil, as if a Junkers 88 had just been blown out of the sky by a squadron of Spitfires.

I was flummoxed. I took a few paces in several directions and then stood still, a rabbit with myxamatosis. I had lost control. Things were bad but they got worse. From out of the ground, from trap-doors in the turf it seemed, leapt a company of East German soldiers, armed with rifles and machine pistols, their faces as welcoming as the Berlin wall on a rainy night. They forced us, with curses and rifle butts, back into the smoke of the bus, even those who had made it halfway to the border post. Never mind the danger, never mind the fumes, never mind the octogenarians and the wheelchair. I had to restrain Oona from starting World War Three. 'It's just meeting the people,' I said, 'except they're in uniform. Remember the brochure, Yorkshire Tours never lets you down. Only we can give you this kind of experience.'

The Jewish woman was beside herself, her face twisted with rage. I can't repeat what she said, but she did lay most of Hitler's war crimes on the head of the sergeant in charge, although there was every chance he hadn't been born until the year of the Normandy landings.

There was nothing for it but to obey. We all stood near the front of the bus, ready to escape at a moment's notice. We were in a mobile Black Hole of Calcutta. Everyone present was talking, and their opinion of the group-leader sank lower and lower. The fumes continued to burst through the floor. 'It's only a hole in the exhaust,' said Snotty, 'that's all.'

At the border post the Prague group and the Leningrad group made common cause and rebelled: they squatted on the ground and refused to move, a decision reached democratically by secret ballot. No one was going any further until the bus was repaired, and the Soviet bloc could go stuff itself.

I felt sorry for the East German soldiers. They'd never seen anything like this. All they wanted to do was get rid of us and continue with their ordinary, hum-drum business of bullying people. Now they had Yorkshire Tours on their doorstep, and looked close to suicide. After a while an officer appeared; he didn't speak English and we had no German. His temper was short and grew shorter.

His face said it all – a summary execution by firing squad was too good for me. He became very angry; he shouted and he stormed, but it did no good. I was defended by Oona, who stood between me and death. I might have been an unregenerate male chauvinist pig but I was her unregenerate male chauvinist pig. For that German officer Yorkshire Tours was a battle too far, a Stalingrad. He retired to lick his wounds.

It was a sunny day and the two groups were happy; they'd been on sit-ins before. This was a piece of cake. They made themselves comfortable and read Aphra Behn novels; they played travel Scrabble and chess and did crosswords. They could have kept going for a month. 'These East Germans aren't anywhere near as bad as the Metropolitan Police,' said Oona and she smiled and called me 'Petal'.

At last the guards surrendered and telephoned across the border for a breakdown truck and we were towed, in triumph, to a village in the free world. There, in the local garage, the exhaust was dismantled and repaired. We, meanwhile, brewed tea, shared our iron rations and played football with the village boys on the sports ground. West Germany 6, Yorkshire Tours 2. We were a fine body of men and women whom nothing could daunt.

We were now running more than six hours late. By the time we reached Zeebrugge our ferry was long gone. We waited through most of the night until another dawn crept up on us, but we had no luck. There was no space on any of the ferries that day.

'We'll go to Calais,' said Snotty, and go to Calais we did,

with me reading the map, standing at the front of the bus. At Calais we waited a few more hours until another day began to darken. I had gone about fifty hours without proper sleep by then and I was beginning to hallucinate. My body felt like it belonged to someone else, and my head was floating a foot or two above my shoulders.

Once we were on the boat Snotty sidled up to me and told me that he was now out of driving hours. 'The moment we land in Dover,' he said with a leer that would have done credit to a necrophiliac, 'I'm off home.' He was delighted. He could simply dump us; this was a *coup de grace* that gave him a deep and satisfying pleasure – it warmed his decaying soul.

On the quayside at Dover we waited for a relief driver to come from Huddersfield; a driver from Dover would have been too simple. The new man was a better human-being than Snotty, but he didn't handle the bus as well, and soon, not only was the gear lever springing out frequently, but it began to stick in just as frequently. We were caught between the devil and the deep blue sea. There was only one way to free the gear-box when it stuck; the men had to disembark and rock the bus back and forth.

Rocking a car out of gear is one thing; rocking fifteen tons of loaded coach is another. It began early on, halfway up the hill out of Dover. We men rushed out of the coach, followed by Oona and her band. Half our number took up stations at the front, half at the back – one, two; one, two; one, two. And so we rocked our way to London, out of the coach every twenty miles or so, the butt of passing motorists, the fingers of scorn pointing at us. Bleary eyed and exhausted we travelled beyond fatigue and touched the shores of despair. At Canterbury we rocked; we rocked at Sittingbourne and Dartford, at Blackheath and Eltham. It was surreal: we were a laughing stock for the south of England and beyond.

The evening rush hour was in full swing when we hit the Old Kent Road. I was sixty or seventy hours without sleep now and would have killed the entire Royal Family for a cat-nap. Then the gear stuck again, right outside Waterloo Station. Thousands of commuters stopped on their way home to gawp at us. Cars and buses came to a halt, a massive traffic jam grew around us, hooters began to blare. Once more we disembarked, once more we rocked the bus, and cheers rose from the pavements around us. And I did something I had never done before, or since: I blushed.

I couldn't get away quickly enough at King's Cross. I rushed into the Underground, I hardly said goodbye, even to Oona. In the weeks that followed I made no attempt to discover if that bus got back to Huddersfield. For all I know it might have become the Flying Dutchman of charabancs, rocking its way for ever northwards, on an endless journey into a land of myth.

When I fell into my bed at last I swore I'd never travel with Yorkshire Tours again, but I did. Yorkshire Tours was a bug, a disease that infected the blood and returned every year, like malaria. Only twelve months after the Prague adventure I was on the road again with another bunch of stalwarts. Christmas and the New Year in Leningrad, Laurie Shaw's type-written brochure said. It was wishful thinking – we didn't get to Leningrad until Boxing Day evening, and had to leave on the return journey well before New Year's Eve. No matter. It was one of the best Yuletides ever: our train shunted into a siding in Vilnius; a foray into the snow-quiet forest to steal a Christmas tree; toilet paper looped over the windows by way of paper chains, and, on Christmas Day, everyone in my group doing the conga, followed by a hundred workers from every country in the Eastern bloc, snaking down the train and up the platform. A party that went on and on...but then, that really is another story.

GREAT MILTON, OXFORDSHIRE

Thirty thousand pounds for the Turner Prize, for an unmade bed, a pile of bricks or a room where the electric light flashes on and off. Not one of them as great in conception as the roof I put on my house. My roof is a work of art and will last a hundred and fifty years, two hundred maybe. It was made of timber I had cut, battens I had soaked in creosote, ancient tiles, and the knowledge of the builders who showed me how to do it. I had been to Blanchford's builders' yard to buy galvanised nails and sacks of cement; I had bought my first claw hammer. There was nothing better than my roof.

The activity of making a roof brings with it all the joy of making a work of art, especially when you do it for the first time. It is art to the roofer even if it isn't art to anyone else, just like the pile of bricks to the artist. You go beyond life for a while, beyond death. You are not quite sure where the work is taking you or what you are going to learn about yourself. It beats Columbus for discovery. I climbed a hundred tall ladders to the highest roofs in order to meet knowledgeable men, searching for instruction. And in pubs I talked with artisans who made celebrity sculptors look fashion-minded and fraudulent. I spent time with builders who carried the wisdom of the tribe with them. And, it came to me as a bonus, I worked out a definition of art on those roofs: art is something you want to return to, something you want to see many times, and not just a one off joke.

Celia and I had each won a year's scholarship after Trinity: she to Tubingen in Germany; me to the École Normale

Supérieure in Paris. Then, in 1967, we came to Oxford to begin working for D.Phils. We rented a four-roomed cottage in Little Milton – thirty shillings a week. We furnished it from chattel auctions; a couple of beds and cutlery came from my mother in Battersea. The cottage had one tap and a chemical toilet that I emptied once a week into a large pit I had dug in the garden. At the rear there was a view over rolling farmland towards the River Thame.

Then Celia's grandmother left her about £7500, a large amount of money – enough to buy a house – so we bought one in the next village: Great Milton. It was a good thing to do, and a bad thing. That house was to rule our lives for many a year. It was a large place, ten rooms, with three stone-built sheds at the back, a tumbledown garage and a walled garden. It had been the village butcher's shop for at least two generations, maybe three, run by a family called Turrill's. Johnny Turrill, the last owner before us, had been a towering figure in village history. The three sheds had been scullery, stable and slaughter house. Rivers of blood had run in the back yard, and there was a special drain for it as well as a pump to wash the gore into a soakaway.

The scullery was the only room that had running water and there we camped for maybe four years; it was our kitchen and dining room. We didn't have much; a sink: a Calor gas stove, a second hand table, a dresser and a few kitchen chairs standing on a patch of rotting lino. To begin with there was only one bedroom that didn't leak. Television wasn't an option, though we sat up in bed sometimes and played dominoes, threes and fives, with a crib board and matchsticks.

Behind the black timber garage was the walled garden, a double drop lavatory and two long corrugated iron sheds full of a century of Turrill's rubbish: butcher's hooks, pulleys made of wood, hand-made nails, tins of screws, chains, old locks and their keys, scythes and sickles and stones to sharpen them; a rickety workbench, a vice, and piles of bent hinges.

'Them Turrills never threw anything away,' they told me in the pub. 'Not a bit of string, not a bent nail. They wouldn't give you the snot out o' their noses, nothing.'

Celia and I were innocents abroad, completely naïve. We simply walked into the front yard and it was love at first sight. It would have been churlish to notice that the window frames were rotten, the doors off their hinges, and that the stone walls were covered in creeper, more than a foot thick, holding the damp in so the rooms smelt of mildew. Nothing had been touched since the 1920s.

'Ah!' we said, 'isn't it wonderful. It has such a lovely feel to it.' And the walled garden? Never mind that it was tree high in weeds. There might well have been rhinos in there and we wouldn't have seen them.

Inside the rooms were gloomy. It was a Boris Karloff house. The stairs creaked, the plaster bulged on the walls and everything was painted in dark brown or green. The sash windows wouldn't slide up or down and the flagstones were wet to the touch. At the front, in the room above the cellar, in what had been the butcher's shop, there was a huge hole in the plank floor where the wood had rotted away. There was no bathroom, no lavatory. It would mean standing up in a tin bath, like at Askern, sluicing each other down in the scullery.

We had no money for a surveyor. The trustees of Celia's bequest (her mother – mem-sahib, Indian Army – was one) would not release any cash until we had actually bought a house. They feared that I might buy a Ferrari with it. 'What is more,' said my mother-in-law, 'Spaniards are untrustworthy foreign fellows, known for their cruelty.'

It wasn't difficult to find a way around the surveyor problem. Great Milton was heavily populated with jobbing builders and I had met most of them in The Bell public house. Freddie Neail was the most approachable, a slight, gentle man who was a cousin of Johnny Turrill's.

'Yes,' he said, 'I'll walk round the house with you.'

He came one evening after work. It was July and it was still light. He stood close to the stone walls and glanced up and down. 'They're straight,' he said, 'no subsidence, no bulging. They're fine, them walls'll be at least eighteen inches to two feet, old lime mortar.' He was right; one gable end was two foot six thick. I know because I had to make three holes in it; one for a kitchen extract fan, an air brick and a passage for a water pipe.

We went down to the cellar where Johnny had salted his pigs. There we found a long trough, lead lined.

'You'll sell that lead,' said Freddie, 'worth a few bob.' He examined the beams that held the ground floor up. I looked at them too, peering over his shoulder.

'God,' I was horrified. 'Look at the worm.'

Freddie sucked his teeth. 'Worm, be buggered,' he said, dismissing the whole universe of worm. He took a large penknife from his pocket, opened it, and passed it to me. 'Try shoving that into that beam.'

I did. The point of it sank in about a quarter of an inch, it wouldn't go any further. The heart wood was as hard as iron.

'There's nothing wrong with it,' said Freddie. 'That beam's at least two or three hundred years old. Probably came out of a ship, or off a barge; older than the house – look at the shape of it. The worm starts on it but then they gives up. It's too tough for 'em. I tell you that beam will last you out, and your children, and their children as well.'

We went back to the ground floor. 'It's damp enough in 'ere to be a ditch,' said Freddie. 'You'll need a damp proof course.' I didn't know what a damp proof course was.

'Yes,' I said.

We went up a flight of stairs where we found three bedrooms. The floorboards were a foot wide and more than an inch thick. 'Elm,' said Freddie. There was worm along the edges. 'You could take 'em out, plane the edges off and put 'em back. They'd look lovely, polished. It won't be easy getting them out.'

It wasn't. I took a cold chisel to them eventually and they split apart rather than come off their rusted nails. It was hard graft.

'Don't worry about the main timbers, the joists and beams will be fine, they used good stuff in them days. You can treat them with worm-proofing if you want.'

In the attic we stood inside the sloping roof and I could feel the ghosts nudging me.

'Johnny never came up here, lived in the scullery his last years and slept in the room next to it.'

There were two dormer windows facing the yard and the weather had got into them. They leant outward, longing to surrender to gravity. The roof had leaked so much that Johnny had covered the floors of all three attics with a treble thickness of horsehair mattresses to catch the rain, preventing it from bringing down the ceiling plaster in the bedrooms below. The dust was thick and mice had been nesting in the mattresses for many a winter. The smell was sickening, like a dungeon where human flesh had been rotting.

The inside of the roof had, in its time, been grandly decorated in lath and plaster, but the rain had got to it long since. Freddie pulled a large patch of it down so that he could look at the state of the roof timbers. I didn't like that. Pulling things down was frightening; I hadn't yet come to terms with the idea that parts of the house had to be destroyed so that I could build them up again. Eventually I carried on where Freddie had left off, pulling the whole lot down and shovelling it out of the window; dust in my eyes, throat and lungs.

The roof was made of peg tiles laid on split oak battens. I remembered them now. The women made battens and pegs in one of Thomas Hardy's novels, though I couldn't remember which. The pegs were wooden, a couple of inches long, the battens nailed to the rafters with wire nails. The pegs had been eaten away, the nails had rusted through: that meant that with the weight, each tile weighing about a couple of pounds, the whole construction was, like the dormers, slipping towards the ground.

Freddie estimated that the roof was at least 150 years old, maybe more. Straw had been laid as thick as could be along the battens and between the rafters, acting as insulation and to prevent driven snow drifting into the house between the tiles.

'There was no such thing as roofing felt when that roof went up.'

He pulled a tile from the roof to show me the weight of it. On the back a date had been stamped with a die – 1804. I have it now in my study. Another carried the imprint of a sheep's hoof, and one had a ship in sail drawn on it. Freddie sucked his teeth. 'You're going to have to do that roof,' he said. My stomach shrivelled against my backbone. People who know nothing about roofs are frightened to death by them. They would rather face Torquemada for a week in a Spanish jail. I tried not to think of it; I filed the information away and consoled myself; a lick of paint and everything would be all right. 'The structure's fine,' Freddie concluded, 'but there's work to do.'

'How much do I owe you?' I asked.

Freddie looked at me like a doctor looking at a madman for whose malady there was no known cure, but then he knew what lay in store. 'Oh,' he said, 'give us ten bob.'

He was right about the work. Had Celia and I had an inkling of what awaited us we would have gone straight to a suburb of Oxford and bought a modern semi-detached. I was an ignoramus. I didn't know the names of the tools I had to buy, the structure of a house, or even the correct mix for cement and sand. 'Needs must when the devil drives.' Soon I was digging drains, installing windows, ripping up floors, and learning how to cut a straight line with a saw – 'measure twice, cut once.' I had twenty years of it, off and on, and at the same time I had to earn enough money to feed the family, buy tiles and cement and pay the plasterer.

I was forced to abandon my D.Phil. – Jude the Obscure in reverse: from intellectual to builder. I didn't have the time to become an academic, which was regrettable as I had found a subject that captivated me. While studying in Paris at the Bibliothèque Nationale I'd stumbled across a fellow called Nicolas Gueudeville: a French monk (circa 1654 – 1721) who had gone over the monastery wall in the late seventeenth century, and escaped to the Sept Provinces where he produced a revolutionary journal called *L'Esprit des Cours*. In his journal, well before Voltaire and Rousseau, he attacked the excesses of the *ancien régime*, even suggesting that the army should mutiny, depose the king and declare the people free. His courage must have been extraordinary. Under Louis XIV criticism of the monarchy was not taken lightly, and many a disrespectful scribbler had found himself kidnapped and dropped into an *oubliette*. With deep sadness I dropped Nicolas into an *oubliette* of my own: some half a dozen shoe-boxes where I kept him and all his cross references. 'Adieu, Nicolas. One day someone will find you and give you the recognition you deserve.'

In fact it was good for me. I discovered that I wasn't cut out to be an academic but I was cut out to be a freelancer. I did anything. I was a tour guide, mainly in France: Bordeaux wine châteaux, the Dordogne, Paris and Provence. When that was out of season I was a dogsbody in the film industry – camera assistant, video assistant, boom-swinger. I drove vans, I ran cable across studio floors. I was employed on interviews, documentaries and commercials, and I often worked for a man called Billy Johnson on audio-visual presentations. So I drove more vans up and down the country, built sets, and even wrote some of the rubbish that company men were obliged to deliver at their annual conferences.

And when the travel company I worked for went bust and I was broke I went on the dole and worked on the lump as a navvy for one or two of the village builders. Ten pounds a day mixing cement, nailing down floors and painting windows. Unsurprisingly roofs became my speciality. By the time I'd finished I'd done six of them: two for me – the sheds and the main building – two for friends and two professionally. Any spare time that Celia and I had was spent on renovating our own ruin: the next room, and the room after that, for by the early seventies we had two daughters, Aimée and Phoebe, and they needed proper accommodation – a bathroom, a kitchen and a play room.

Maybe we should never have bought the house, but I learnt a lot from it, mainly about myself. I could do it. I had the energy and the grit and the village had real people in it. They saw what Celia and I were doing, with very little money, and they helped.

'It's nice to see young people in that house,' said one of the old ladies of the village, looking up at Celia and me on the roof. 'Be careful you don't fall now.'

It was simple. We bought the house because it had a feel to it. Never mind the work. The rooms, though damp and dark, exuded love; never mind what had happened and what was to happen within those walls. Life and death happened there, as in every house, but love was the strongest – it seeped out of the walls and out of us. We would add our own blood to the mix and the house would suck it up like wine, and those that followed us through those rooms would feel sadness and love too, three hundred years of it. Love and sadness, you didn't get one without the other.

After Freddie's visit Celia and I talked things over and decided to buy the house, if possible. It was to be sold at auction, and we calculated that we could go as high as five thousand pounds. Celia's bequest was £7500 but there was stamp duty to pay and a thousand pounds worth of central heating and damp-proofing on top of that, and we needed some money to live on as we moved in.

We dressed up to the nines for the auction which was held in The Bell. The public bar still had its barrels on trestles and the ale was poured without benefit of pumps. The saloon was different: it had just been refurbished and given Formica counters and carpet tiles. None of the locals liked it but that was where the auction was held. The auctioneer, a Mr Messenger, thought it was more fitting, more suited to the gravity of the occasion.

The landlord of The Bell was called Bob Gurton, a big, solid, slow moving man with a wide leather belt that held in a vast stomach, bulging with force. Had it been released it would have rolled forward like an avalanche. Bob Gurton had a broad brow that sloped backwards, an oval face tipped on its side and a soft voice. He always dressed the same: a striped shirt with no collar and loose trousers that flapped about his legs. When he smiled his lips disappeared inwards as if there were no teeth to stop them. For all his size he was a gentle man. He too was a builder and every day he worked with Freddie Neail. There were four pubs in the village in those days: The Bell, The Bull, The King's Head and The Red Lion. The wives ran the pubs at lunchtime, the men in the evening when they returned from work. The Bull was a car mechanic; The Red Lion an electrician, and the King's Head worked for Post Office

Telephones.

I arrived at The Bell in my one and only suit, light grey and beautifully cut in Savile Row. Celia was elegant in her smart coat. I stood at the bar, where it made a corner with the wall, talking to Bob Gurton. I wrote a western a couple of years later and I made Bob the owner of a saloon called 'Gurton's Gaiety.' I had forgotten to bring any money with me.

'Can I have a pint on tick?' I asked him.

Bob smiled his disappearing smile and poured. He had pumps now in the saloon bar.

There were five groups interested in buying the house. There was a speculator; a builder; a local landowner named Gale-Taylor who owned half the village, and a couple of families.

The auction began slowly. Everyone, apart from Celia and me, sitting primly round the edges of the room like wall-flowers at a school dance. The auctioneer and his clerk had a desk. The bidding started at £2500. It was not enough; a similar sized village property had sold for £4000 the week before.

The bidding went up in hundreds until it got to £3800. Then it slowed down. Everyone there, except me, knew that the house was a complete ruin, that the roof was scary and also that it was Grade II listed which made things even more difficult. I didn't even know what Grade II listed meant. Messenger wasn't pleased; he wanted to get the sale going again, and he brought the bidding down from hundreds to fifties, then to twenty-fives.

I stood quiet in the corner, my back to the room, showing no sign that I was interested in the proceedings until the bidding had crept, reluctantly, up to £4200. Then I turned slowly, raised my hand and spoke, fighting to keep my voice cool. 'Five thousand.'

It came as such a surprise to Messenger that he missed me.

'Who? What?' he said.

I turned towards him. 'Five. Over here.'

The bar went as quiet as a mausoleum, all faces pale. Messenger tried hard and went down to lots of ten. It was no good. I had taken the wind out of every sail, I could see them flapping against the masts: they were in the doldrums. I might just as well have said: 'There is no God and I have slept with all your daughters.'

'Masterly bidding,' said Messenger, as we signed the papers, and Bob Gurton shook his head. 'I dunno,' he said, 'spends five thousand and takes two pints off me.' We didn't know it, but Celia and I had taken the first step to becoming roofers.

We found a whole pile of deeds and waxed indentures in the attic, in perfect condition. They dated from 1726 when the house had first been mortgaged, though the local history mentions a date of 1690. The building was then described as a cottage with garden and orchard. It had been nameless until the 1920s when the Turrills had called it 'Oxford Cottage', a name that Celia and I disliked. The first names on the first mortgage were Alice and George Tallis and so we named our house after them; we wanted all the ghosts on our side. 'Alice Tallis's Palace.'

Tallis House was next door to the King's Head. Like all the pubs in the village it was a quiet pub, even on Saturday evenings. There were dart competitions and dominoes, though best of all were the Aunt Sally evenings. There was a high wall separating our garden from the pub and there was a profound pleasure to be had by listening to the sounds of an ancient game being played in the cool of a long summer evening: the voices rising as the consumption of beer rose; the applause when a player scored with all six sticks; the sound of wood striking wood – 'a doll, a doll.'

If the building work hadn't tired me out I would often drift into the King's Head for the last hour of opening time in order to smoke a cigar in company and be a villager. That last hour was always good, the public bar crowded with characters from a country novel: the Headmaster of the village primary school; the husband of the local hairdresser who always came loaded with gossip; men from the Cowley car works; a poet on sabbatical from a university in Connecticut and an Oxford don, a reader in anthropology, as daft as only dons can be. There was also a legion of the Wise family: George, who told stories about the war, with poaching the only way to feed his family; Ron, who rode a tall black bike which he pushed home, very carefully, after an evening of ale; and Herbert, who ambled about the village, staring at the sky, mumbling to himself – 'Looks like rain, look likes rain' – his overcoat buttons fastened all skew-whiff, the wrong buttons in the wrong button-holes, so that even now my children call it 'doing a Herbert'. And Willoughby Wise, a man with a cloth cap, a bony face and a nose like half a pound of nails in a brown paper bag. He knew his building though. He told me that half my garden wall was going to fall down that winter – and it did – but at least he didn't crow too much and showed me how to rebuild it.

Bert Hayes used to drink there too. He chopped half his thumb off once, in his garden, and suffered the eternal ridicule of the public bar because he hadn't rescued the amputated piece and taken it to hospital to get it sewn back on. 'It weren't my fault,' he'd say after a pint or two, 'bloody magpie came down and flew off with it. I couldn't fly after it, could I?' And Evelyn, an ancient agricultural worker, one of the last in Oxfordshire. He was a huge man in tweeds and a pork-pie hat and boots like barges. I watched him lay a hedge once, up on Gale's Hill, his hands as wide as shovels, fingers as thick as salamis, bending the saplings to his will, making a fence that was a delight to look at, straight out of the previous century. A poem in trees our poet called it.

But it was Roger Cope who got me up onto the roof the first time. He was a tall willowy man in his thirties, with a long face, and short blond hair. A travelling salesman for a stationery company, he had purchased, with his wife, a row of five Victorian cottages and, in an indolent way, was doing them up. He didn't spend much time out on the road. A couple of sales in the morning and he was home for lunch. His afternoons were spent doing a little work on his cottages and chatting to anyone in the village who would chat to him. As soon as The King's Head or The Bell opened he would be off for a packet of cigarettes and a pint of beer, and more often than not forget to go home. At eight or nine the door to the pub would ease open and his wife's tiny face would appear, her voice plaintive across the bar: 'Oh, Roger, your dinner's ready'. But he was a man who had done his own roof. 'It's a piece of cake,' he told me.

'We'll start on your scullery, that's where you are going to live. I'll come over Saturday.'

Although the scullery was a single storey building it looked like a skyscraper to me. While waiting for Roger I went up the ladder to the pitch of the roof and looked down the other side. It was as steep as an alpine pass and my resolve melted. I couldn't do this, it was total foolishness. Then Roger arrived, a ladder on his shoulder, beaming, happy to be pulling something apart. He climbed the ladder to the top and began lifting the tiles from their battens, sliding them down a scaffolding plank to me at the bottom.

'Stack 'em properly,' he said, 'otherwise they'll crack under their own weight.' I stacked and worried; worried and stacked.

In no time that section of the roof was clear. Then Roger took a claw hammer and began breaking the battens, throwing them down, removing their rusty nails. At last all that was left were the rafters, all sound save for one or two. 'You see,' cried Roger. 'Easy, easy. Job done, down the pub.'

He was extraordinarily generous was Roger. He neglected his own cottages that week, not to mention his salesman duties. I ordered battens, roofing felt, galvanized nails and anti-worm spray. I toiled away all that weekend and the week that followed, and Roger came home from work earlier and earlier to help me. He showed me how to do the double row of tiles at the bottom of a roof, how to keep bond like a brick wall, how to set the ridge tiles, and how to cut half tiles for the gable end. I was filthy every day, washing in the zinc bath, and we celebrated every evening at Bob Gurton's, just to let him know how we were getting on. And, from time to time, Roger's wife popped her head in at the door to announce dinner, and always to no avail.

I learnt my roofing on the sheds. I still look up there and see the mistakes I made. But the main job was still to do – the roof of the house, colossal and three storeys high. I used to gaze at it in fear every time I went down the yard. It wasn't going to be easy; I would need scaffolding, and Freddie Neail, once again, was the man.

'There's a heap of it in my garden,' he said. 'Scaffolding clips, too.' It was old-fashioned gear, heavy and rusty, and I had to ship it from one end of the village to the other, on a borrowed flat back lorry. I had never erected scaffolding before, and Celia and I struggled to get it up; and it wasn't too steady when we did. To make sure that it didn't collapse I ran a pole into each window and strapped a crosspiece onto it, inside the house. It wasn't professional but it worked.

The roof took nearly three months, day in, day out. A real roofer would have done it in two weeks at the most. We worked from seven in the morning until it was dark. I had school kids of fourteen rushing home to join me, bringing up tiles, cutting battens. They loved every moment of it and I paid them pocket money: two shillings here and there – Brinley, David, Lester and Geoffrey. Two of them still live in the village; now into their fifties, with grown up children of their own. There is still a special camaraderie when we meet, us roof-boys, and I know if I needed to replace a tile they would climb the ladder with me, happy as kings, cheery as cherries.

It was a dry summer that summer of 1970 and the tiles were off for a long while. I trusted nature too much. A huge storm rolled up one night in August and in the middle of a cloudburst I climbed onto the roof to nail some plastic sheeting onto the rafters to keep the weather out.

It was a tempest. The rain was torrential and seemed to go on for hours, lightning flickered around me. I was shaking with cold and fear. I was the highest living thing within a radius of a mile or two, a steel hammer in my hand, and several thousand volts were searching for me, eager to burn my flesh. I got down to ground level as soon as I could and found the yard a foot deep in water; it poured through the front door and down the steps into the cellar. I seized a shovel and tried to push the water away from the house. The lightning never stopped, burning the rain; the smell of brimstone filled the air. Then there was an almighty explosion, very close, in the yard it seemed, my head spun. A thunderbolt had hit the electric sub-station just over the road and every light in Milton went out. That was it. If another thunderbolt landed it would be my light going out. I was stupidly vulnerable, standing there soaked to the skin, holding a metal shovel and over my ankles in water. I was not being sensible; let the cellar flood. There was a soakaway down there wasn't there?

The following day I saw Sam Howard, one of my neighbours, in the King's Head. He had the whole pub laughing at me.

'Some storm,' he said. 'I goes to my window, 'bout three in the morning, it was. And what do I see?' He gestured at me with his pint. 'I saw this maniac up on the roof, light as day it was, rain and thunder, trying to nail plastic down in a force ten gale. I couldn't believe it, I called the wife over to look. "Them bloody students," she said.'

Slowly the roof progressed and my knowledge increased, though there were some things that were too much for me. The two dormers had to be replaced and the valleys and purlins needed repairing; work that would call for proper carpentry. Fortunately there was a man called Hans Pacsoska, an extraordinary man. Hans was lean, with a high forehead. There was nothing he couldn't do; intelligent and bright as a button he worked and moved fast. He scoffed at my efforts and called me 'Hammer Strangler' and 'College Boy', yet he taught me everything. He had a heart of gold and a short temper.

He'd been brought to England as a German prisoner of war; shot through the left hand and captured by the Americans in Brittany in 1944. He'd been sixteen years old then. ('I joined up,' he always insisted, 'I wasn't conscripted.') After his capture he'd been shipped off to the States to work on a farm for a couple of years, then brought back to England for some more of the same. After a while he'd met and married a local girl, Eva. Now his four children were grown up and spoke with broad Oxfordshire accents.

He must have been totally self taught: carpentry, plumbing, central heating, bricklaying, glazing, roofing, tiling, car mechanics. No wonder the Wehrmacht was so hard to beat. He built my kitchen for me, coming to Tallis House in the evenings after work, designing the cupboards, plumbing in the sinks, and never asked for a penny. He was just a friend who wanted to see me get my house finished. He was a diamond.

But perhaps Bernard Cross was the king. 'Scorcher' Cross they called him in The Bell; that was because he was a plumber, and plumbing had to do with sweated Yorkshires and blow-torches, flames and molten lead. He hadn't begun life as a plumber. Silver haired, brawny and tall, he looked like a heavyweight boxer. When he came into a pub he brought a hundred seasons with him, and the country air stuck to the weave of his coat; winters, autumns, summers and springs. A host of remembered people followed him everywhere, their families and their stories, and all of them had lived within a twenty mile radius of Great Milton: farm workers and farm owners, scandals from the past, lovers long dead, adulteries best forgotten. And he knew the name of every field in the Milton hundreds, names now lost to memory and maps as the meadows were robbed of their hedges and copses. And the tales he told went back through the war, back to the twenties and thirties. He was a link to a different life, a life disappeared, a world from which it was possible to glimpse the countryside of the eighteenth century, the perfect pastoral.

He'd lived in Little Milton as a boy and his mother had run the Lamb public house. (Her chairs now live in my kitchen). He'd begun work on the farm. 'Thirty workers at least then, only two now.' He'd been a stable boy, then a groom, and as he'd risen through the ranks he'd been given a horse and made a stockman.

'I'd ride out at dawn, to check the herds. I was a prince,' he'd say. 'Sat up there on my horse, Milton to Haseley and back again, through the mist, the fields all grey-green like the sea. I could box a bit too, I was a big lad. I was pushed up against a wall once, by a cow, fully grown, nearly killed me. I swung a blow at her that cracked one or two of her ribs. They had to take her off to the slaughter house. Well, word o' that got round, yer see. I had no trouble with anybody after that, even though I was promoted over the heads of a few of them. I loved it, but then farm work became scarce after the war, so I took an apprenticeship in plumbing, and now I toils away at the Cowley

159

works. It's regular, but it ain't like riding your horse over a thousand acres.'

Bernard could talk for hours. 'I used to get sent out to block up foxes' earths, the night before a hunt like. I was creeping down the bottom here, pitch black, by the brook.' He tilted his head westwards, as if the wall of the pub didn't exist. 'At the bottom of Harris's Farm, I heard some noises, strange noises. It weren't no fox, I can tell you. Well, I won't tell you no names. No names, no pack-drill, I always says, but I will.' He laughed at his own joke. 'It was Mrs High-and-Mighty Fitz-Albert, with one of her house guests, up against a tree, at it hammer and tongs.'

Bernard's laugh was joyful, looking back over his life and relishing every moment of it. The door of Tallis House was always open and every time he went by he came in for a beer and gave us a story, or left cabbages on the step. He would check on my building prowess too, and make sure I was doing the bathroom right. He installed my taps when we got that far and taught me how to flash a chimney; that was plumber's work, cutting lead and shaping it with a wooden mallet.

'Pity you didn't meet Johnny Turrill,' he said often. 'He was a character. He was the first person to have a car in the village; your garage at the back, that was the first garage too. Everyone knew Johnny. He had a sister called Annie. They never married; there was a brother as well, he went off to America somewhere. We all had a pig at the end of the garden, specially during the war. We fed it on scraps, potato peelings and such. When it was ready we drove it down to your slaughter house and Johnny would poleaxe it. We'd pull that head down to the block, and we'd hold it tight so it couldn't move, and Johnny would swing the axe at it. Never forget the sound. Crack, right through the skull and into the brain. He never missed – wallop. Then he'd cut it up. Blood and guts all over the place. We ate every scrap of that pig, we did: black pudding, chitterlings made from the guts, backbone pie, hams of course; lard in jars, sweetbreads, kidneys, and that liver was luvly – fresh, melt in yer mouth... and we'd simmer the head for days to make brawn, and you could slice that up and stick it between chunks of bread. That used to keep the winter out.'

* * *

I wrote my first book at Milton. I don't know where I found the time but I did. In fact I wrote five between 1970 and 1981, when I was at my busiest as a builder. I had a portable typewriter, an Olivetti Lettera 22, which my mother had bought for me in Battersea by cashing in one of her insurance policies for twenty pounds, a lot of money in 1953. She knew I had dreams of becoming a writer. I had hoped she would live to see one of my books published, but she didn't, though I suspect she would have had trouble dealing with such an event. I can just imagine her reaction – 'I can't read it, Mick, I'm too nervous, it would give me stomach-ache.'

I'd sketched out an autobiographical novel that described my early days on Lavender Hill. It was resolutely refused. Then, in desperation, after a trip to the cinema, I wrote a western: *The Redwater Raid.* They publish westerns, don't they – wholesale? My brothers had read 'cowboys' all the time at home: *Sudden Rides Again* by Oliver Strange – *The Law of the Lariat.* I will never forget the first line of my book. It has a certain ring to it, provided that it is read in the correct accent: *'The town of Redwater, Arizona, was hardly a town at all.'* My brothers read thrillers too: James Hadley Chase; Peter Cheney; Mickey Spillane. Those were my literary horizons to begin with. Unfortunately the brothers never found their way to Dashiell Hammett or Raymond Chandler, but luckily for me Battersea Lending Library was at the end of the road I lived in; there I could stretch my wings and soar a little closer to the sun.

The Redwater Raid was accepted by Hodder and published as a Coronet paperback. I was paid £250 for it. There was happiness in Tallis House, such a lot of money at one go. They were, the publishers said, going to turn me into their house western writer; could I write some more? I wrote the second, *Sweet-Tooth Jones,* and the synopses for several others. Okay, so I would become a western writer; not really what I'd had in mind as a literary career, but with some travel and film work on the side I could make a living maybe. Travelling and writing; the two best things. That would do nicely. There was even a Hollywood film producer who bought an option in the book – for all of eleven pounds. Gosh and golly, but I had a lot to learn.

And learn I did. I learnt how publishers (with very few exceptions) and literary agents for that matter, treat unsuccessful writers. Hodder had a meeting, changed their corporate minds and threw me out. Not for the last time I was asked to write a book and then told it wasn't wanted. At least a year of endeavour had been wasted.

And so the years in Great Milton slipped by; twenty or thirty of them: work, writing and love. My children grew faster than roses on the wall; picnics by the river at Cuddesdon Mill, teaching them to swim, canoeing expeditions. And me loving them every minute, watching, hoping they would turn into friends one day. Learning how to get through adolescence again; second time for me, first time for them.

But how rapidly everything changed around us: pubs closing and converted into houses, no stories told at the bar, a whole generation of old builders dying off, with Wheatley, the centre of our universe, suddenly a different place: the butcher's now a suite of offices; the greengrocer's a chemist; the ironmonger's a massage parlour; and from nowhere two hairdresser's, an antiques shop and an Indian takeaway. I learnt, as everyone does, that sadness comes with age; so prepare for it, I told myself, and anyone who would listen – fill your haversack with memories and as much love and friendship as you can lay your hands on, just so there's something for you to enjoy when you take your last picnic by the side of the road, and make sure you order up the best bottle of wine you can think of, you're going to need it.

There is a photo of me sitting high on my roof with it all finished, looking out over the village, every tile in place, snug and safe, not a leak, gutters doing their job and smart lead flashing at the chimneys, and the house below me all neat and tidy, each daughter with her own room. And there was even carpet on the stairs at last and Aimée was content: 'We're posh now, aren't we Daddy?' I even had an office in the attic, but I was torn between writing and travelling; there was so much I hadn't seen.

There's a definite connection between travelling and the imagination. Perhaps travel, real or imaginary, is simply a question of breaking out, getting fresh air, testing the mettle of our own way of life against the steel of another, a tempering of our soul. Most authors have written well about their travels and much of their best work was inspired by their voyages. They all come home to tell their stories of triumph and failure. Yes indeed. But on the other hand, how far did Jane Austen travel? But I wasn't Jane Austen and the odds were that I would never make a living by writing.

My family was eating, but only just. The film business was shrinking, technology changing fast; two-man crews replacing four-man crews, and the travel firm I worked for in France had gone broke. Then, luck struck again. At this point my literary agent, an attractive and sharp-tongued woman known to some as Miss Whiplash, sent one of my books, *The Provençal Tales* – an account of my life with the shepherds – to the editor of the travel section of the Sunday Times, and I was offered an occasional job writing lead articles for that section.

The god of freelancers had come to my rescue. I was on the road again but I was able to choose, more or less, where I went and when. In fact I wrote about sixty articles over a period of twelve years or so. And I was able to work intermittently, three or four months of the year. I filled in with any other work that came my way and so earned enough to put bread on the table. The rest of my time I spent with Celia, watching the children grow.

Suddenly I was a Sunday Times travel writer – it was an offer I couldn't refuse, and in no time at all I was in India.

Nasik

'The time of the gods is now,' said Vanita, and we boarded the bus, a pale green affair with white stick-people painted all over it and with flower baskets hanging from the luggage rack. It was my first visit to India since I had ridden that motor bike down the Grand Trunk Road on the Marco Polo Route Project thirty years previously. Vanita was a local guide and I was travelling with a group of eighteen people – half of them English, half American. We had come up from Mumbai, north to Nasik on the road to Trimbakeshwar, and whatever time Vanita thought it might be it was two o'clock in the morning for us. We were all jetlagged, our eyelids heavy. We had been travelling for thirty-six hours.

Vanita was a woman of flaming energy. On the journey from Mumbai she had told us stories from the holy books, shown us yoga exercises and read my palm too. But on the rough roads, where we bounced around the bus like marbles in a can, she told us another story – the story that had brought me all the way from Heathrow.

'Once upon a time,' said Vanita, 'many thousands of years ago, the gods and the demons fought a great battle, fighting for a kumbh – a jar of precious nectar. This jar lay at the bottom of the ocean and the conflict was so fierce that it threw the waters into turmoil and huge waves rose high into the air. The war was long and bloody for it was known that whoever drank the nectar would be granted eternal life. At last Lord Vishnu seized the jar, but the demons did not give up easily; they pursued him and the struggle went on for twelve years, until finally the gods defeated the demons and achieved their immortality. And during the battle four drops of the nectar fell from the heavens to the earth in four different places – Allahabad, Hardwar, Ujjain and Nasik, and since that time a mela or festival is held in each city in turn, every three years, a twelve year rotation. This year is the turn of Nasik and Tribakeshwar, and tonight is the holiest festival of them all.'

Some three million pilgrims and twenty thousand holy men, the sadhus, had come to Nasik to take part in this, the greatest of the Kumbh Mela. On the night of our arrival, the sadhus were to walk in a great procession with music and garlanded elephants. They had come to dip themselves in the holy waters of the temple pool at Trimbakeshwar, waters that flow from the mountain-side, the source of the Godavari, a sacred river that flows clear across the country to the Bay of Bengal.

As we neared our destination the crowds on the highway became so dense that our bus could no longer advance. 'Out,' said Vanita and we climbed down into the road to join the throng of pilgrims. 'You will take off your shoes,' we were ordered. 'Trimbakeshwar is holy ground tonight.'

Very soon the track narrowed and my feet were soon wet, the ground was stony. From time to time we passed an elephant, docile, waiting to take its part in the great ceremony. In dark spaces of waste land sat platoons of policemen, cuddling their night sticks. Further on we were halted by an official; he gave each of us a name-tag and then told us how to behave.

'There will be no smoking from now, this is a most holy of occasions, not a tourist event. The sadhus will be naked when they dip, so will some of the women. Be reverent because they are in a trance, and if you upset them there is no telling, but they will dip and sip and that will be good kharma.'

Vanita led us past the man and into a steeply descending street where whole families slept on the narrow porches of their shanty shops. The street twisted and turned until suddenly we came out onto an open square where the high branches of a huge banyan tree spread like a roof above our heads. To one side was the holy pool and beyond it stood the temple with a portico of carved columns along the water's edge.

We went towards the temple immediately, passing under yellow lights that made the skin of my companions look malarial. Then we went by a group of military men, officers, standing very Sandhurst, tapping their calves with swagger-sticks. In the portico we were given wooden chairs to sit on, not more than a foot or two from the pool's edge. The water was murky green and looked solid enough to walk on. I knew that one sip of it would have done for me entirely; for the sadhus it was desirable and holy. They were, no doubt, made of stern stuff.

On the scum of the water floated several inflated motor-car inner-tubes, each one moored to a column by a length of cord. They must have been put there for those sadhus who couldn't swim. In the shadows of the temple were a dozen or so life-guards dressed in white T-vests and swimsuits, their arms crossed professionally on their chests. The pool was deep and in a trance a sadhu could drown, pushed under by his colleagues in a moment of fervour.

Beyond the yellow lights, and invisible to us, were two hundred and fifty thousand believers, tense and expectant, and that tension lay tangible across the night air. We sat and waited for four-thirty to arrive, the auspicious moment that the sadhus had chosen. Every now and then the officers strutted up and down. Their corporals came and went, bearing messages. The special hour arrived and as it did so the tension tightened to breaking point. Vanita touched her holy necklace for reassurance. She looked nervous. We should have heard music by now, the sound of voices raised in adulation. There was nothing but silence. Vanita glanced again in the direction of the two hundred and fifty thousand. 'They have been waiting since yesterday morning,' she said, 'just to see their holy men. I hope they don't get angry. They could tear us to pieces.'

The sky began to pale. A group of Norwegians on the far side of the pool got up from their chairs to leave. At last the electric lamps were turned off and a tribe of monkeys began to brawl in the trees above the temple roof. A soldier brought a message. The sadhus had quarrelled amongst themselves and there would be no mela. The auspicious moment had passed and a twelve year wait had dwindled down to nothing. 'When sadhus fall out,' said Vanita, 'they wouldn't take a dip or a sip for Vishnu himself.'

We returned the way we had come. Daylight was in the streets and we pushed through the host of pilgrims, still immobile, still hoping. We cut through an alley where the shutters were opening on the shops, the day beginning with the violent hawking that comes up from the stomach and beyond, with the spitting phlegmatic and fulsome. Outside a shanty we found our official drinking tea. 'No mela,' he said, 'well then, that's your tough unluck.'

At last Vanita led us up a steep path, through the hordes of men, women, children and livestock. We halted by a door where a crowd stood. Somehow Vanita had obtained an audience with some of the most important sadhus present at the mela. We removed our shoes once again, ducked into a low-roofed hut, and sat cross-legged on dusty carpets.

There were three sadhus before us, in saffron robes and sitting on mats alongside the rear wall: one of them awake, the other two asleep. The hut contained an audience of thirty or so people, sometimes talking, sometimes not. Pilgrims came and went freely, approaching the holy trio with reverence, touching them with humble hands. The sadhus were fine looking men, thin, aged and with wise beards.

Through Vanita we asked questions. It had been a quarrel over precedence. A committee of sadhus representing some ten groups had decided on an order of march but one group had not been happy, and had decided to take a dip all by themselves on the twenty-third, a night of full moon. This decision had not pleased the remaining sadhus; they had talked the matter over and declared that the twenty-third was not propitious – there would be no dip on that day. In the end the rebels refused to agree to anything and the discussion grew so heated and prolonged that a riot threatened. The police and troops prepared themselves for trouble. Then, the propitious moment passed and the procession to the temple became impossible anyway – the whole thing was cancelled.

Outside the crowd went by, a never ending stream of worshippers; cows and water buffalo and children too. On the porch of the house opposite the men who slept there rolled over and yawned themselves awake. Drums were tapping from somewhere close at hand and smoke from a rubbish fire drifted in through the open door bringing other smells with it; incense, food and a rising warmth from the earth.

The sadhu who was awake sighed deeply. Yes, it was shameful that so many pilgrims had been disappointed, but the twenty-third was not a good day. It had cost a lot of money – the flowers, the elephants. He gestured with his hand and every finger was loaded with rings. At any rate at the next Kumbh Mela the rebellious group would not be allowed to participate, that much was certain.

We stood and joined our hands before us, palm to palm, and bowed. We went out and threaded our way back through the crowds, past the elephants and past a band of naked sadhus who stood behind a roughly built wooden lattice, like animals in a cage, their skin covered in ash and dust, their bodies indistinguishable from the darkness of the hut they stood in. Around their heads floated long strands of hair, grey, stiff like banners; their eyes stared at another world. We were silent; my companions had taken the night's disappointment in their stride. They had not seen the holy dip and sip but they had learnt a great deal about India, its people, its religions, its timelessness; and so had I.

Back at the crossroads the Norwegians sat on a wall and waited for their mini-bus. 'I came a long way,' said one, angry. 'And I paid a lot of money, for nothing.'

I was amused, detached from such thoughts. This scene, this night had nothing to do with money. I was high on the experience, the noise, the voices; it happened all the time in the sub-continent. I looked around me at the multitudes; thousands of pilgrims washing and cooking and thousands more setting off for a new destination. Then I looked across the valley and saw where they were going; an unbroken line of worshippers climbing countless steps to the top of the mountain so they might drink the waters from the very source of the holy river: a procession of white dhotis and bright saris caught in the early sun of the morning, brilliant colours shining against the dull and misty green of the hillside.

As we climbed into our bus, all of us ready for sleep, the angry Norwegian raised a hand in farewell.

'Don't go too far away,' he said, and his voice was bitter. 'There'll me another Kumbh Mela in twelve years.'

I smiled at him. 'I know,' I said, 'it's hardly worth going home, is it?' and the door of the bus closed behind me.

* * *

I had written a book called *The Borribles*, while still working on the house in Great Milton. I only knew one publisher personally in those days – Judy Taylor – who was in charge of children's books at the Bodley Head; not that I was sure that *The Borribles* was a child's book. Judy had relatives in the village and visited frequently. I simply shoved the manuscript at her one day and didn't hear from her for two or three months. I discovered later that no one at the Bodley Head, except Judy, liked the book and she'd had a hard time pushing it through. Her colleagues considered my work far too strong and violent, subversive even, but eventually it appeared in hardback and was well reviewed by most national and provincial newspapers, except The Guardian of course:

> *It creates a convincing sub-culture, which could become a cult, of tough, petty criminal Peter Pans in the less idyllic parts of south-east London.*
>
> *The Borribles are against everybody; and everybody – cause or effect – is against them. They are against 'normals' (that is real children, which Borribles once were). Against adults, against Woollies (the police), and above all against the Rumbles of the desirable London suburb of Rumbledom. They are as ferocious about the Rumbles as some people*

are about the Jews, or the blacks or the middle-class.

There were better reviews, luckily:

'*...this juvenile* Clockwork Orange *projects a gripping story through slam bang action.*'
Los Angeles Times

'*...the book has a deadly glint and a sophisticated appeal.*'
Kirkus

'*London's answer to* Watership Down, The Lord of the Rings, *and* The Guns of Navarone...*try* The Borribles, *warts and all, before they become a legend.*'
The Times

'*It's a brilliant invention and no more horror-filled than, say,* Treasure Island *or* King Lear *or any other great work.*'
Publishers' Weekly

'*Granted* The Borribles *won't win friends among the starry-eyed or squeamish; all the same they are the offspring of a singular imagination.*'
The New York Times

There was much more in the same vein, very flattering, and I thought I had made it at last. The 'phone rang continually for a few weeks – films, television – and I puffed out my chest and began to spend the millions I was about to earn. Then the would-be film producers read the book and decided it was indeed too subversive for them; so did the paperback publishers. Ah well, back to freelancing.

FROM LENINGRAD TO ST PETERSBURG

I saw Tania from about a hundred yards away. She was staggering in huge swoops from one side of the road to the other, avoiding the passing cars in a way that showed me that the Gods loved her. It was raining hard and what few pedestrians there were had their heads down. It was dark too and the lights of Gorky Street seemed far away. I was tired; I had spent four days walking the streets of Leningrad – it was still called Leningrad – and a couple of days in the Hermitage. Now I was in Moscow, ready to board the Trans-Siberian Express.

The moment I'd arrived in Moscow I'd gone straight down to the parliament building, for this was August 1991. There had been a coup against Gorbachov and Yeltsin had taken over, haranguing the crowd from the top of a tank. Outside the 'White House' – the seat of the Supreme Soviet – were the remains of half a dozen barricades; lumps of concrete, paving stones and barbed wire, but all now decorated with flowers. On muddy stretches of ground stood groups of people, old and young, staid and hippy, bleary eyed, arguing, deciding the fate of Mother Russia. A young couple stood silently to attention, dressed in overcoats that looked as if they'd been roughly cut from ancient army blankets. They stared into the distance, guarding the future. Behind them were tents for the demonstrators to sleep in. Everyone looked stern and serious; revolution was in the air.

Before long I was on the point of overtaking Tania, and her staggering had become Homeric. As I approached her I could see she was no bag lady. Well-dressed in a smart coat her hair was clean and neatly piled above her face. She'd been to an office party perhaps, or a wedding. Two sailors laughed at her, some children pointed.

I accelerated to pass her but Tania swooped once too often and walked into a wall. She swayed and I took her arm to prevent her falling over. Her face swivelled on her neck and she stared up at me. She was about fifty-five, a good solid tram of a woman with brown eyes and bulging rosy cheeks like Cox's orange pippins, not a wrinkle to be seen. A wisp of hair fell across her face.

'Taxi,' I suggested. I had no Russian so I waved a few roubles under her nose thinking she might be broke. Tania's eyes brightened and she seized my arm with both hands and staggered closer to me. She was twice my weight and now, when she staggered, I staggered, mimicking her dangerous long swoops.

'Come,' she said, in English, 'Come,' and with her head bumping against my shoulder we fox-trotted into Gorky Street where the tarmac shone in the headlights.

In Russia nearly every car is a taxi. The private owner can only pay off the heavy cost of his motor by moonlighting. He picks up fares on his way home and negotiates a price. So I stepped into the stream of home-going traffic, arm in arm with Tania, and held a hand in the air, waiting for my destiny to work itself out.

After a few minutes a Lada saloon zipped to a halt in front of us. The driver, a man about Tania's age and looking very much the worse for wear himself, leant over and opened the rear door. I pushed Tania inside and followed. I knew then, or thought I knew, that Tania lived a kilometre or two beyond my hotel. 'Hotel,' I said slowly, giving the name; 'Hotel.' I held up ten fingers. 'Desyat roubles, ten roubles.'

'Da,' said the driver, and with the all-knowing leer of the perfect pimp stuck on his face, he drove back into the centre of the road.

Tania patted my hand and shifted her buttocks on the seat in the randiest of fashions. I smiled a frozen smile, noticing the spark of lust blazing deep down in the clinker of her soul. Before I could protect myself Tania had thrown her iron arms around my neck and delivered a rough kiss full on my mouth; a kiss heavy with halitosis, and laced with vodka and tobacco and the remains of several meals she had lurking in the crevices of her teeth. 'No hotel, you come me, sleep.' So that's why she was reasonably well dressed and spoke a smattering of English – she was on the game.

I panicked at this, especially as the driver took Tania's words as a command, turned from the bright lights of Gorky Street and drove off into more gloomy precincts.

'Hotel, hotel,' I was beginning to worry.

'Home, sleep,' said Tania.

I seized the driver's shoulder and shook it. 'Hotel, hotel,' I shouted, keeping it up until the car was back on the main road.

Then the driver took up his own refrain. 'Ten dollars,' he said, 'Ten dollars.'

'Roubles,' I insisted. 'Roubles.'

'Dollars,' said the driver, twisting his head to glare at me, letting the Lada navigate itself.

'Home, you, me,' repeated Tania and this three way chorus persisted until we came to rest in a side street.

I'd had enough. I thrust ten roubles into the driver's hand and escaped from the cab, out into the blessed rain, hiding as soon as I could behind a nearby tree. I was curious to know whether the driver would take Tania home as contracted, or indeed, if he might supply her with the night of passion which she had been expecting from me.

No such thing. Tania pushed the car door wide with her stubby legs and wriggled into the open. She got one foot on the ground but then caught the other on the sill. Her luck had run out at last and she tripped and fell flat on her face, into the wet mud of the pavement.

Now the driver got out and advanced unsteadily around the front of the Lada. He pulled Tania to her feet and, with his hands, attempted to wipe her down in the area of her bosoms. She pushed him away and headed back in the direction of Gorky Street. I followed her as far as the nearest corner. There two men appeared, walking with the gait of those who know where and how to find more than their permitted vodka ration. Tania greeted them like old friends, and the three of them talked, circling each other slowly, convinced they were standing still.

It was time for me to go. I went down some broken steps into an underpass, an underpass steaming with the night and the smell of stale urine. A beggar with a stump for a leg was sitting on a box. An old lady held out her hand, her eyes too deep to see into. She had matrioshka dolls in a plastic bag. She opened the largest: inside Yeltsin was Gorbachov; inside him Brezhnev, then Lenin and inside Lenin a tiny doll of Margaret Thatcher. Symbolism of a high order. The world was changing, too fast to keep up with.

On the far side of the underpass, back in the rain, were the old ladies selling flowers. There had been about twenty of them that morning, now there were only three or four, determined not to go home until every last bunch had been sold. You can buy flowers everywhere in Russia, and in a way it is reassuring; it's as if the flowers want to make up for the underlying sadness they took root in. I stood in the rain enjoying the feel of it on my face. On the other hand perhaps the flowers were blooms of despair, adding to the sadness they were meant to dispel, their very beauty working against them; an ode to melancholy. In any case, those old ladies should've been at home, in the dry. The bunches were no more than three or four roubles each and I bought them all, an armful. I was catching the Trans-Siberian the next day and the flowers would decorate my compartment.

*   *   *

Ludmilla, the Intourist guide, paced along the platform at Yaroslavl station, a green umbrella held high above her head. There were twenty four of us in her group – tour 38. We did not know each other at that stage but were destined eventually to bond together in a kind of siege solidarity as we undertook the longest train journey in the world.

Slowly the seventeen coaches of the train backed down the

platform towards us. Two carriages were ours, next to the restaurant car; two travellers to each four-berth, first-class compartment. I was sharing with David from Wales, handsome son of Sandra and Michael, next door. He was eighteen years old.

I arranged my provisions on one of the spare bunks: three 3-litre wine boxes, a bottle of Stolishnaya vodka, two hundred cigarettes to give away as presents, and some cans of food that I had brought along as iron rations – two tins of beans, two tins of tuna in mayonnaise, corned beef, Horlicks tablets, and vitamins with cod liver oil; and, of course, loo paper. On the table I arranged my flowers and my books: Gorky's autobiographies. So we settled in and made our beds, and the carriage quietened as the first of 5000 miles began to slip by, the train lurching as it rattled over a vast network of points.

My first visitor was the accountant from Guildford, popping his head through the open door. 'There's a stirrup-cup party,' he said. 'Or is it a soon-to-be-crossing-the-Urals party, into Asia? I don't know. It's Russian champagne.'

I went along to his compartment where the guests were already assembled: there were two English nurses working in Saudi; the Welsh family who worked for their local council; two town planners from Oxford; two boys from Basildon, reading Turgenev; a married couple from Walsall, and a teacher nicknamed 'Mastermind' in recognition of his deep knowledge.

As we drank our champagne the shining domes of Zagorsk rose up, then drifted away; a monastery with blue and gold cupolas all decorated with gilt and silver stars. We leant in a line against the windows of the corridor and some more of the 5000 miles clattered beneath us. Small wooden dachas went by, looking like dolls' houses, the detail of their fretwork shutters and carved gable-ends picked out in bright paint. And as we watched, the sun darkened and changed the colours of the leaves on the birch trees; the first thousands of the millions that were to come.

There were few Russians in the restaurant car that evening. Most locals on the Trans-Siberian travel relatively small distances and carry their own provisions with them. The company was international: two Japanese couples, and an American girl who had just finished a D.Phil. in medieval history at Oxford and was going home via Tokyo – about thirty years old she had bright blue eyes set in a face full of intelligence.

A young waiter looked after us, slim and slight. He was aided by a powerful woman in her forties whose shoulders were huge slabs of muscle. She had raw red hands like sides of bacon and a barrel chest which swept down to great columns of legs. Her short bob of black hair framed a broad face which in turn surrounded a wide and mournful mouth, and her eyes were full of fatigue. She was dressed in a dirty white button-up overall and her name was Vayucka. At every table she was offered drink and never refused, throwing it down her throat in the high Russian fashion. After every glass she shouted 'Zahvash darovyah' and her voice was as rough as coal on a shovel.

Our first meal was garlic sausage, tomato and onion salad, dark brown cabbage and chunks of meat, followed by a small peach. As we ate the train slid to a halt in a small station about four and a half hours out of Moscow, and within the square of my window a scene floated into view, illuminated by the yellow lights of the platform, a light that was soft and subaqueous, unreal. I had a glass of red wine in my hand and it stopped halfway to my mouth. Three drunks were being rounded up on the platform and thrown into the back of a police lorry; one old, one docile, and one angry. The angry one lashed out at a policeman and was booted hard in the stomach. He lashed out again and was booted again, harder this time. Once more he tried to fight and was beaten. The old drunk clambered into the lorry on his own; he was a man who had been arrested many times. The docile drunk attempted to wander along the platform but staggered into a fence, was led back and thrown into the lorry. The angry man made one last attempt to get to his feet and land a punch but, hopelessly outnumbered and with his face all bloody, he was thrown into the lorry on top of the others. The train moved on and I lifted my wineglass to my mouth.

As the coffee was poured we crossed the Volga and the night

settled over the forest outside. Rain rattled against the windows like handfuls of gravel. But if it was dark and forbidding outside, it was warm with life inside. The samovars at the end of each carriage were bubbling; the compartment doors were open, and the six-day conversation was just getting into its stride. The man from Walsall was at home to the Japanese, and the Welsh contingent was trying to explain to a Russian workman where Wales was.

'It's 5331 miles from Moscow to Khabarovsk,' said the accountant, 'and we cross seven time zones.' He took out a calculator. His wife was knitting. 'Six days, divide by 24...do you realize that's 37.026 miles per hour, on average?'

At every stop the platforms became social worlds of their own, and it was easy to discover why. Little old ladies, the fabled *babushkas*, were always waiting for us, night or day, sitting on boxes behind their wares, touting for custom, selling from meagre supplies: carrots, onions, plums, damsons, cakes and, of course, flowers. But this commerce was never just one way. As the train screeched to a halt the staff rushed to the doors of their carriages and sold, as fast as they could, every scrap of merchandise they had purchased in Moscow. The local inhabitants came in crowds, bargaining for what they could get: shampoo and toothpaste, skeins of wool, a cardigan, socks and a shirt. Even in the restaurant car, boxes of pastry and other provisions changed hands at every opportunity.

'I don't like it,' said one of the boys from Basildon, 'I bet that's goodbye to tomorrow's dinner.'

At the beginning of the journey Ludmilla had told us, with a certain amount of *schadenfreude,* that the small lavatories at either end of each carriage would soon become unpleasant; a quagmire, she said, proud of the word. So at four, on the second morning, when the corridor was deserted and the whole world seemed asleep, I decided it was time for a complete stand-up strip-wash before such a thing became undesirable.

I locked myself into the nearest lavatory and removed my dressing gown. There were two taps but both gave out cold water. That wasn't too important; just outside the door was a samovar and I used my tea mug to convey the hot water to the basin. There was no plug for the basin but, forewarned by the Trans-Siberian handbook, I had brought my own.

Face, chest, armpits, abdomen and then the tricky bits. Next I slipped a foot out of its shoe (it was foolish to go barefoot) and up into the basin. The train lurched and water slopped onto the floor and filled the shoe. My right buttock was stabbed by the door knob. I squelched the first foot back into its shoe and washed the second. The train lurched again as we swayed across some points and my elbow caught the edge of the window. When at last I could dry myself, I counted the beautiful bruises that had begun to bloom like mauve and yellow flowers on my skin.

Back in the corridor I made myself a cup of coffee and opened a tin of beans. I ate them cold from the can with a spoon. Nothing moved in the train. Outside the sky lightened and the dawn crept up the sky. Gradually the birch trees appeared from the gloom and then, some time later, I began to see the deserted mud roads rising and falling between the dark settlements. Little by little the pale light invaded the corridor, and one by one the compartment doors slid open as the faces of my travelling companions emerged gingerly into the day. After a while, and politely taking their turn, they made their way, sponge bags at the ready, towards the dangers of the morning wash.

One afternoon David, my room-mate, returned from a sortie along the train with a new friend – Sonia, an ex-gymnast, journeying home for her sister's wedding. She was young and beautiful in the way Russian women are beautiful, and we all fell in love with her. She was large-limbed, her skin transparent and she had eyes as blue and as wide and as deep as Lake Baikal. David cultivated her with a trembling and desperate determination, his Russian phrase book held just in front of his panting chest. She was a quiet girl, and spent the whole of her journey, day and night, clad only in a mauve towelling dressing gown of which she was very proud, even wearing it for her platform walks every time we stopped. When at last she left us, in Irkutsk, David was heartbroken, and his voice lilted with Celtic sadness whenever he spoke of her in the days that followed.

'How I longed to see her out of that dressing-gown,' he chanted time after time, sounding like Nogood Boyo in Under Milk Wood, 'but never did I, more's the pity.' And he would gaze to the far end of Siberia, and sigh.

At Sverdlosk the generators powering the restaurant car failed and the Captain of the train and two of his engineers set about running a cable from an adjacent carriage into the kitchens. These repairs took two hours and were only partially successful. During this time we were able to stroll around the town square, take in the station buffet and do some exercises.

'This is where the Czar and his family were murdered,' said Mastermind, 'only the town was called Yekaterinburg then, after the Empress Catherine. And Gary Powers was shot down here too, in his U2 – 1960 – it seems a long while ago now, doesn't it?'

After Sverdlosk the afternoons settled into a routine: some doors firmly shut on a private world of siesta, while others were left open to encourage visitors. There were card sessions, exchanges of books, and leisurely conversation at tea-time. And all the while Russia went on and on; trees, wooden houses, geese and goats, shacks, and mounds of hay. And in the gloom of the fearful forests, roaming packs of feral dogs loped through the trees with a vicious and lupine intent. In her compartment Ludmilla gave a five o'clock class in the Russian language, and made us do an hour's study a day, working beyond the call of duty, setting homework and marking it.

And Radik, our carriage attendant, took to appearing at last, late in the afternoon, at apéritif time, his face looking like a steak tartare from the effects of the on-going birthday party he had begun days earlier in Moscow. For a train that in theory had no drink on board there was plenty available, and other workers from other carriages came to wish Radik a happy birthday, bearing lemon vodka and salted cornichons: Igor, Marina, Olga and Alexei.

The accountant was not to be fooled. 'They are having us on,' he said. 'I bet they take it in turns to have birthdays so they can all have an excuse to drink, and they can take it in turns to take the lead role and get into our drinks supply.'

'Omsk,' Mastermind informed us as we drew into it. 'A fortress town and HQ of Cossack regiments. Dostoyevsky did four years' hard labour here, for political crimes. He was twice flogged, first for complaining about dirt in his soup; and second for saving the life of a drowning prisoner. He was six weeks in hospital recovering from this second beating.'

'Only two thousand kilometres to go,' said the accountant one day, beaming at his wife, who was still knitting.

Our social life went on, highly organised. The two nurses entertained us with caviar and games of whist, while the boys from Basildon, still reading Turgenev, told me how parasitical travel-writers were: always on freebies in five star hotels, eating the best of the food available and never telling the truth about the women they'd seduced. I ignored them and listened instead to the American D.Phil., who had soft pools of lavender under her eyes, massaged my feet and said; 'You know, Michael, men of my age are frightened by women like me – we're far too intellectual.'

In the mournful twilight a goods train clanked by, forever long, cutting off the view; and the two locos whistled to each other as they passed, and the sound echoed along the Khilok river, out across the empty valley and its wide meanders, dark-edged with sand, the black hills rising beyond with the low sun glinting on the marshy ground.

On the last evening the restaurant car took on a festive air, and out came my iron rations and those of my companions. Boxes of red wine, Russian champagne and brandy appeared from under the seats we sat on, alcohol suddenly and easily available, as if some philosophical customs' barrier had just been crossed. The lights failed as we ate but it didn't matter. A riotous sing-song exploded out of the gloom, and candles were lit. We, the English, did the usual ditties: songs from the music halls, 'On Ilkley Moor', 'Jerusalem', but our songs were poor compared to those of the Russians – they were not to be outdone. The Captain of the train sang, then Olga, Irena, and Radik, still celebrating his birthday. But it was Vayucka who dominated the evening, her voice booming as she drank her way up and down the restaurant car, clutching men to her bosom, a vast expanse of flesh capable of asphyxiating a regiment. She held me against her at one point and, as she sang, her song vibrated into me through her soup-stained overall, resounding in my head like an aria by Chaliapin. And such singing: dark, rough and beyond God; dangerous and unformed, like Russia itself. The tears rose in Vayucka's eyes as she stood there, singing sad songs for us from the depth of her being, and tears rose in our eyes too. Our hearts went out to her and to the vast spaces that lay beyond her, and then we were silent.

I got up in the middle of the night to visit the lavatory and walked into a staff party in a compartment a carriage away. It was a quiet and reflective gathering: the train clanking gently on: Olga, Irena, Alexei, Igor, Radik and Ludmilla. I was invited in and a tumbler of vodka was handed to me.

'A thousand kilometres is nothing to travel, a hundred roubles nothing to spend and a litre of vodka is nothing to drink,' said Radik, and raised his glass.

'Happy birthday,' I said.

'There were queues under Brezhnev,' said Irena, the carriage cleaner, 'but at least when you got to the end, there was always something to buy. Nowadays, who knows? We haven't been paid for three months.'

'And we do not smile much,' said Olga, 'too much in our heads has been destroyed for smiling. The smiling has been knocked out of us.'

'Gorbachov knew the coup was coming,' said Ludmilla. 'I think he set it up, so the old guard could take over and they could go back to communism, but then when Yeltsin took over, Gorby jumped the other way; but then is Yeltsin to be trusted?' There were nods all round, and glasses were refilled, vodka from mineral water bottles – so that was how they carried it.

The dark was thick outside, only a slight gleam of yellow fell on the tracks from our windows. We were somewhere north of China.

'The land out here is only half made up,' said someone.

'Not even started,' said another.

There was sadness that night as addresses and souvenirs were exchanged. There was no sign of David when I went back to my bunk and my sadness wouldn't go away and kept me wakeful. In the hour before dawn the door to my compartment slid open. Against the starlit window of the corridor I saw the silhouette of the D.Phil., the endless birch trees drifting behind her. The door clicked closed and I heard the lock fall into place. A hand reached out in the darkness.

'Are you really twice my age?' she asked.

'No,' I lied, 'not quite.'

*   *   *

At Khabarovsk, Ludmilla marshalled us on the platform. She had seven more days with us – seven days to shepherd us back to Leningrad, by plane via Ulan Ude, Irkutsk and Lake Baikal. While she went in search of a bus, the staff of the train disembarked to stand with us for a moment. We embraced our farewells and the train pulled slowly away and cleaners, cooks and samovar attendants climbed back on board. The honey-blond head of the D.Phil. protruded from a window. She didn't wave. My compartment went by, already occupied by strangers, beneficiaries of my flowers.

We grabbed our bags and trudged towards the station exit, all of us swaying, the movement of the train still pitching in our heads.

'My God,' declared the accountant, 'but we live in momentous times.'

'Yes,' I said, only just holding back my tears, tears that were for Russia. 'And Leningrad will be St Petersburg by the time we get there.' And so it was.

THE GROSVENOR, PARK LANE

'I wonder if anyone has ever had a pee up here,' I said. Billy Johnson and I were perched on top of the Wellington arch at Hyde Park Corner, hidden beneath the quadriga – the four bronze horses and chariot that crown the Iron Duke's monument. The view was wonderful: to the right, we could see out across the park while behind us was the sweep of Piccadilly. Our video camera stood on its tripod and we were taking shots of central London, cine-excerpts for a huge audio-visual show we were doing at the Grosvenor Hotel, Park Lane. I was acting as stage manager and general dogsbody; my job was extremely well paid and, once again, I needed the money.

Billy looked at me. 'The guys who put this statue up here must have,' he said. 'Why? Are you going to?'

'I most certainly am,' I answered, 'it will be my only claim to fame.' And with that I peed against the southernmost wheel of the chariot, staring down into the gardens of Buckingham Palace, hoping the Queen would appear while I was doing so.

I liked Billy a lot. He was a generous spirit and gave me work when I was broke which, over the years, I often had been. He didn't mind when you called him a lunatic; he just grinned, it was his way of admitting it. Billy was a big man, almost too big to live with. He was six and a half feet tall, with a wide stomach that leant out over a leather belt and pulled the rest of his body along, making the feet run. His face was bizarre, the size and shape of a rugby football on its side; brown hair swept his shoulders. He had a big mouth and he could stick a great grin on it and make it work. It was the grin of a boy caught scrumping the reddest plums in the orchard, yet all the time knowing that he was too young and too lovable to be punished.

In his eyes, and not too far away, there lurked a gleam of madness.

He was about forty when we first met. I had just come back from one of my trips and a friend of mine put me onto him. 'He wants some writing done,' was all I was told, 'audio-visual stuff.' I didn't know what I was getting into but was glad, ultimately, that Billy had come into my life; there are not many guys like him in the world. I once saw him deal with a stroppy Maître d'Hôtel. We, about twenty of us, had been working all night and all day in some conference rooms, and had eaten very little. The Maître D. refused us entry to the restaurant because we had come straight from building the sets and were dressed in old jeans and wore no ties or jackets. Billy grabbed the fellow by the lapels of his dinner jacket and swung him from the floor.

'Look,' he said. 'I'm spending a hundred grand in this hotel, in just one day. I don't care where you put us, you can put a screen round us or feed us in the kitchen, but feed us you will or your bereaved wife will be planning her second marriage.'

'Yes, sir,' said the man, 'come this way.'

And once, when reception had lost his room key, and couldn't find the pass, or a spare, Billy simply went for his tool box, and took the door off its hinges. That done he got into bed and ordered room service to bring up steak and chips and a bottle of red. Billy lived hard, and didn't have time to waste.

So Billy was difficult to keep up with. He was powered by a thriftless energy. He had strong shoulders and the thighs of a giant. He argued all the time. He was child-like, exasperating and exhausting. In Billy's house doors slammed, voices rose and people left for ever, only to return the next day. Billy's wife had left him a hundred times; living with Billy was like giving up smoking. His mind had the vitality of a bullock: he didn't mean any harm, but if he ran at you he would knock you down into the mud, and it hurt if you didn't get out of the way.

Going to work with Billy was always frightening; you never knew what might happen. He hauled you from sleep, threw clothes at your head, thrust breakfast into your stomach and stuffed money into your pocket. He lifted you and the camera gear into the Volvo estate and aimed it into the middle of the road and he stayed there, defeating traffic by ignoring it, grinning through the windscreen.

The car was part of Billy, and it carried everything: telephones, recorders, movie cameras, still cameras, and booze. He dressed cleanly, fresh jeans and shirts every day; for business meetings he wore loose, well-cut suits. He liked his women fashionable, good-looking, big-bosomed and middle-class; above all he wanted them to have style. What he meant by style in a woman was something she had that made other men look at her and envy Billy; it didn't matter what that something was.

There was no in-between with such a man, you either loved him or you hated him. You went out to do a day's filming with Billy, just for the wages, and you ended up with a leading role in a French farce or a Greek tragedy. He was a good employer if you could stand him; generous and dangerous. Time spent with him was like being in a room with no door, while a monster smashed the furniture and threw it at you, piece by piece.

In the early days, Billy had been a sound recordist, then freelance film-maker; prestige documentaries and commercials, mainly. That work dropped off and Billy was forced into the audio-visual game. He organised trade fairs at first and then moved into business conferences. He established a firm called Magic Lantern, and discovered he had a special talent for disguising other people's shortcomings, making nonentities look good. He began to make a lot of money, and everyone working for him, me included, made a lot of money too.

I used to talk to him a great deal, discovering what made him tick. He meant to be a millionaire by the time he was forty-five, he said. He wanted to make enough money to retire on, to stop working and take it easy, as if Billy could ever take it easy. I never once saw him sit down with a friend, or read a book. I never once saw him stay in one room when he could get up and go out of it. What he really wanted was to produce good films, features, but he had to get rich; good films could make a lot of money, the trouble was that to make the films you needed the money first. 'I've got to get there,' he used to say, 'I don't want to die a worm, I'm better than that, I've got to get out of the ruck.'

So Billy ran everywhere, worked all the time, earned heaps of money, and then spent it on things like mortgages and mistresses, food and drink, cars. His overdraft grew like honeysuckle over everything he did. Billy was a big power station glowing in the sky, day and night, burning coal to make electricity, using the electricity to dig the coal – and always his dream stayed beyond the reach of his arm. So Billy threw himself into the A-V game. He ran a little faster, ran a little further. He brought enthusiasm, knowledge and imagination into a business that badly needed it. Conferences had been dull affairs, but not after Billy came along; he changed everything.

An A-V production cannot exist without several tons of equipment: electric cables, amplifiers, scores of slide projectors, and something for showing movie inserts. It also needs thousands of mounted colour transparencies, especially created for rippling across enormous screens to the accompaniment of well-chosen music. Such a show also calls for tape-decks, decoders, conference rooms big enough for trucks to drive into, and crazy technicians who don't mind working a month of sleepless Sundays when they must, and if the money is right.

The money Billy paid me on that Grosvenor Hotel job was generous in the extreme. It made me rich for the rest of the year, but I earned it. I began by writing scripts, but that soon changed; I drove vans, I laid cable, helped build the sets, and was stage manager as well. I had never seen anything like it.

The main ballroom of the Grosvenor is as big as a football pitch, with a wide balcony all the way round it. The client was Morley Products (USA) and it was the biggest show that Billy had ever tackled. The whole circus was costing millions of dollars and Billy had a big bit of it. The Morley Corporation did pyramid selling, and was one of the largest organisations in the States. They pushed vitamin supplements and elixirs, meant to keep people young, and they put the elixirs into everything they could think of: shampoos, toothpaste, face cream and even boot polish. Morley had shipped over two thousand of their best performing salesmen (and their families) on a 'thank you' holiday, a holiday that was thinly disguised as an on-going sales conference in order to avoid certain taxes.

Billy had been engaged to organise seminars and educational lectures every day that Morley was in town, but in the evenings there had to be 'happenings'. The Morley conference ran for ten days; and we, the crew, were in the hotel for a week beforehand, getting it ready. There were twenty to thirty of us: electricians, riggers, carpenters, set-designers, projectionists, cameramen and recordists. We didn't sleep much, grabbing an hour here and an hour there in the penthouse suite on the top floor. We survived on steak sandwiches and bottles of Bordeaux.

The set filled one end of the ballroom, and represented a stretch of 'England's green and pleasant land'. Stage right was a small church with a pointed steeple and a real pulpit on the outside wall; it faced the audience and was there for the speech-makers. Behind the church was a foreshortened scene of rolling fields, drawing the eye to haystacks, hedges, trees and bushes; a gentle eighteenth century landscape, canvas on a wood and metal frame, painted as bright as spring.

Above was a sky made of five or six large screens which were to carry the visualisation of the Morley message. Stage left was a small thatched cottage modelled on Anne Hathaway's. There was a long castellated wall too, and in the middle of it a wide drawbridge. Across the stage ran a moat, real water in a plastic ditch; when it reached the church it tumbled prettily down a tiny cascade of coloured rocks into a pool, and was returned stage left in a pipeline, electrically pumped without a sound. 'First time it's ever been done,' said Billy.

We worked ourselves to a standstill. Every day and every night the show had to go on. Rehearsals, conferences with screens and recordings and graphs, and then a show in the evening; half a dozen acts maybe – music, dancing and singing. All coordinated with the serving of dinner at long refectory tables.

We crew members ate together, when we could, in the dark shadows of back-stage, where my stage-manager's desk was situated. That was where I sat for the duration of each show, and took instructions through the headphones from Billy, who hovered high above everything in a control kiosk front of house. Those meals were the best moments – they were medieval: all of us crowded together at a trestle table, always exhausted but enjoying a rare camaraderie, ribald and warm. We toiled and drank our way through the ten days, until we came at last to the last show, the last meal.

And above us as we ate loomed the ultimate surprise for the Morley faithful: a huge statue of Professor Morley himself, the founder of the Morley Corporation. The statue was three times life-size, one index finger pointing to the sky; the other hand carrying the books of wisdom the Professor had written. Behind him floated his jacket, unmoving in an imaginary wind, as he strode purposefully across the hemisphere, bestriding it like a colossus. When the show ended and the light of a new dawn was powered up by our electricians, the word Morley would be written across our indoor sky, and we would unveil the Professor – a figure carved with skill out of a material that would outlive granite and bronze – fibre glass, smooth and metallic, but light and cheap to air-freight anywhere in the world. It was a statue that four of us could have lifted and carried on-stage, but that wasn't it: for the Morley people we had to make it look as solid as stone: weightless, it had to appear weighty. So we fixed it onto a hotel trolley, the heaviest we could find. At the right moment we would pull it on with ropes, and push from behind with exaggerated effort. We were masters of illusion.

It was just ten minutes before the show. Our last meal had been joyful and sad; the task was nearly over, though we all knew that it would take another two or three days to clear the ballroom of our gear. Behind the set I had about a hundred people to shuffle into order, and I had two 'wingers' to carry messages and instructions – two blonde secretaries from Billy's office. Against the back wall leant a score of bandsmen, drinking beer from brown bottles, and the members of the Welsh Choir joined them – they couldn't sing a note without whetting their whistle. I sat at my desk in a pool of light that spilled from a small lamp, enabling me to read the script. Sitting beside me was a woman with a boa constrictor in a bag, an animal that was a good twelve feet long.

'How often do they eat?' I asked, remembering stories of these animals swallowing goats whole. I was thin in those days.

She smiled at my nervousness. 'About every fifteen days.'

She waited for the obvious next question.

'When did it feed last?' I shifted my chair slightly to the right, away from her.

'About two weeks ago.'

Billy did Morley proud that evening. As the Morley people came down from their rooms and through the foyer they found themselves in the middle of an Olde English Fayre, with side shows and stalls that led all the way down the sweep of the stairs to the ballroom, where there were even more booths offering every entertainment imaginable: coconut shies; hoop-la; dart throwing; rifle ranges; strolling players singing Greensleeves to the accompaniment of their own lutes; and drum majorettes marching every which way, their thighs flashing and bosoms swinging gorgeously left and right in time to the music. There were archers too, Robin Hood and Will Scarlet swinging on ropes from balcony to stage. We had a fire-eater, twelve feet high on stilts, who fell over in the foyer and broke his leg; a sword-swallower and a small merry-go-round for the children. Green branches and armfuls of flowers decorated the hotel doorways and dining tables, and every waiter and waitress was dressed in a plastic-leather jerkin decorated with a gold letter M, sprayed from a can. An armoured knight on horseback rode around the balcony. The Morley bigwigs had wanted 'historicity' and Billy gave it to them in spades. I had even written a script that proved that Sir Oswald Morley had been one of Henry's knights at Agincourt and was an ancestor of the Professor. There had never been such a show.

Then the Morley dinner was over and Billy's voice came through the cans.

'I'm bringing the grams up,' he said. 'Coffee's gone, liqueur glasses are being cleared; the waiters are leaving. Stand by: house lights down, Mike, get the trumpeters in position; sparks, light them, stage left, Mike. Okay fellas, it's back on your heads.'

And so the show proper began, and the trumpeters gave a fanfare for every act: the brass band; the marines counter-marching; the Welsh male voice choir; a troupe of Scottish dancers dancing to their own pipers; the drum majorettes again, and the archers shooting at targets and scoring bulls' eyes.

Not far down the show I told the snake lady to prepare herself for her entry on stage. I can't remember what her part in the spectacle was, but the snake came out of the sack and I forgot my fear of it. I was too busy for fear, that was, until I felt the tail end of the boa-constrictor's body wrapping itself around my leg, under the table, working upwards from my ankle. I was terrified. I jumped several feet into the air, and a solid stream of invective poured into my mike and into the ears of the other twenty crew members listening on cans. They thought it was the funniest thing in the show.

'Steady, Mike,' came Billy's voice, 'keep calm, concentrate, we're bringing on the statue in five or six minutes.'

'I can't effin' concentrate,' I screamed. 'Or keep calm. I've got a Black Mamba climbing up me leg, and heading for me balls.'

Then the grand finale – the statue of Professor Morley, towed on stage by half a dozen stagehands, another two or three behind, making a great show of pushing an enormous weight, me directing. And then the whole cast: bandsmen; Welsh Choir; drum majorettes; trumpeters and all crowding on stage to raise their arms in a salute to the Professor, worshippers every one.

And, at the moment the statue appeared, the recorded sounds of the Morley music surged up to meet us, Billy winding the decibels to full blast. The Morley acolytes rose to their feet, cheering, clapping, laughing. The Professor was their God. From the balcony a hundred hands threw flowers down to the tables and onto our heads, garlands made from pink and waxy petals, flown in at the speed of sound that day from Hawaii. The audience snatched at the odourless blooms and sang the Morley hymn and cheered and laughed and clapped again, intoxicated by their own devotion. Now the Professor's statue was centre stage, and the audience climbed up to be with the cast – drunken reporters, dumpy ladies from Minnesota, clerks from Wisconsin: and they pushed and scrambled their way to the statue and touched it for its holy powers and placed their garlands around our necks and thanked us for the best show they'd ever seen. And they wept with happiness, tears molten on burning cheeks, eyes aflame; believers spinning in delirium, like dervishes, carrying their God to the temple. '*My name is Ozymandias, king of kings. Look on my works, ye Mighty, and despair!*'

* * *

The Morley show was such an amazing experience that I wrote a thriller based on it – *The Bunce* – with Billy as the main character. It was based on a true story in which the Billy character was instrumental in recovering some stolen bullion, and expected to receive a reward, but in the end was swindled out of it. It was a romp of a book, well reviewed and short-listed for The Golden Dagger award, a prize that was in the gift of critics of the genre. I was pipped at the post by a book that was much more conventional than mine. I even got into paperback as well, though once again, the money was negligible.

A while later I wrote the second volume of *The Borribles* and presented it to the Bodley Head. Unfortunately for me my champion, Judy Taylor, had moved on and a woman called Margaret Clark had taken over her desk. She accepted the book, which she hated, with a bad grace and brought it out as a trade paperback, and reviews were hard to come by. It was yet another disappointment for me in the writing game; but there was some good news. Three American independent film producers came out of the woodwork and asked if they might option *The Borribles* for a film. I was to travel to Los Angeles to see them and discuss things. That was exciting and once again I began spending the millions. But reality dogged me, rather like the slave who stood behind Roman emperors in their chariots as they progressed in triumph across the city, whispering in their ear – "Remember, thou art only a man." The reality was that I had to pay my own air fare. That wasn't too bad. I talked the Sunday Times into sending me to New

York to do a piece on the St Patrick's Day parade; that got me halfway there.

SUNDAY MORNING IN HARLEM

It was just before eight on a Sunday morning and Madison Avenue was empty – empty except for a roller-blader, a girl skating in boots that at first sight looked like ice-skates, only here the blades were four small wheels in line, making friction non-existent. The girl went by me at the speed of light, all alone, racing southwards, leaning forward, bent at the waist, arms swinging in a slow rhythm, her mouth half open with expectation and enjoyment. About eighteen, she wore black jeans, tight to her thighs, and a flowered shirt tucked in at the waist, her figure shown off to advantage. Her hair flowed free behind her. She sang to herself though her voice was loud enough for me to hear as she passed. She was attractive, full of life, and mad – like New York itself.

I carried on across town, on to 54th Street and Broadway, just north of Times Square. I was wearing a jacket under an overcoat; a jacket because I was going to church – to church in Harlem, on a bus.

The bus was full but we were not all tourists, nor were we all white. I sat next to a black woman in her mid-thirties. 'I've lived in New York all my life,' she explained, 'and I've never been to Harlem.' She wrote westerns for a living. 'They're all about a Texas Ranger,' she said, 'only I'm not allowed to kill him off, dammit.'

The bus took us uptown on Eighth Avenue and the smell of slumber weighed heavily across the apartment blocks. 'The city that never sleeps' was certainly snoozing, though in Central Park to my right the joggers were busy, weaving quick patterns

193

of colour against the dark green. Further north we entered Harlem and our courier, a young black man, switched on his microphone.

'There are more churches in Harlem than anything else,' he said, 'almost a church on every block. And here's St Nicholas Avenue and the house where Duke Ellington lived.'

The streets became tougher, graffiti crawling over the landscape like the trails of silvery spiders, abstract webs spun from aerosol cans. There were abandoned buildings in plenty, spilling garbage into the open spaces between them, scarred by fire at the doors and windows, like faces with the eyes gouged out, the blood dark. The long sidewalks were desolate.

'Absentee landlords,' said our guide, 'found they couldn't get enough rent for these places, so they burnt down the houses for the insurance money. The Lord knows what happens inside them now.'

Then suddenly we were into Striver's Row. Long lines of elegant 'yellow brownstones', mansions with wide patrician steps up to broad entrances with wrought-iron railings on each side, and delicate balconies decorating the fronts like lacework.

The bus went on – into Nat King Cole Street, turning a corner named for Sugar Ray Robinson and so into 125th Street where there was a Sunday morning market. At last we stopped outside the Baptist Church of Mount Morian and the courier spoke again.

'Do not wander off in this area, you might not come back.'

There were two other busloads apart from ours, and slowly we filed through narrow doors, about a hundred and fifty of us. Inside, the church resembled a theatre, with a wide sweep of stalls and a low, spacious balcony supported by slender columns that descended in swirls of brown and cream paint. There in the balcony we sat and waited.

Below us was a stage and behind it, empty of water, a green tiled pool for baptisms; on stage were two or three lecterns, seats for two wings of a choir and a podium for a pair of electronic keyboards. In front of the platform were five people, male and female, thinking their thoughts out loud, unashamed, singing 'Hallelujahs' from time to time and naming the name of

Sweet Jesus, encouraging the congregation to advance as they entered the building, greeting their friends; 'Thank you, Jesus, I'm here, Jesus, I'm here.'

The men were neat in dark suits and ties, and their black shoes glittered. The women, for the most part, were in white – white skirts, coats and broad brimmed hats, and the ushers wore white gloves. They held the doors open and the congregation kept coming, one of them an enormous woman, hardly visible under a hoop of headgear, and submerged in waves of golden frock that rippled down over the ripples of her body to touch her ankles. She looked up and her smile embraced the world. Her hands were held at shoulder height and revolved on universal joints, like flowers turning towards the sun.

As the congregation grew the quintet at the front of the stage began to warm up with hand-clapping and improvised song. Shouts came from the back of the hall: 'Pray now, friends, pray now, join us, join us.' Two acolytes arrived on the platform; the Pastor followed. He too was clad in white, a burly man in a full flowing smock.

The electronic piano began to pick up a relaxed rhythm, something like an old fox-trot, and through the doors at the rear of the auditorium a choir of about forty men and women appeared, the men in suits, the women in white like the others but with black squares or mortar boards on their heads. Now the two hundred voices of the congregation were raised in earnest, good strong voices that knew how to sing, and the choir advanced down the aisles, moving in a slow march and swinging from side to side on the beat. The hand-clapping became more and more enthusiastic and the calls and responses became more insistent. The choir divided in front of the Pastor's lectern and each half took its own way and climbed the steps onto the stage.

Soon the pace and sincerity of the music began to work, but still I felt like some kind of voyeur. I had paid my 35 dollars and was looking down into somebody else's life. I felt awkward – an eavesdropper about to be discovered – and I could see that the others with me in that balcony felt the same; self-conscious and out of place.

The Pastor read from his bible and an acolyte began to preach; the congregation was moved in its soul and called out. Then a woman came to a microphone. 'Will our visitors please rise.' We did as we were asked, sheepishly. The woman raised her arms. 'You are all welcome here,' she said. 'You are welcome to our service. We want you to join with us in our praise of Jesus. We hope you enjoy what you see and will join in the songs. We hope the Lord has said something to you today and we want you to come again.'

We sat and the singing took off once more, gaining in passion and rhythm as it went, working on us as powerful music does. Those who had come to stare were stirred instead and, though still self-conscious, we began to sway to the music and even to clap our hands.

A young pastor came from the centre of the platform and took over the keyboard in mid-song. The temperature rose and the voices with it. He stood at the keyboard, pumping all his belief into his microphone and the choir sang with him, the congregation too. 'Do you really need a miracle before you can believe in the Lord?' he sang, 'then look at me, 'cos I'm one of the Lord's miracles, just like everyone.' The congregation went wild and applauded this sally, laughing at the humour of it. The old Pastor smiled and raised his hands towards us and we were no longer voyeurs.

The service seemed to have no ending, yet after about an hour and a half our courier appeared and beckoned us away. We stood, but hesitantly, not wishing to leave. Only fear of missing the bus perhaps, or being marooned in deepest Harlem, made us move. At the door the big woman in the rippling satin waited, a collection plate in her hand.

'You all come back soon,' she said, 'and remember, you saw the Lord today.'

Outside in the silent street the buses waited to take us away.

*   *   *

In the event I didn't pay my air fare to Hollywood. Bernard, a sound engineer I had known since childhood – in fact we had grown up in the same Battersea street and had been projectionists together in the Festival Gardens – was working on a comedy film in Hollywood with a British star called Max Boyce. Max was a Welsh actor, singer and comedian, who stood five feet nothing and was training in California with the Dallas Cowboys, an American football team, each one of them over seven feet tall. That was the comedy.

Bernard needed a sound assistant for six weeks. It wasn't exhausting work – boom swinging and fixing radio mikes on sweaty chests. It was much easier than being a camera assistant and the film crew were, like they generally are, a good bunch of men. We ate in excellent restaurants, drank very good Californian wines and played cricket on the beach at Santa Barbara, much to the puzzlement of our American audience. 'The outfield's a bit wet,' said Max, as he stood up to his neck in the Pacific Ocean.

One day when I wasn't working the three would be producers – it turned out that they were show business lawyers who wanted to become film makers – invited me out to lunch. They arrived in a huge convertible, hood down in the Hollywood sun – two suited men and a well-dressed woman – and drove me off to the Beverly Hills Hotel, spinning past the homes of the stars on the way and showing me the theatre where the hands of the great are imprinted in concrete. The second we arrived at the hotel, uniformed lackeys spirited the car away and we were led, escorted and followed, into the restaurant. It was all pink table cloths and napkins, soft-focus like in the movies, and hosts of people talking big deals and looking over their companions' shoulders in case there was someone more important at the next table.

I can't remember what we had for lunch, I was far too excited. I had arrived; those millions were glinting on the horizon once more, and I would never work again. My lawyers told me the names of the other diners and what they did, and the woman told me that she had once seen Fred Astaire in the cocktail lounge and had been overcome with the joy of it. Not to be outdone I mentioned that I had seen James Stewart and Gloria Grahame in the grill room of The Savoy Hotel, London.

I didn't admit that I had slaved in the Bill Office there and, in reality, had passed them on the stairs.

The conversation progressed, to and fro, until The Borribles was optioned for £8000. It had a nice ring to it – £8000. They drove me around Hollywood some more and left me finally at the Sheraton, where the film unit awaited me – drinks on de Larrabeiti. I was floating, but just to keep my feet on the ground, as it were, I read Montaigne in the 'plane on the way home: *"Just as our mind is strengthened by contact with vigorous and well-ordered intelligences, so too it is impossible to overstate how much it loses and deteriorates by the continuous commerce and contact we have with mean and ailing ones. No infection is as contagious as that is."*

I was wrong about never working again. The £8000 was slow in coming and the film never did. I went to Papua next.

PAPUA NEW GUINEA

I was in the Ambua Lodge Hotel when I got the message, high in the southern highlands of Papua where I found myself travelling, by chance, with a dozen Americans. We were up to see the Birds of Paradise and then to cruise down the Sepik River to Madang. The message had come by radio, the only way the hotel had of communicating with the outside world – 'Mr de Larrabeiti to depart Ambua 06.45. Travel by Cessna 206 with the baggage: Tari to Green River.'

We'd arrived at the hotel in the late afternoon, a long day of travel completed, the air cool and quiet. We'd ordered apéritifs and taken photographs of the Tari Basin, a mysterious valley where the evening mist rolls in like an ocean and the hard blue of the mountains stands out like island peaks. From the native villages below us the thick smoke of a hundred evening fires climbed the sky and drew the clouds down to earth. The light faded and soon there was nothing left to see but a gleam of gold, followed by a last flourish of crimson, and the night came in from the forest and covered the world.

Tari airfield was nothing more than a hut and a palisade. I watched as the Cessna 206 landed on the dirt strip and four or five Taiwanese businessmen, natty in suits and ties, disembarked and got into a waiting car. The Australian pilot, Gary, ran a hose to the plane and sluiced out the cockpit.

'Sorry about that,' he said, 'a couple of them threw up on the way here. Don't know why, it's lovely up there. No worries, it don't smell that bad.'

I helped Gary load the Americans' luggage into the Cessna,

leaving just enough room for the pair of us to sit up front. The Americans themselves were to follow in the twin-engined Otter which stood ready for them.

'See you at Green River,' I said, and Gary and I took off.

'It would be nice to have two engines.' I suggested, once we were airborne. Gary laughed; he looked all of sixteen. 'You sure gotta be mad to fly over this kind of terrain in a single-engined aircraft. There's nowhere to land and if you did there's still cannibals in some of those valleys. They reckon a Rockefeller son got washed up here from a yacht a few years back, they never found him. That must have been the most expensive meal ever. Pass me that map, I haven't been to Green River before.' I did and he placed the map on his knees.

'But don't you worry. I bought this plane off a Bishop, so it has a special relationship with God.'

I gazed at the altimeter: 9000 feet, it said. The mountains around us were much higher than that.

'They certainly are,' explained Gary. 'I just fly down the valleys and go over the passes. It helps when the sky's clear. Even I don't like it when it's cloudy.' I watched the soft terrain unfolding below me; midnight blue in the shadows, purple to olive green along the great looping rivers. Then, an hour and forty minutes later, we banked and I saw the airstrip.

That's all Green River is – an airstrip and a hut, about 15 miles from the border with Irian Jaya. There I caught up with the Americans – the Otter had overtaken our Cessna – and helped unload the luggage. The coolness of the mountains had been burnt away; the air was hot and stuck to the skin. We climbed into jeeps and were driven for an hour over mud tracks until we arrived at the great sweep of the Sepik river and found a sea-going catamaran waiting for us: 17 cabins, four suites, a bar and a restaurant, all bright and white against the primeval dark of the forest. On board it was a little world of air conditioning and gin and tonics and, for me at least, a feeling of guilt came with the comfort. I was showered, cool and clean, leaning against the rail and staring as villages floated by me, huts on stilts, places where nothing much had changed for several thousand years. The natives we saw looked much poorer here than in the Highlands; their clothes were worn and filthy, the children had traces of fungus on their skins and the pot-bellies of malnutrition. In the dark doorways old women sat and smoked tobacco leaf, I suppose, in cigar-sized cigarettes rolled in newspaper. 'The air mail Times is best.'

That evening a pale and hesitant light came down over the Sepik. A heavy flurry of rain swept over us, and the river turned menacing, the rain drops pock-marking its surface so that it resembled the scarred skin of a crocodile. The trees crowded to the water's edge and parakeets screeched unseen in the forest. Fruit bats, as big and as evil looking as crows, flapped across the sky, while others hung upside down in the branches, like gorged vampires.

The Americans, bird watchers to a man (and woman), told me what I had seen that day: a White-Bellied Sea Eagle, a Whistling Kite and a Palm Cockatoo – 'worth $40,000 to a collector back home.' And a Ulysses butterfly, brilliant blue with a black border around wings that were as big as my hand.

Two days into the trip I went down with dengue fever: headaches that made me scream and temperatures that gave me the shakes hour after hour. 'It can't be malaria,' said the old hands on board, 'you haven't been in the country long enough. Don't worry. Dengue fever does kill people sometimes, but you'll be all right.'

I didn't eat and I didn't sleep for five days, and there was no way I could get to a doctor. In fact I wouldn't find one until we reached our destination – Madang on the edge of the Bismark Sea. I had a bad time of it, and whatever the old hands were saying by way of comfort, I was convinced I was dying. There was nothing that could be done for me and I was left to my own devices. On the last day I tried to do my packing but was so weak I had to perform the task on my hands and knees, lying down every few minutes to regain my strength. I wept with fatigue and pain, and at Madang I was half carried off the boat and into the hotel.

It was an hour before dawn when we got there and a dark rain blurred the lights of the town, making them indistinct, runny, like a watercolour. A doctor was called. He took a blood slide but couldn't find anything. A day or two later the fever broke and I limped into the restaurant. The American group had journeyed on and I was on my own.

Next to me at the long table was a big man with furry arms and huge hands, hardy and full of energy.

'George,' he said, and crushed my limp hand in his. George had seen action in the Solomon Islands during the war, and had come back to indulge his passion – tracking down B17s. He knew all there was to know about the warplane and the information was catalogued, in detail, on his computer. 'There were 12,731 built,' he said, 'and I know where 8900 of them ended up and who was on board. There's one just up the coast here.'

'My father flew it,' said the girl sitting next to him, George's niece.

George jerked a thumb over his shoulder. 'There's a lot of stuff went down in this jungle...and there's guys in the States pay good money for photographs of these wrecks.' He sat up straight, suddenly proud. 'I fly a B17,' he explained, 'in Arizona. We call it The Confederate Air force.'

An Australian helicopter pilot leant across the table. 'I found a B17 on New Britain,' he said. 'A village headman took us to it. Only a few yards off the track, that's all, so overgrown we didn't know we were near it until we were standing on the wing – upside down in the bush, it was. There's a line of Japanese tanks too, abandoned, take some finding though, it's rough country, real jungle. Ships are easier. I dive down to a Jap destroyer pretty often, into the kitchens, I've got some rice bowls and plates. They say there are sixty ships at the bottom of Rabaul harbour.'

*   *   *

At Madang airport I waited for the plane that was taking me to Rabaul, the capital of New Britain, and watched a three year old boy play rugby with an empty beer can. He threw it hard along the floor and then scampered along in pursuit and, while the can was still bouncing, he fell upon it, down amongst the feet and the cigarette butts, scoring a try. Then he did it again, while his father, a player himself, stretched his neck as proud as any bird of paradise.

'Rugby's very big in PNG.' There was an Australian sitting next to me, name of Joe. 'It's a good place. I left Adelaide thirty years ago, to see the world, the whole nine yards, and this is as far as I got.'

On the plane Joe kept talking, pointing through the floor of the Fokker F28 in the direction of the Bismark Sea but meaning to indicate the whole of Papua New Guinea. 'It's the Stone Age meets the twentieth century. The natives still fight, still get wounded, attack the police and up in the Highlands pigs is still power. Bride price is about thirty – so they make the women work looking after the pigs, breed more pigs, gain more wealth, buy more women, breed more pigs, so it goes.

'There's a notice outside the hospital at Mendi: "Bed for one day, six kina. Bed for a week, thirty kina. Spear and arrow wounds, sixty kina." My doctor grew up in a village on the Sepik and has just won a scholarship to Harvard, but his father, just one generation, is all scarred back and front with old spear wounds, and he took Japanese heads during the war, to prove his manhood...I love it here. No one gives a damn whether it's today, tomorrow or this afternoon. Things are changing though. A lot of tribesmen have come in from the hills and set up shanties in the towns, that leads to petty crime, it's a problem. Different when I first came. I was hauled in front of the District Commissioner once because I wasn't wearing starched shorts and shirts, white of course, and knee-length socks the same colour.'

I shook hands with Joe at the airport. 'Lukim yu behain,' he said in pidgin. 'See you later.'

I had been told that Rabaul had the most beautiful setting on the west side of the Pacific. It lies along the edge of Simpson Harbour which is formed from the huge crater of a volcano, the remains of its vast rim standing high behind the town. The sweep of the bay is breathtaking; the green of the hills soft and sedate, the waters mother-of-pearl. The volcanoes, however, still rumble: Tavurvur, smoking gently, and Vulcan, giving no sign of life, though it had last erupted in 1937 killing more than 500 people.

Very few tourists visit Rabaul in any one year and ten of them were at the Hammas Hotel when I got there, all of them from the States, spending their pensions and led by a young New Zealander. 'I've wangled us into a village fire dance tonight,' he said. 'Why don't you come?'

We left after dinner and were soon out of town and into the shapeless dark of the forest, a darkness barely touched by the headlight beams bouncing across the track. The drivers of the two 4 x 4s lost their way a number of times and the vehicles lurched and swayed as we dropped down steep banks and forded stony streams, ducking our heads when low branches scraped across our windscreens.

The village too was dark, forty kilometres out of town maybe. Just a few huts, black against black and no light save for our torches. The women and children of the place sat to one side, the old men next to them but on their own. After waiting a while, not knowing quite what to do or even how to hold ourselves, the men in our party were gathered together and led into the trees by a young native. Our women stayed where they were, by the 4 x 4s, not allowed to see what we were to see – the preparations of the dancers.

We set off in single file, deserting the women without a qualm, and went down into a rustling obscurity of jungle, tripping and sliding until finally we came to a muddy hollow where the dancers were. The grass was trampled and soggy underfoot.

In the light of a portable gas-lamp I could see that the young fire-dancers, the initiates, were almost naked. They stood quietly, about a dozen of them, close together, helping each other to daub their bodies. Two or three younger boys were kept busy as acolytes, and what talk there was in the group was subdued and kept to a minimum, though from time to time we heard loud bursts of nervous laughter, which was not surprising because this was the way into manhood for these dancers. We outsiders were privileged to be there; indeed the charm of the occasion was its total naïveté and the knowledge that, for those involved, this dance and this night came only once.

The grown men were in the process of smearing clay over their bodies; black clay on the torso and abdomen and white clay from the groin downwards. The boys crouched and tied long leaves to the dancers' legs, from the knee to the ankle, to protect them from the fire. From the men's shoulders fell great woven lengths of coarse grass, cascades of it like heavy cloaks, yellow and green, ghostly in the wavering gaslight.

Most of the men had a finer grass woven into their pubic hair, and it was combed forward into a kind of bag to cover their penises. Others wore a disc of bark, like a mushroom the size of a dinner plate, with the stem covering the penis and held fast to the body by means of a length of creeper tied around the waist so that the whole contraption bobbed up and down as the men walked. And then, when all was ready, the dancers settled enormous headdresses onto their shoulders, so that their heads were covered with the wild faces of birds and butterflies, fierce-looking with cruel beaks and wide ringed eyes.

The men's bodies reflected what little light there was, gleaming with earth and ochre, but to make their skins shine more brightly the acolytes knelt again, filled their mouths with bush honey from bottles and blew and spat silvery gobfulls of it over the buttocks and thighs of the dancers. 'It saves their legs from burning,' someone explained.

When the preparations were almost complete we were led back through the trees to the village. A huge fire of wood and brush was burning now in the open space between the huts. The women and the old men had not moved from their places but the tension had increased and the air was full of the screams of children as they ran around the glow of the fire, keeping it fed with branches, making the red sparks fly upwards into the darkness like swarms of fireflies.

About a dozen men provided a simple music; hollow bamboo poles striking against wooden planks, while everyone chanted and sang to the rhythm they made. Now at last the initiates emerged from the forest, led by a man wearing a large rectangular piece of bark, a huge and rigid envelope for his body, all painted in violent swirls of red and black, with streamers of creeper and leaves floating like banners from his hands. He pranced up to the musicians and the initiates followed him. In the firelight I could see the costumes and masks more clearly – a cockerel with a head that was half-bird, half-man, large gaudy plumes nodding on its crest; and a vulture stared at me from a one-dimensional skull, a mop of straw for hair above it.

The children screamed again and again, somewhere between terror and delight as the monsters advanced. The women laughed and held their children close when fear surprised them, covering their faces. More branches were thrown into the flames and the sparks renewed their flight, garlands of them, but brighter this time, enticing the dancers back to weave their way around the fire, until plucking up courage and one by one, they began to run at it, charging and leaping across the highest part, their legs and feet trailing yet more sparks behind them.

The shouts became louder, everyone caught in the excitement of the evening, laughing helplessly as the dancers hesitated in fear, trying to be brave. At last after more than two hours, the blaze was allowed to die and the dancers set themselves to run, as slowly as possible, across the red embers, their feet still bare. The boys who would be men, followed them, kicking out at the glowing branches in their bravado. Then it was over. The dancers disappeared back into the jungle and the women hauled their children into the huts. In a little while nothing remained but the smell of smoke and a kind of breathing redness at what had once been the heart of the fire.

* * *

The next morning the New Zealander took me, together with his group, to Rabaul market. Just beyond it was a Japanese bunker, concrete exits and entrances bursting through the turf. This had been the headquarters for the Nippon war effort in the Solomon Islands and the Coral Sea. Eighty thousand Japanese troops had been based in Rabaul alone, and they had sheltered in miles and miles of underground tunnels, all excavated by slave labour. Half an hour later we drove on, up a hill to a gun emplacement that gave a commanding view of the harbour and its sleeping volcanoes. In the centre of the emplacement stood an abandoned artillery piece, pitted deep with rust but smothered with bougainvillaea and hibiscus, the flowers making the gun seem absurd and ludicrous.

'Some guy, that Bougainville,' said a woman from New York. 'He had an island and a plant named after him. So who the hell was Hibiscus? Some Portuguese sailor?'

Along the road at Kopopo we found the East New Britain Museum and yet more detritus of war: rusty weapons resting on bright clean grass; a 150mm gun, a searchlight, a three-man tank, a hydraulic bomb-loader, a motor-bike and an American Jeep.

Inside the museum was an example of B17 nose-art, lost in combat and then rescued from deep in the jungle. Beside it were faded black and white pictures of the crew and a typed resumé of their story. It was calm in the museum, conversation stilted, and a breeze that drifted in through the open windows somehow made the pity of war a real presence, like someone standing too close behind you.

Only the navigator had survived the crash of the B17; the other crew members had been shot up and had perished with the plane. The navigator, badly wounded himself, had endured three hellish weeks in the jungle before being captured by the Japanese, spending the rest of his war as a prisoner in Rabaul. More photographs showed him on a return trip, many years later, standing by the nose art that I now stood in front of, visiting his plane in the jungle with the natives who had saved his life. 'Naughty but Nice,' said the nose art, the words winding around the painted picture of a chocolate-box girl whose face was still bright and smiling, teeth like tombstones, gazing inanely down the years, ignorant of death.

Outside I met Bill from Wisconsin; he was leaning against a tree, a man in his seventies. He was reading from a guide book. 'Rabaul is where Admiral Yamamoto spent his last night,' he said, 'before his plane was shot down over Bougainville Island.' Bill read some more, a quote from the son of a PNG porter who had worked for the Australian army. '"My family got nothing,

nothing at all. They owe us. We carried their wounded on our backs, and their bombs. We slept on dead Japs and drank the water they were rotting in.'''

Bill gazed at the silver skeleton of a Japanese bomber, its back broken, its wings crumpled. It glittered in the sun against the untarnished grass. A gardener moved silently across the scene, his bare feet making no noise as he swept the fallen leaves into tiny piles and tidied them away.

Bill stared at the crucified plane but was seeing something else – his own escape from a premature death. 'I flew thirty missions in a B17,' he said, 'out of East Anglia. Thirty in four and a half months. It was only meant to be twenty five but the figure was raised, they kept on raising it...that meant a death sentence for some guys. I did five missions one week, I was a wreck.' Bill was talking to himself, not to me. 'We got drunk every night and used to crawl into those B17s so hungover, it was a disgrace. But we'd switch on the oxygen supply and breathe that in for all we were worth. I tell you in two minutes we were as macho as hell.'

'I was a kid in the war,' I said, 'some of it in London, during the Blitz.'

Bill lifted the book and read from it again. '150,000 Japanese soldiers were killed in New Guinea. When General Adachi surrendered at Wewak, he wept: "My soldiers fell like petals in the wind," he said. 4000 Aussies died too – no one counted the natives.' He put the guide book back into his pocket and sighed. 'You end up knowing you know nothing,' Bill went on. 'When you think of the sweat, pain and death that's gone on in this world, it just seems too beautiful to be here, like this.'

'Yes,' I said, and looked for the last time at the view where the volcanoes slept, out of sight, under the calm waters of the bay. There had been a lot of war in my life, though I'd never fought in one: the ghost of a grandfather from The Great War, and the tales my mother had told of him; World War Two as an evacuee, brothers in uniform; the Malayan emergency: Korea; Vietnam; Gulf War One and Gulf War Two...and there would be more coming as I grew older.

We turned then, hurrying to catch up with the rest of the

group who were waiting for us in the bus, politely patient. We climbed up the steps and sat down. 'Sorry,' said Bill.

THE CHARITY BALL

I was old enough to know better, but I was into trouble before I'd realized. The sun was shining and it's an enjoyable walk from Great Milton up to Cuddesdon, a couple of miles. Across a pasture, down to the river Thame, where the mill and the mill house are; a solitary game of pooh sticks on one of the bridges, and then up a footpath, across more fields, before coming out on the Wheatley road, opposite the seminary. I was on an afternoon visit to my doctor, John Hughes, who was also a drinking companion. I wasn't ill, it was a social call.

It was one of those summer days that make you feel that you never want to travel again; why leave home when Oxfordshire was paradise? There was a light breeze, a clear sky and tar bubbling in the road. Looking down from my bridge I could see silver fish floating motionless in the current, and a reflection of myself and the trees behind me. The grass in the meadows was thick and rich, and a herd of cows stood unmoving, like cardboard cut-outs, up to their bellies in the bright waters of the river, cooling themselves, too lazy to move.

I found John sitting in his extensive garden with a friend of his – the 'Mad Dentist.' I think they'd been students together. I forget what they were drinking – chilled Beaujolais perhaps, but there was lots of it. I was welcomed, and the conversation went this way and that; the wine came, bottle after bottle.

'I'm down here for the charity ball,' said the dentist.

'Yes,' said John, 'a bloody bore, but I have to go.'

I didn't like charity balls, and said so. 'Why don't them toffs just stay at home and send the money? There'd be more to go round if they did.'

'It's at the manor, Little Milton. Twenty-five quid a ticket.'

I became angry – it was the Beaujolais in my blood. 'I've a good mind to gatecrash it,' I said.

'Not easy,' John shook his head. 'There's some big names from London, local celebs too. There'll be a lot of security.'

'It's a piece of cake,' I said. 'I'll dress as a woman, security people always look behind you for the bloke who has the tickets.'

'Bet you can't get in.'

'Bet I can.'

'We'll bet you twenty-five quid each for the charity that you don't.'

By then I had a serious drop taken, and the bet was made.

'Done,' I said. My dander was up. I was the tipsy man on the Clapham omnibus, ready to strike a blow against Charity Balls. Strangely I didn't know then, nor do I know now, what the 'good cause' was. It might well have been for Depressed Fox-Hunters or impoverished Range Rover drivers – it was the principle of the thing.

I don't remember getting back home. Perhaps the 'Mad Dentist' drove me. My daughters were there, and my wife, I ranted and I raved. 'I am determined to get in,' I said, 'there's fifty quid in it.'

There was only one woman in the village who was tall enough to have a wardrobe of clothes that I might choose from – Cynthia D'Anger, who in spite of her name was a local woman born and bred and lived in a house just over the road from me. She took no persuading. We fished about in her cupboards and came up with the proper gear: a black evening skirt, full, with fringes all the way down it; a silver lamé bolero jacket; a frilly blouse; stockings, and a tiny handbag in gold sequins hanging from a string. Luckily, my feet being aristocratically small, she even had gold evening shoes I could get into.

Still pleasantly tipsy, I carried this booty back to my daughters and they began on my make up. It took a long while; however hard they tried I still looked like a bloke. It was a bit better when we got the wig on – short chestnut curls. My double D bosoms were two aluminium colanders joined together and held in position by a capacious brassiere. Then it was time to go. I had sobered up a bit by now and the escapade did not seem so hilarious. Never mind! It was the principle of the thing.

I drove a mini in those days, and felt decidedly odd swishing into it dressed as a woman. It was also my first experience of driving in high heels. My daughters waved me goodbye and my heart suddenly felt like a lump of lead. I had no idea how I was going to get into the manor and didn't feel confident enough to drive through the main entrance like those who had been invited. Besides it was late now and they would all be taking apéritifs in the marquee.

I parked the mini at the back of the manor where a steep grass-covered bank rose to a high stone wall which surrounded the estate. I tottered from the car, scrambled up the bank and, hitching my skirts to the knee, managed to climb to the top of the wall. I laddered my stockings on the way, but was soon in a position to allow myself to drop to the ground on the far side. The first objective had been gained; I was inside the forbidden boundary. Unfortunately I had dropped into a small forest of stinging nettles. The toffs obviously could not afford a gardener. The stings were extremely painful and I thought of beating a retreat but my dander was still up. I had to go on.

I straightened my wig, settled into my bolero jacket and adjusted my false bosoms which had slipped a little. I scouted out the back of the house, slipped across a kitchen, into a cloakroom and looked at my reflection in its mirror. I made an ugly woman. I would have to find John as quickly as possible, claim my reward, and get off home.

I peered from the cloakroom; crossed a corridor and the raised voices of drunken conversations guided me to where the action was. It would be easy, surely; they would all be standing around some kind of buffet, wouldn't they? I would be able to sidle in, unnoticed, spot John from afar, touch him on the shoulder and then disappear without being noticed.

There was a covered walk leading from the rear of the

house and on into the enormous marquee that had been erected in the garden. I minced past the two security guards who stood at the entrance, men with bulging muscles and tight suits. Either my theory was correct or my mincing was excellent. They didn't give me a second glance. Then came the horror. Instead of casual groups of people eating on their feet, the guests – three hundred of them – were all sitting down, about a dozen to each table. Three hundred pairs of eyes turned my way and stared at this extraordinary woman. But then, being English, their eyes turned away again. I was into the marquee now and obliged to mince on, my handbag on my wrist. I knew that if I didn't spot John first time round I would have to walk the length of the tent – bad enough in itself – and then walk back again, straight into the podgy hands of those security guards.

Luckily John was stationed near the main aisle and I fluttered my eyelashes at him from close range. He and the 'Mad Dentist' were still carrying a cargo of Beaujolais from the afternoon and leapt to their feet, ordering another chair, and sitting me down. The assembly now felt free to stare at me, down their noses, for as long as they liked. The hosts themselves were mortified, and had it not been for John Hughes would have evicted me for sure. I felt nothing but relief. The worst part was over, except for one thing. I had never been in drag before, and would never do it again, but cross-dressing does affect people in strange ways. On that particular night I was approached by more women than I could handle, insisting I dance with them, fondling me as they held me close, their eyes blazing with a daring intent. The men too were excited by the situation, their hands wandering. In fact my colander bosoms were dented by one drunk who punched me very hard in the chest and thought it highly amusing. It certainly hurt me but perhaps he thought I was his wife.

The Tatler photographer was there and I appeared in the magazine the following week: a picture of me looking very stunned: '*Mr Michael de Larrabeiti was so excited he decided to come as a woman.*'

The Oxford Mail was kinder:

A top-selling author dressed up as a woman and gate-crashed a swish autumn charity ball for a bit of fundraising fun.

Armed with a long dress and make-up Great Milton writer Mike de Larrabeiti scaled a stone wall to get into the ball at Little Milton Manor.

He was challenged by his friend, Wheatley GP Dr John Hughes, who bet he couldn't get in undetected.

So he did what his top-selling creations the Borribles – top favourites with children – would have done.

He borrowed a long dress from neighbour Cynthia D'Anger, and his two teenage daughters, Aimée and Phoebe, set to work on the make-up.

He said: 'Have you ever tried to climb a high stone wall in drag? It was very spectacular.'

He got into the grounds expecting to find everyone eating and dancing – but got a shock.

The assembled 300 guests, including newsreader John Craven, were seated eating a full meal in a huge marquee.

'I had to walk the full length of the marquee to some very penetrating stares, but I saw John Hughes and claimed my reward. He paid up straight away.

Then I was made very welcome by the guests and had a great evening.'

Dr Hughes said: 'I was flabbergasted when I saw this creation coming up the marquee. I just flung my arms around him; it was marvellous to see him and I paid up. It was

great fun.'
One man who missed the joke was
organiser Hugh Buchanan. 'I did not know of
any gate-crashers,' he said. 'I had a lot of
security, like guard dogs, to prevent that
happening.

And my daughters? They treated me like a hero when I eventually got home, lipstick smudged, the following morning. My wife was a little more circumspect.

❋   ❋   ❋

The Borribles option money kept me going for a while, and provided the finance for a couple of family holidays and the leisure to write the third *Borrible* book, *Across the Dark Metropolis*. Sometime in the 'eighties I met Stuart Mungall in a wine shop on West Side, Wandsworth Common. He was an actor/stage director, and a fervent fan of *The Borribles*, and when he was given the Young Vic theatre to run he decided to do a stage version of the first volume – *The Great Rumble Hunt*.

He avoided recruiting children from drama schools and instead restricted auditions to kids from comprehensives. It made his work more difficult but it made it more fun also. The show was ragged but enthusiastic and the cast never let us down; lots of hard work and no tantrums. We were a happy band of brothers and sisters. There were songs too, and the kids sang them wonderfully, full of energy and cheek. Billy Johnson recorded them for me, and my own children still love them even now, twenty odd years later. The last night was a riot and impossible to get those kids off stage; they sang their way through the songs again and again, marching up and down and round the auditorium. There were tears in my eyes and I was given a long round of applause: "Author, author," they shouted, bless 'em. It was the nearest I ever got to the West End.

My adventures with the third *Borrible* volume were not so enjoyable. The 'Wicked Witch of the West', Margaret Clark, had moved into complete control at the Bodley Head and she had never liked the series. 'It's far too long,' she said. 'It needs 10,000 words taken out of it.'

I worked on the book for about six months solid, day in, day out, taking three or four lines off each page. It was a virtual re-write and it broke my heart to throw that stuff away, stuff that I'd worked on for weeks and months. But I did the work, and re-submitted. She didn't even look at it: 'I don't want it,' she said. 'Try somewhere else.'

Given that the Bodley Head had published the previous two volumes it was unlikely that another house would accept the third book of a trilogy refused by the original publisher. Surprisingly Collins picked it up and took me out to lunch in Albemarle Street – a good sign in itself. I wasn't counting my millions again but I was pleased. After all, Collins was much more dynamic than the Bodley Head of Margaret Clark.

Then there was a serious riot on The Broadwater Estate in Tottenham and a policeman was killed. It wasn't long before I received the following letter, sent to my agent and forwarded to me:

COLLINS – PUBLISHERS

THE BORRIBLES: Across the Dark Metropolis.

After the events of Brixton and Tottenham we have had to look at The Borribles in a different light.

Those of us here who were enthusiastic about the book a month ago now feel (unanimously) that the present climate of urban Britain is not the climate in which we would wish to publish this book.

No matter how exciting the story (and Michael de Larrabeiti is a wonderful storyteller) it is a novel that pits a gang of lawless young people against the police. We told ourselves originally that this was OK because the story was an 'urban fantasy', that Borribles were not real children (even though the blurb says the author has two 'borribles' of his own), that the police were not real but comic characters, that the Borribles were moral characters who lived by their own moral code. Nevertheless the battle between the law and lawlessness is glamorized and given a status, which we cannot appear to condone in children's literature now that Britain has entered a new era in which this battle is a daily reality.

I am enormously sad to have to withdraw from this venture for these reasons and I do hope that Michael de Larrabeiti will try to understand our decision. I think if he still lived in Lambeth he just might.

Yours sincerely,

Linda Davies
Publishing Director

No one wanted the book now, except Pan, but only as a paperback. It appeared eventually in a blaze of apathy, attracting no reviews whatsoever in spite of the controversy, and it died the death. Being a travel journalist was definitely more straight-forward than writing books and, more to the point, my £8000 wouldn't last for ever. Once more I set off for foreign parts.

MADAGASGAR

'Once upon a time there was a huge continent called Gondwanaland.' Alexander spoke slowly, addressing me, the ignoramus of the party. 'It was made up of Africa, South America and Australia...and Antarctica and India. Madagascar drifted off on its own, maybe eighty million years ago...so 80% of its flora is endemic, all of its mammals, half of its birds and 90% of its reptiles...except those introduced, of course.'

I was dazed by numbers and Malagasy beer. I had come to Madagascar to write an article and had been attached to a group of experts who seemed to know everything. 'You are having me on,' I said.

Alexander shook his head. 'You can trust me, I'm a herpetologist.' And so he was, a man of great experience leading fifteen of us, for a fortnight, through the wonders and sadnesses of Madagascar – a former rugby player with a wide knowledge of his subject, a zest for life and a Rabelaisian sense of humour that he used with a practised sophistication.

Robert Louis Stevenson had long ago discovered the words for Alexander and his sort: noting that 'enthusiasm and special knowledge are the social qualities, and what they are about, whether white sauce or Shakespeare's plays, an altogether secondary question'.

We were sitting, that first evening, at the bar of the Hôtel Colbert in Antananarivo, submerged in the roar of a hundred conversations. Through the din ran white coated waiters, trays shoulder high, the sweat silver on their faces. This was the watering hole for ex-pats from all over the world: businessmen, professional conservationists, and a handful of villains who worked the same territory.

'See that man over there,' said Alexander, 'he's the biggest illegal animal dealer in the world, there's a fistful of warrants out for him in Europe, he should be hanged, drawn and quartered. There is so much stuff smuggled out of this country – chameleons, snakes, everything. The other man, in the fawn linen suit, drinking g and t, he makes his living by nicking orchids - for collectors, you understand. More than a thousand species of them here, orchids I mean. It's rough and it's tough, and there's lots of money in it. A couple of smugglers got shot last year, shot dead. They were discovered *in flagrante*.

In the morning we left for Andasibe, everyone but me a genius in something, and they had all travelled the world several times over. There was even a professor of zoology, now a consultant, and a nematologist, bubbling with enthusiasms. It was only fitting that he was called Cassius and he made it his delight to tell me stories of parasites and what they could do once they were inside my body. 'There's one in the Amazon,' he said, 'that swims up your stream of urine and anchors itself in your penis; once there you never get it out.'

I swallowed hard. 'That's nice,' I said. I wasn't good at parasites.

Along the road to Andasibe, the countryside looked fecund and green, but beyond the rice paddies and the terraces of cassava the hills were bare; patchy like the back of a moulting dog. Almost everywhere the forest had been cut down for firewood or to make charcoal, and the undergrowth burnt so as to encourage new grass for the humped zebu cattle to feed on. And so it will go on. The population has doubled since 1960 and will double again by 2015, and every man, woman and child on the island needs a kilo of wood every day, just to keep the cooking pots cooking.

At Andasibe we were housed in thatched bungalows and ate in the Buffet de la Gare, a piece of provincial France from the late 1930s. Lying halfway between the capital and the east coast, the building is restaurant and railway station in one, with a welcoming atmosphere and an impressive rosewood bar. But

Alexander would not allow us to linger and, as soon as lunch was done, we headed into the forest and never mind the heat.

Underfoot the rotting vegetation was soft and springy and we were content, scanning the terraces above our heads, binoculars busy: a paradise flycatcher on its nest; a giraffe beetle on a leaf, its body red, its legs and neck long - and out came the macro lenses, and the cameras clicked. All around us was a richness of flora, not all of which could we recognise: camellia, wild rose, malanga, jasmine, pandanus, palisander, the Malagasy periwinkle and wild orchids growing on high branches, delicate and strangely aloof.

'Epiphytic,' said the professor.

And then my first chameleon: very large, a light metallic verdigris colour with dark markings – a *parsonii*. It moved slowly along a branch, pretending not to move, pretending it was a large twig.

'And a hunter wasp.' Cassius was pointing, sandboy happy. 'It's a predator. Stings its prey, paralyses it, oviposits and then buries it. Then the egg hatches and the larva eats the host while it is still alive. Wonderful.'

We went on, stepping quietly, until at last, on the slope of a thickly wooded hill, we saw five indri lemurs, high in the terraces; the adults about three feet tall with black and white fur, vestigial tails and faces that looked permanently surprised. We had found a whole family - two parents, two grown-up offspring and a young one. They seemed not in the least disturbed by our presence, but their territorial screams rang out nevertheless, powerful and clear, echoing a mile or two across the forest; a scary noise, haunting too, like the sound of whales recorded under water. Then the lemurs moved on, sailing through the treetops in great exuberant trampoline leaps, bounding about as if in glee. They were highly trained acrobatic clowns, their sense of humour fully developed, careless and foolhardy yet sure and steady, thrusting up and over with long, powerful hind legs, covering great distances and landing with aplomb on slender branches that bowed and then sprang up with the weight of them. We followed until the family rested, still unperturbed, settling down to lie on shady boughs, their legs casually looped and stretched, their arms languid, like gentlemen in a Pall Mall club, snoozing in leather armchairs.

'Oh, it's so beautiful, I could weep.' That was Lorna, videoing madly. In the next instant she screamed and we turned to help, but there was no need. 'It's very difficult,' she went on, 'holding a camera steady when there's a lemur piddling in your face.'

In the town of Antsiranana the smell of the fish factory made my eyes water. The Hôtel de la Poste was out of Conrad's *Heart of Darkness*, and in a corner of the restaurant there was an ultraviolet box that made cracking noises every few seconds, killing flies as efficiently as the carnivorous and endemic pitcher plants we had seen earlier that day. After a hard night's sleep in steamy rooms, we set out in a procession of rusty Renault 4s and drove to Amber Mountain – one of the best examples of moist upland forest in Madagascar. At the entrance to the reserve we happened on one of the villains from the Hotel Colbert. 'Watch out for leeches,' he said.

'And black widow spiders,' added Cassius, his eyes widening with anticipation as mine closed in fear.

That afternoon we came to a small waterfall, white foam tumbling into a deep, three-sided hollow to form a sunken pool. The walls of this cavern were thick with fern and moss and a strange red flower that none of us could name. Trees grew horizontally from the steep sides and the water in the pool was black, too opaque to reflect the warm grey clouds that formed the sky. Round to the right was an overhanging cliff, a proscenium arch where a curtain of water slid down slabs of stone and, as we stood looking, the rain came in low, altering the light, making it mysterious and magical.

But there was more. Down a steep leech-laden slope we came to a huge volcanic lake, ringed with mauve rock and fringed with forest. Here the gloom was ancient and untouched, and my companions looked small against such size and silence; vulnerable against a vertical backdrop of purple and green. They gazed in wonder, now and then photographing both flora and fauna, and Cassius progressed steadily along the edge of the water, turning rocks over, hunting for bugs. This was a spot that was far away from the world; the gateway to a fantasy, down through the water and into a tale by Jules Verne.

I found a flat boulder and sat, watching, and close to me a malachite kingfisher made elegant forays across the lake, showing off, darting out periodically with neat economic swoops, taking a fish each time and revealing lightning flashes of his azure wings.

Suddenly there was a call from Cassius, impatient and imperative, and he waved me over to him. Under one of his rocks, as promised, he had discovered a large black widow spider, a rectangle of brilliant red across its body telling the world that it was dangerous and fatal. 'Poke it with a stick!' shouted Cassius, his excitement attempting to get the better of my cowardice. 'It's got its legs all folded up, I can't get a decent shot of it.'

We stayed at the lake as long as we dared, but the clouds came in low and covered the hills. We raced the darkness back up the slopes to the mud-soft track where our Renault 4s waited, and there we sat on the ground to remove our boots and socks and pull the leeches from our legs, the blood glistening on our ankles. 'Another good day,' said Alexander and grinned, his legs the bloodiest of all.

* * *

'Hmm,' said Cassius, at Toliara, 'entomologically speaking, this is the most interesting airport we've seen.' He led me outside and showed me a pair of insects, a bit like dragonfly, three or four inches long.

'One of the family of neuroptera,' he explained. 'It's carnivorous, called the antlion; its larva makes funnel traps in the sand, catches ants and then eats them.'

The track from the airport to the hotel was deep rutted and there was at least thirty kilometres of it. This was zebu cattle country: herds on all sides, and pairs of them pulling carts under heavy yokes. The ground was dry and sandy with sisal, prickly pear and scrub; a landscape laid waste by slash and burn techniques, the trees cut down by charcoal burners, the stumps finished off by goats and pigs. Towards the end of our journey the track turned along by the ocean, with here and there a scattering of lonely dwellings made of cane and leaves and thatched with swamp grass. Our bus threw up a smoke of dust as it advanced and grit settled on the villagers as they squatted by their huts, their cooking fires small sparks of gold in the dusk; and against the horizon – a flame sunset all daubed with grey – the crested terns took fish from the surface of the sea.

By eight-thirty the next morning the heat lay unmoving across a solid sea, and I took to the shade by the edge of the Mozambique Channel. A waitress brought me breakfast. Alexander had led the dawn walk through what had been, just two years previously, a flourishing forest, but was now nothing more than a dusty degradation, denuded by the quest for fuel, with only a few baobabs growing, together with some thickets of the cactus-like didiereaceae, its spiky branches like Rastafarian hair, twisted against the sky.

By nine-thirty the air felt dangerous, scorching the skin, and I became even more indolent, watching my companions as they hired a twin outrigger and set off for the coral reef. Cassius, for once, had chosen indolence too and he appeared from his bungalow bearing a jug of iced tea and two glasses. He sat beside me, stretched his legs and leant back in his chair.

'Then there's the lancet fluke,' he began, *dicrocoelium lanceolatum*. It's a fascinating generation cycle with a change of hosts. It starts with sheep; they distribute the fluke's eggs by their excrement. This fluke is able to swim or float and swims off in search of a snail so that the snail may take in the fluke's eggs with its food. In the snail's digestive gland the fluke's first larval generation hatches – *miracidium*, it's called. It gets into the lung and the snail surrounds it with a mucus layer which is expelled as a tiny ball of snot.

Now this mucus is highly attractive to meadow ants, *myrmica*, which eat them. The larvae grow in your ant's abdomen but one of them gets into the ant's head. There they attack the ant's nervous system and cause a change of behaviour and they become what are called *zombie ants*. The ants become crazy and begin to do crazy things. They climb up plant stems and attach themselves, with their mandibles, to leaves and grass, waving their legs in the air. The grazing sheep must be attracted to these waving legs; they eat the plants, and the ants of course, and thereby infect themselves with the liver fluke. Once inside the host the larvae change into the fluke's adult stage, they reproduce sexually and then lay eggs that are excreted by the sheep and the cycle begins again.'

'Amazing,' I said. 'Where does all this happen? In darkest Africa?'

'Well no,' answered Cassius, enormously pleased with himself. 'In England actually.'

*   *   *

The sailing contingent returned from the reef three hours later, fulfilled and crimsoned by the sun. 'Coral like rose petals,' they said, 'and brain coral, like brains of course, and stag's horn and parrot fish, turquoise like the sea, with green and orange and yellow markings.'

'And I saw a tang fish,' said Alexander, 'all powder blue, coloured lemon around the mouth with the palest and most delicate of fins, and as I followed it so it swam into the sun and all its colours shone from within. I was taken by the beauty of it and gasped, and took in a lungful of ocean. I nearly drowned.'

Late that evening, after dinner and in farewell, four or five fishermen came from a nearby village, their women with them. They carried guitars fashioned from the planks of fish boxes, each instrument sporting only one string, and that made from string itself. They played bright music for us and a woman blew a chrome police whistle in time to the beat. Three other women danced, and such a dance: their arms did not move, nor their legs nor their heads. Only their buttocks shivered, leading lives of their own; bursts of muscle control with the flesh rippling, a triumph of carnal enticement so rapid that paradoxically, the movements seemed as stately and as stroboscopic as any chameleon's.

When we flew home a few days later, I gazed down as we

climbed into the sky so that I could see where the bright red earth of the Great Red Island stained the sea like a halo of blood, the precious soil washed away from the deforested hills, day after day, year after year. Cassius leant over to look through the same window. 'They say,' he mused, 'that there's only a thousand hectares of galleried forest left in the whole of Madagascar. You know, it could be an offshore Sahara in twenty years' time, and that's the sadness of it.'

After a while the stewardesses brought the food and as we ate Cassius told me the story of the French nematologist and the tapeworms. 'Nobody could work out their life cycle,' he explained, 'so this chap fed the eggs, at various stages, to condemned prisoners and then dissected them after they'd been guillotined. In that way he was able to find out how far each worm had developed...a good bit of research that.'

He regarded me steadily but I carried on eating my fillet steak, unruffled, and opened the Bordeaux. Two weeks in Madagascar had toughened me up no end.

CARTHAGE

'If Aeneas did have an affair with Dido,' said the young man opposite me, 'then he would have been 500 years old at the time.'

I was drinking a beer in the Café de Paris on the avenue Habib Bourguiba in Tunis. It was a barn of a café, crowded from wall to wall and the roar of the crowd lay over everything; a rough, intimidating noise like a dangerous undertow dragging down a loose wash of pebbles on a stony beach. Under the high ceilings, the sound was trapped for ever and, on the marble floor, the wooden chair-legs were scraped back and made the flesh creep, like fingernails scratching a slate blackboard. The waiters shouted their orders and cigarette smoke, thick and blue, hung motionless in the air, great swaths of it. There were no women to be seen, save for two antique *grandes dames*, archeological vestiges of French colonisation, their skin stretched and starched, stiff with rouge and lipstick, their blonde and ginger hair brittle with lacquer. They did not talk but gazed steadily into the street, into a past that was too distant to see.

'Dido came from Phoenicia and built Kart-Hadasht in 814...BC, of course.' The young man eyed my beer. 'And Aeneas escaped from Troy in 1250 or thereabouts. Virgil's story was that they fell in love, but Jupiter had a master plan – Aeneas's destiny was to establish Rome – so he went on his way and Dido stabbed herself and jumped onto a bonfire. That's why Carthage and Rome never hit it off. Then Rome razed Carthage to the ground and, even when they rebuilt it, the

Vandals came along, then the Byzantines, the Arabs and the Ottomans, and they all stole stone for their own monuments – Roman stone, Carthaginian stone. Carthage is just a suburb of Tunis now. All you have to do is take the TGM railway, get off where you like and you'll see what's left in half a day.' He leant forward and recited the station names, and I took pleasure in the romantic sound of them: 'Carthage, Hannibal, Amilcar, Byrsa, Salammbo.'

'So you've read a lot of history?' I asked.

He shook his head. 'I come from here, but I married a girl from Tottenham and she's made a study of it. She's an expert. I came back last year to visit my parents and I was pulled in off the street...I'd forgotten to do my national service.' He smiled sadly, like someone remembering a bad joke. 'Still, I finish next week. I can't wait to see Spurs versus Arsenal at White Hart Lane. They don't pay us soldiers much – you could buy me a beer.'

I bought him the beer and paid the bill. As I rose to leave the young man raised his glass. *'Delenda est Carthago,'* as Cato used to say – 'Carthage must be destroyed.'

The Tunis-Goulette-Marsa railway runs across the Lac de Tunis on a causeway; past the port, with its oil-storage tanks, its warehouses and cranes, and then northwards along the coast of the Mediterranean. Beyond La Goulette the scenery improved, and I disembarked at Carthage-Salammbo, a station that was clean and whitewashed and decorated with dwarf palm trees. I crossed the main road and went into the suburban streets that lie between the railway and the sea. It was quiet and there were few passers-by, the white villas decorous behind white walls, their shutters and wrought-iron gates all painted in a gleaming royal blue. In amongst the villas were a few concrete apartment blocks and, occasionally, a corner shop selling groceries and sandwiches. This was Carthage.

At the rue Hannibal I turned left and, as I did so, a small man on a square framed bicycle, at least sixteen hands high, glided to a halt beside me. He wore a grey sports jacket and a red *sheshia* on his head. One of his eyes was blank and blind, though it shone as brilliant and as blue as any local shutter. The eye stared at me for a second as the man braked; he dismounted as best he might, allowing the bike to fall sideways until one of his feet touched the ground. He leant the machine against a palm tree and took, from an inside pocket, a much folded rectangle of newspaper. He opened it with care and displayed several coins, holding one up at last for my inspection.

'This is a Hannibal coin,' he said. 'See, this is Hannibal, his head, see.'

I peered down. The coin was black and oval and seemed to have been sprayed with copper sulphate to make it look mouldy with verdigris. I shook my head. The man touched me on the arm and spoke with a finality and wisdom that was meant to brook no argument; irrefutable proof was on its way. He turned the coin slowly. 'This coin is genuine Punic, 2000 years old. See, on this side there is an elephant. Hannibal had elephants.'

'Don't they make these coins in Naples?' I asked.

'Four dinars,' he said, his impatience beginning to show. 'For 2000 years old, this is nothing.'

'No thanks,' I said, '*je ne suis pas acheteur.*'

A little further along the rue Hannibal, I came to the entrance of the Tophet, the sanctuary of the Carthaginian gods – Tanit and Baal. I paid the man at the gate and went into a small patch of wasteland, unlovely and unkempt. The ground was rough and uneven, and scruffy grass fought for its life in the dust. To my left lay a copse of Punic headstones and some bits and pieces of columns and capitals and, at the back of the site, there was a hole in the ground where, it is said, Carthaginian children were ritually sacrificed.

It was a horrible place. A damp breeze came in off the sea, and the day was dull and overcast. The ground smelt as if it were rotting, an odour of rankness, and the palm trees leant together, their leaves dark and sinister. A blackbird clattered away from its bush, and an owl stared at me. The Tophet, with its atmosphere of death, made me uneasy and it was impossible to stay there long. I made haste to be on my way, my departure ignored by the custodian, untroubled and happy in his hut, his newspaper held high between him and history.

Not far from the ruins of the Roman theatre, on a dusty

playing field of sorts, I watched two teams of boys playing football. Their goalposts – piles of coats in my day – were made from little stacks of archaeological debris, shards from carvings and shattered pillars. Just inside the entrance to the theatre the caretaker and his assistant were playing belotte on a rectangle of stone – a chunk of foundation worn smooth by the hands of generations of card sharps. And down by the main road a man was hanging out the family washing at the rear of his house, his garden furniture perfect – a section of Roman column with a round capital served as his table, and three other column lengths of a lesser size did duty as chairs, sunk into the ground until they were the required height.

Evening was rolling in from the sea as I made my way to the Antonine baths; several acres of land laid out like a small park with narrow untidy paths meandering among the excavations. In a secluded spot, under some trees, I came upon a mosaic lying open to the sky: four cupids dancing, a rope of flowers held in their hands, linking them together. Their feet were raised to a forgotten music and their eyes were strangely serious. Red heart-shaped blooms and green leaves formed a background to the dancers; above them a cupola, with columns on either side, as if to make a stage. It was a postcard from the past, an image of delight and gaiety, and its joy had not faded.

By the seashore a row of crumbling columns looked out over the Bay of Tunis, all that was left of great walls and arches, now all denuded of their marble cladding; and the domes, which in their glory had been as high and as wide as those of any cathedral, fallen and vanished; a ghost of empire.

On my way back to the railway station I came to an expanse of water that had once been the military port, and beyond that a second port used by the merchant ships in the great days of Carthage. Both harbours had been excavated with pick and shovel, 220,000 square yards of earth and rock; the headquarters of the greatest navy in the ancient world, with space for more than 200 warships. But now the famous waters are silted shallow, shrunk to insignificance, with not a single boat, of any size, to be seen – 'the weapons of war perished'.

A woman and a child went by, hand in hand, and

disappeared into one of the villas on the other side of the road. The man with the walleye circled me once more and came to a halt. He found it hard to believe that I could have so much money and refuse to give him any. Puzzlement deepened the lines on his face. He showed me a 'Punic' oil lamp, carved in stone.

'Two dinars,' he said. I shook my head and he turned away. I followed the circle of the military port towards the sea. The villas followed on my left and, to the right, the gravel fell away to the water's edge.

It was not a long walk and I came, in a while, to an open space close by the shore. The man with the bike was still shadowing me. A few labourers were building a garage in breeze blocks, adding them to a house of breeze blocks. On the rim of the sea, where a few rocks had been thrown down to act as a breakwater, I at last found a boat – a wooden rowing boat with two young men sitting in it, talking softly and mending their nets. Three boys of eleven or so stood nearby and threw stones into the water, their movements listless, the ripples made by the stones were small and tired. As I stared at the horizon, another boy carrying a long loaf and a can of something ran up to the fishermen. A couple of idlers strolled by. The builders and the boys watched, even the man with the bike watched, there was nothing else to do.

One of the fishermen cut the loaf along its length, opened the tin and spread the red contents into the bread. Then he broke the loaf in half, gave one part to his companion and offered the other to those who were watching. They shook their heads, but I was hungry. I nodded and the fisherman tore about five inches off his loaf and passed this smaller section to me. The onlookers smiled, and with reason; the bread had been laced with the hottest *sauce piquante* I have ever tasted. I was immediately in tears and my nose began to run. I waved my hands up and down and sucked up cool air to dampen the fire in my mouth. Now the fishermen smiled.

'It is good for the insides,' they said.

I lay back on a flat rock to recover, my head resting on my rolled up jacket. I had done a lot of walking over the previous few days and was soon asleep. Not for long. After about ten minutes, someone shook my arm and I opened my eyes to see one of the fishermen leaning over me. While I had slept he had roasted half a dozen fish on a driftwood fire. He offered me one, fat and long, lying across the palm of his hand, a whole feast, the head and the tail hanging down, all black and burnt from the flames.

It smelt delicious. I took the fish from him and we crouched together on the sand, the three of us, picking at the hot flesh with our fingers, eating our fill with more bread brought by one of the boys. And the idlers and the builders continued watching, and grinned at the world and the things that were good in it.

When the meal was over, we washed our hands in the sea, and the fishermen pushed their boat out of the shallows and rowed away from the land until they were small on the pale water, their oars hardly disturbing the surface, the foam of their wake dying as soon as it was born. Then they were gone, an arm raised in farewell. By the embers of the fire a feral and scrofulous cat ate the skeletons of the fish, and the man with the bike shook his head, worried by my outlandish behaviour. Small wonder that he could make little profit from the likes of me. He climbed on to his bike and rode sadly away.

Then there came a call from the sea, one of the fishermen, bidding me adieu, his voice echoing across two thousand years. The Romans would have been pleased, I thought, to have seen what I had seen, one row-boat being all that was left of the Carthaginian navy; *Delenda est Carthago* indeed, but then, where was Cato's fleet?

*　　*　　*

By the time the millennium arrived I had written fifteen books; three unpublished, two thrown away, ten published. Although *The Borribles* had been out of print for some years it had gone on to be optioned four times, though the film had not been made. Then I met a couple of decent publishers – it was about time – Peter Lavery of Macmillan, who brought out *The Borrible Trilogy* in one volume in 2002; and John Hale who published *Foxes' Oven* and *French Leave* in 2003. I immediately began writing two more books and gave up the travel writing. Even so, there was one place I had to see – Samoa, and the house and the tomb of Robert Louis Stevenson.

SAMOA

I have a friend called Richard who once asked me where and how I wanted to die, if I could choose. 'We're getting to that age,' he added, 'when it needs to be considered.'

The answer to the question came to me easily enough. 'I'll spend a couple of weeks wandering around Samoa,' I said. 'Visit the house that Stevenson lived in, then when I'm ready, I'll climb Mount Vaea to his tomb. I'll take a light picnic with me, a bottle of Burgundy or Bordeaux of course, which I will share; half for me, half as a libation. I'll enjoy the view for an hour or two, then lie back and await the painless heart attack.'

So I came to Samoa at last. I'd been to a lot of other places by then; I'd ridden the Copper Canyon railway in Mexico; I'd crossed Canada, Halifax to Vancouver; sailed down the Yangtze; drunk coconut milk on the Backwaters of Kerala; sailed up Doubtful Sound in New Zealand; and had climbed aboard the most graceful sailing ships in the world – the Buginese schooners of Indonesia. But to visit Samoa had been my hidden ambition, and I seized the first occasion to do so that presented itself. Not because I wanted to tempt Providence or because I felt close to death…well, no closer than usual – after all, the Grim Reaper is notoriously unreliable when it comes to timing – but because I wanted to climb the hill to Stevenson's tomb while my knees were still in good working order.

I fell in love with Samoa immediately. At the airport, in the arrivals lounge, a grand name for a small one-roomed building, a guitar player sang songs to his own accompaniment. I suppose someone looked at my passport but I wasn't aware of it. The sunrise air was soft and succulent; a few taxis and hotel buses waited for custom and it was a hotel bus that took me to Aggie Grey's. Dawn had come and brown cows stood in pools of mist under palm trees. On a field of dust a man practised penalty kicks with a rugby ball, his goalposts made from misshapen saplings. Open-sided dwellings were dotted along the roadside, family tombs beside them. Away to my right the hills were covered with forest. Closer at hand there were hibiscus and banana plants. Not a breath of wind, not a leaf stirring.

Apia, the capital, also stole my heart. The town wanders carelessly along the shore, with a handful of streets running inland towards foothills that seem within touching distance. Traffic is light and the buildings low, not many of them over two storeys, the ancient ones made of timber, with porches and verandas in front like battered old go-downs. Almost every passer-by makes eye contact and smiles, pleased to see you, happy to chat. The girls wear bright dresses and have flowers in their hair. And the men, even the policemen, are clad in sarongs, which in Samoa are called lavalavas.

On the edge of town I found a fish market, an open sided construction furnished with wide concrete slabs for displaying the daily catch. Here the sun slanted under the roof, cutting across the gloom, and a salt laden breeze blew in from the Pacific. There were fish exotic, fish elegant and fish frightening, scales striped and daubed – turquoise and crimson, orange and green – their dead faces mournful with pouting lips. And there were more of them strung out like washing on a line, string threaded through their mouths, and they gazed at me with black, dead eyes, their bodies giving off the smell of a deep and secret sea.

The fishwives sat behind their wares, waving away squadrons of kamikaze flies with green-leaved twigs; and in dark corners and on empty slabs, lay weary fishermen, stranded high and dry after their night's work, like landed fish themselves, surveying a half-speed universe out of half an eye.

Beyond the market, in the full blaze of the sun, was the bus station, an open square. Along one side was a roofed shed giving shade. There the passengers waited with their bundles, packages wrapped in dark green leaves. Their dress was gaudy and joyful: cotton skirts, baggy shorts, shirts and sarongs. Babies slept on generous laps, schoolchildren fluttered and chattered like sparrows, and the buses came and went, their superstructures painted in fairground colours, the roofs too, vulgar colours like the acid drops of childhood. Their window spaces were unglazed and their rear axles were a foot or two higher than the front ones, giving them a provocative high-buttocked look, as if suffering from steatopygia, as were a good percentage of their passengers. Destinations were written on squares of cardboard and propped in the windscreens; names that brought to mind the titles in Stevenson's collection of island stories: Falelatai, Satapuala, Solosolo, and Tafitoal; Motootua and Siumu.

I lazed in Apia for days; I was eating lotuses in amazing quantities. I talked to anybody who would talk to me, went to the public library, bought three lavalavas, ate in most of the restaurants and even went to a prayer meeting. I should have gone straight away to Stevenson's house, Vailima, and climbed Mount Vaea to his tomb, but I postponed the pleasure. I wanted to get the feel of the whole island, meet more people; I wanted to know more about Samoa, and to discover if what had attracted RLS to the place would also attract me.

At last I shook myself from indolence and hired a car from two jolly girls in a ramshackle hut. 'My brother-in-law plays rugby for Bedford,' said one of them. At the main police station I paid ten tala to a sergeant in a blue lavalava and he validated my driving licence. He was a five-storeyed apartment block of a man and he moved with the steady grace of a traction engine, irresistible once in motion. 'Take care,' he said.

I drove out of Apia, past the harbour. Two coasters lay at anchor, their hulls streaked with rust. Once out of town an exuberant vegetation came close and high on either side of the road, leaves shining under the touch of a sweaty rain. Here and there were square clapboard dwellings with porches, but no windows. Samoans do not need windows. And there were the traditional houses too – the *fale* – oval constructions raised up on short stilts, some three feet off the ground, roofs thatched with palm leaves. These *fale* had no walls; Samoans do not need walls.

I followed the coast, not another vehicle to be seen, the white waves breaking on the reef to my left, back-lit, a brilliant silver, the sound floating in through the open window of the car. There were black volcanic rocks along the shore and black sows rooting in the sand, lines of piglets following them, moving like clockwork toys. Chickens strutted arrogantly where they would.

In the village of Solosolo there was a lean-to emporium and post office. There was a boy in charge, his elbows propped on the counter, his chin in his hands, his dreams so far away that he hardly saw me. I bought pot noodles for lunch and the owner of the shop invited me to sit with him in his house. He was a man built like a wine vat, vast and round; the mayor of Solosolo, ready to chat through the afternoon, sitting with a friend as vast as him. They reclined at ease in their chairs and stroked an acre or two of their sun-warmed stomachs with a cold can of beer. A light rain moved in and pattered on the roof. The afternoon drifted as planned. We talked of New Zealand, rugby and Stevenson until I thought about leaving.

'How far is it to Saleapaga?' I asked the mayor.

Notions of distance are not strong in Samoa.

He considered the problem for a short lifetime, then pronounced his verdict. 'It'll take some while,' he said, and continued to cool his stomach with his beer, inside and out. I did likewise. There was no hurry. Stevenson was my guide on this trip and his words were never far from me: *'I travel not to go anywhere, but to go. I travel for travel's sake.'*

A few miles further on I stopped to give Roki a lift. In Samoa you just keep on meeting people. Roki was a pastor, his face lit from within. He was spotless in a fawn lavalava and wore a shirt as crisp as an arrowroot biscuit. He had missed the bus to Taelefaga. I didn't know where Taelefaga was but what did that matter? That's where I was going now; keep saying 'yes', and things will happen.

We turned off the main road and lurched into a rough track

that dropped steeply and suddenly to skirt the rim of a precipice. Streams of water burst from the cliffs, rushing out of black rocks to carve deep ruts in the road. I was a fair way down this track when I came upon a bunch of about ten men blocking my way, resting a while on their long march out of the valley. They looked untrustworthy, Mexican bandidos from a Hollywood western; they stared at me, they stood unmoving. I stopped the car.

I thought I might be in trouble; I had no idea where I was, and no one else in the wide world, except the pastor, had any idea where I was either. They smiled, but then bandidos in westerns always smiled, just as they drew their pistols. I looked at the pastor; he smiled too.

'It's all right,' he said, reaching into one of his shopping bags. 'They are some of my parishioners. All they want is some cigarettes, and a box of matches.' He distributed a pack or two and the men waved their goodbyes, beaming even harder than before.

I ground on in second gear, so steep was the descent. I was in a circle of hills, thick with vegetation, a precipice on my left. Before me I could see across the land to where the endless ocean had submerged the rest of the planet. It was Samoa the wild here, and poor too, at least wilder and poorer than anything I had seen on the island until now. Down, slowly down, then at last we came into the village of Taelefaga, on the edge of Fagaloa Bay, a village that was nothing more than a poor scattering of shacks and *fale* on the edge of a rocky coast, dull and dirty, listless, with an ashen grit underfoot. It was a lost part of Samoa, in a bend of a track that went nowhere else much.

A bunch of ragged children broke off their game of cricket when we arrived, and skipped around the car as I drove Roki to the very door of his church.

'Bye-bye,' they cried by way of greeting. They were barefoot and wore an assortment of cut-down adult cast-offs; T-shirts and loose shorts. Their faces were beautiful, grubby and smeared with mud.

Inside the church were seats for fifty or sixty worshippers;

half a dozen pictures of Jesus, three guitars and a Casio
keyboard. It was a single storey building, rectangular and clean.
'There are 2000 churches in Samoa,' Roki told me. 'With a
population of 160,000 that means one church for every 80
inhabitants.' I whistled through my teeth – it was obvious. This
was the missionaries' revenge for being brought to the boil in so
many cooking pots.

My duty done, I wandered into the village, followed by half a
dozen children who found me more interesting than a game of
cricket. There was a handful of broken down shacks by the
seashore; black sand where it was dry, black mud where it was
not. One of the *fale* sheltered a pool table. It was covered in
sacking, cues standing in a rack, the coloured balls hanging
from the ceiling in a plastic bag. The plank floor was slippery
with sand and a sow and her litter lay, slumberous, under the
table. The village inhabitants squatted in their houses, staring at
me, as motionless as the sow. Games of pool and sermons on
Sundays – that was it.

I drove back to the main road and headed west and then
south. The hills above me were daubed in great splashes of
green – greens that were purple, and greens that were
fluorescent. I thought of what RLS had said about describing
green:

> *Never dare to tell me anything about green
> grass. Tell me how the grass was flecked with
> shadows. I know perfectly well that grass is
> green. So does everybody else in England.
> What you have to learn is something different
> from that. Make me see what it was that
> made your garden distinct from a thousand
> others.*

Not as easy as it sounds.

On the horizon the high ridges of the hills were hard and
scalloped into outlandish shapes. I headed on past Saleaaumua,
Malaela and Ulutogia, following the sea-shore. The sky became
mottled and lifeless and dusk rolled in from the forest to the

very fringes of the road, and those fringes were peopled by families enjoying the cool of the evening: bands of children, girls carrying babies, and women squatting in groups, dangerously close to the wheels of my car.

There were large sows also, just as careless of their lives. They trundled across the road, their heavy dugs swinging, each one followed by piglets that were no bigger than the piggy banks they give their name to. They made their way between the scattered black volcanic stones, down to the flat streaks of sand at the ocean's edge, and there the sows began to root for I know not what, and the piglets crowded around giving tiny leaps of excitement. The Pacific was flat, colourless, not a wave breathing between me and the horizon. The clouds were soft powder-puffs of white and caught the pale honey colour of the dying sun.

The road turned to the north at Cape Tapaga and the islands of Nuutele and Nuulua rose out of the sea, black and huge, and I began to search for a *fale* to sleep in. Stevenson nudged me again: 'To travel hopefully is a better thing than to arrive', but for once I disagreed with him – a meal and a night's rest were beginning to look pretty desirable.

At Faofao I discovered what was needed – a shanty of a shop and, nearby, a large *fale* the size of four living-rooms, with the mother of all mothers occupying a large broken-backed sofa. A young man, the matriarch's son, led me to the beach where five or six small *fale* had been built in a line, a few yards from the ocean. A sign said, "Canoe for Hire."

One of the *fale* was mine for the night and the young man set about making me comfortable. He ran a cable across the road, high up, between two trees, and provided me with a single light bulb. In its yellow gleam I watched him lay out a mattress and a mosquito net. Then he disappeared, returning after twenty minutes with a chair, a table, bottles of beer and some food – a meal that was a strange mixture of rice, vermicelli, peppers, slices of mutton and small pieces of beef. After the meal I opened a second beer, and picked up my book – *Lorna Doone*. The perfect end to a perfect day.

I sat alone in the dying light, the pleasure was enormous and

I wallowed in it. I had several thousand square miles of the earth's surface to myself. I could see life stretching out before me – a rosy twilight – and me with a new career as an indolent bum, clad always in a scarlet lavalava with sand for ever between my toes, a dozen dusky hand-maidens eternally within earshot. So this was why the crew of the Bounty had mutinied and why Stevenson had chosen to live here. He had been unable to do otherwise: '*Few men who come to the islands leave them; they grow grey where they alighted; the palm shades and the trade wind fans them till they die...No part of the world exerts the same attractive power upon the visitor*'.

So much I could see was true, but then I had callers, one after the other. Samoans would hate you to think they were not welcoming. First the son, who told me about his O levels; then his sister, her husband and an assortment of children. We chatted until my eyes become heavy; I had not driven very far in European terms, but I'd stopped frequently, given lifts, and talked and talked.

At last I was alone; I plumped up my mattress, lowered the mosquito net and switched out the light. I could hear the ocean on the reef; the air was warm and the sound of the waves beyond the lagoon drugged me to sleep and inspired my dreams. When I came awake the six o'clock bus to Apia was revving up its engines just behind me on the road. I rolled over and watched the stars vanish and the clouds unwrap themselves from the islets of Nuutele and Nuulua. The rising sun brushed the sky and picked out the diamonds in the spray that drifted up as mist from the reef. There was no one to be seen; not even a canoe crossed the sea.

I swam; the Pacific's only swimmer. The water was limpid and revivifying; serene too, untroubled by my presence. It was an element that yielded to my body without a ripple and closed behind it without a sign of disturbance. Then a woman appeared on the shore, an orange lavalava tied around her breasts, her feet bare, singing as she came through a gaggle of palm trees that leant careless against the sky. She placed my breakfast on the table while I towelled myself dry; three fish sandwiches in bread cut solid as doorsteps, and gallons of black tea in a chipped enamel pot.

For days I dawdled along the coast, the hours passing in gossiping and drinking; giving people lifts, driving them up dirt tracks to lost villages and spending afternoons in their *fale*, talking endlessly. I stopped in almost every settlement I came to, invited for tea into house after house. I had lobster and beer for breakfast with Gregg from Australia and Lulu, his Samoan wife. On Paradise Beach, where Gary Cooper had filmed in 1953, I got a puncture and Tulia Malosi and his whole family, seven kids and their mother, helped me change the wheel so that it took twice as long as it might have done otherwise.

And I joined in a game of Samoan cricket somewhere, played by a gang of children and their elder brothers, every innings a burst of hilarity, the fielders full of energy, adept and agile, scampering around their grandfather's tomb; a flat rectangle of cement surrounded by a low wall, and used by the spectators to sit on; a cricket pavilion that even the dear departed could enjoy. Wherever it was Grandad's spirit would have been content.

My exploration of the island could have gone on for ever; I wanted it to. The time passed in easy pleasure and delightful encounters. I was in no hurry; I didn't have to go anywhere – I was where I wanted to be, every day. In the end I simply ran out of road and drifted back to Apia; the car dusty and bedraggled, the back seat a second hand shop of clothes and picnics. I was ready for my visit to Stevenson's house, and for the climb to the summit of Mount Vaea, to the tomb of the master – never mind the danger of the kindly heart attack at the summit.

So, a couple of days after my return to the capital I caught a gorgeously decorated bus, painted entirely in primary colours, and lined inside, every surface save the floor, with a furry pink carpet. Above the driver's head was a framed picture of the Virgin Mary, the seats were metal framed, and a knotted cord ran the length of the vehicle so that passengers could ring a bell for request stops. Not many of them paid a fare and when they did the money was never scrutinised but thrown carelessly onto the carpeted dash.

I descended at the gates of Stevenson's house. There was a

grocer's stall-cum-shop at the bus stop. 'Talofa,' said the man; 'welcome.' He sold potatoes, soap, onions, long life milk and cigarettes; even a beer named after Stevenson's villa – Vailima. Though it was morning I took one in celebration of my arrival.

At the gates was a notice telling which birds I might see, and their pictures: Samoan fantails, wattled honeyeaters; black and red cardinals; yellow breasted whistlers; crimson crowned fruit doves, and although I did not spot any of them there was a cascade of bird song all around me. I walked through a fine spray of tropical rain; the air comfortable like a warm coat. To my right and left huge flower beds contained bibiscus, red ginger, gardenia, tamarind, mango, breadfruit, paw-paw and lilies.

RLS arrived in Apia in December 1889 and fell in love with it immediately, buying 300 acres on the slopes of Mount Vaea and building a house there. The Villa Vailima was virtually destroyed by a cyclone in 1990, but was repaired and restored and opened as a museum in 1994, exactly 100 years after Stevenson's death. None of the original furniture remains, but, by using old photographs and sketches, the restorers have managed to endow the house with an approximation of the old ambience, though it is now much larger than it was. Stevenson gave the house a library; a double bedroom in Californian redwood; separate quarters for his mother; a great hall, an imposing staircase, and even a fireplace to remind him of Scotland.

In the museum pictures show the Stevenson family assembled on the front porch and there is the man himself, rigged out as a hidalgo in a wide-brimmed hat, white trousers tucked into riding boots and, in true artistic fashion, a floppy cravat. He was adored by the local chiefs and in return he became their champion in disputes with the colonial power – Germany at that time. The friendship with the natives was strong and before long, as a gift, they widened the track to his house at Vailima and made it into a coral covered road, and they called it *The Road of Loving Hearts*.

Although Vailima feels unlived-in it is spacious and full of light. It is easy to linger in the rooms and enjoy the sweep of the wide staircase. I glowed with contentment. Ever since I first read *Treasure Island* I have dreamt of going to Samoa. I saw only two other visitors in the house, a pair of young 'Round-the-Worlders' from England; he was called Jim and she, because of an infected eye, was wearing a black patch. Perfect.

When Stevenson died, opening a bottle of Burgundy so the story goes, the chiefs who were his friends cut a zig-zag path up the side of Mount Vaea to the very top, hacking it out at night. And when the work was done they carried the coffin on their shoulders to the burial place. I set out, at last, to follow them.

Mount Vaea is not really a mountain, but it is a steep climb, a hill covered in thick forest. The air continued warm, made visible by clammy shreds of cloud. Towering trees bent over me, their huge leaves glistening in a light rain, leaves of many shades, from bright yellow to sombre mauve. Birds started away at my approach. A band of woodcutters dressed only in lavalavas passed me, bearing logs on their shoulders, their brown torsos glistening like the leaves; their teeth amazingly white in the gloom as they smiled a greeting. Geckos, as big as dogs, judging by the sounds they made, rustled across the forest floor, and sad-sounding doves cooed ceaselessly as if in madness; monotonous and sickly-sweet like honey dripping from a spoon. Before long I was climbing hard, my heart banging against my rib-cage, my clothes steaming.

Then, sooner than I expected, suddenly in surprise, the path gave a last turn and I was out on a flat grassy knoll and there was the tomb in front of me. My heart gave a leap of pleasure. I had made it – the ambition of a lifetime.

The rain had stopped and I caught glimpses of wooded mountains through gaps in the trees. Grey clouds almost covered the sky, though there were blue streaks behind them. But in a while the sun appeared and the clouds soared away; light filtered through the canopy and the grass was bright. From the far side of the knoll there was a tree-framed view down to the bay of Apia and the town itself, the sun glittering on the sea and on a thousand corrugated iron roofs.

The tomb could not have been simpler: a coffin-sized oblong of mortar resting on a rectangular base, similar to the grandfather's tomb where I had played cricket, similar to most of the tombs that can be seen all over Samoa. They are made for sitting, so that families may keep their ancestors close. And this one was wide enough to lie on. I stared at the horizon and attempted to imagine Stevenson enjoying the same view; and then I conjured up the day when the chiefs carried his coffin here, and I felt that sadness for an artist perished too soon, his work unfinished. I looked at Apia again, and then I read the bronze plaque that carries the epitaph:

> *This be the verse you grave for me:*
> *Here he lies where he longed to be;*
> *Home is the sailor, home from sea,*
> *And the hunter home from the hill.*

At last I was alone on top of Mount Vaea, my desire fulfilled. I stretched out on the tomb and gazed at the sky through a lattice work of branches and leaves. I was going to disappoint my friend, Richard. My heartbeat was good and slow and, now that I had recovered from the climb, I felt as right as a trivet. I had every reason to believe that I would not be joining the Immortals that day, and I was glad of it. I ate my picnic and poured the libation. Burgundy – for the bottle Stevenson hadn't opened – half for him, half for me.

My travels had taught me many things but, above all, they had brought me a host of obligations. I was to remember them, and to value the snapshots of the past that I carried in my mind. I was not to allow fear of the future to frighten me out of my memories, nor was I ever to allow the meretriciousness of the present to paralyse me, or to freeze my thinking.

But there was something else. I had debts to pay, so many debts. I was in debt not only to Stevenson for bringing me here but to all the others – regiments of them: Stendhal, Hardy and Fielding; Dickens and Balzac. And all those poets and painters and composers too, who had sweated out their lives to give me pleasure and knowledge and a little wisdom. I owed people, not only for the lobster breakfasts of Samoa, but for many other things. That farming family who had taken me in off the road as a young hitch-hiker, in France, a night of no moon and much storm. And those folk I had met, miners and steel-workers, shepherds and coach-drivers, they had been generous too. And generosity from women – mothers, friends, lovers – who had given me moments of tenderness and understanding; kindness everywhere, and wit and laughter. And friendship was the best of it; friendship and love. '...*the best that we find in our travels is an honest friend. He is a fortunate voyager who finds many.*'

I owed the living and the dead. I had been nourished by everything that had preceded me – there was no such thing as 'before my time', all time was part of me: the seasons, the rain and the wind, snowdrops and autumn leaves, and wars I had not fought in. I was heavily in debt and there was only one way to get out of it. It was pay back time, difficult though it was, for I did not possess much capital – I could tell silly jokes, I had the gift of making my friends laugh, I could spread a little knowledge and some love and friendship in my turn, and perhaps – only perhaps – I could leave a few decent books behind me. That wouldn't be too bad – picture postcards from the past, thank-you letters addressed to those who read them. It was the best I could do.

EPITAPH

Bright is the ring of words
When the right man rings them,
Fair the fall of songs
When the singer sings them.
Still they are carolled and said –
On wings they are carried –
After the singer is dead
And the maker buried.

Low as the singer lies
In the field of heather,
Songs of his fashion bring
The swains together.
And when the west is red
With the sunset embers,
The lover lingers and sings
And the maid remembers.

RLS

Printed in the United Kingdom
by Lightning Source UK Ltd.
119761UK00001B/29